Better Homes and Gardens®

RECIPES FROM PRIZEWINNING COOKS

BETTER HOMES AND GARDENS® BOOKS
Editor: Gerald M. Knox
Art Director: Ernest Shelton
Managing Editor: David A. Kirchner
Editorial Project Managers: James D. Blume, Marsha Jahns,
  Rosanne Weber Mattson, Mary Helen Schiltz

Department Head, Cook Books: Sharyl Heiken
Associate Department Heads: Sandra Granseth,
  Rosemary C. Hutchinson, Elizabeth Woolever
Senior Food Editors: Julia Malloy, Marcia Stanley, Joyce Trollope
Associate Food Editors: Linda Henry, Mary Major, Diana McMillen,
  Mary Jo Plutt, Maureen Powers, Martha Schiel, Linda Foley Woodrum
Test Kitchen: Director, Sharon Stilwell; Photo Studio Director, Janet Pittman
Home Economists: Lynn Blanchard, Jean Brekke, Kay Cargill, Marilyn Cornelius,
  Jennifer Darling, Maryellyn Krantz, Lynelle Munn, Dianna Nolin, Marge Steenson

Associate Art Directors: Linda Ford Vermie, Neoma Alt West, Randall Yontz
Assistant Art Directors: Lynda Haupert, Harijs Priekulis, Tom Wegner
Senior Graphic Designer: Darla Whipple-Frain
Graphic Designers: Mike Burns, Brian Wignall
Art Production: Director, John Berg; Associate, Joe Heuer;
  Office Manager, Emma Rediger

President, Book Group: Fred Stines
Vice President, General Manager: Jeramy Lanigan
Vice President, Retail Marketing: Jamie Martin
Vice President, Administrative Services: Rick Rundall

BETTER HOMES AND GARDENS® MAGAZINE
President, Magazine Group: James A. Autry
Vice President, Editorial Director: Doris Eby
Executive Director, Editorial Services: Duane L. Gregg
Food and Nutrition Editor: Nancy Byal

MEREDITH CORPORATE OFFICERS
Chairman of the Board: E. T. Meredith III
President: Robert A. Burnett
Executive Vice President: Jack D. Rehm

RECIPES FROM PRIZEWINNING COOKS
Editors: Linda Henry, Martha Schiel
Contributing Editor: Marlene Brown
Editorial Project Manager: Mary Helen Schiltz
Graphic Designer: Stan Sams
Electronic Text Processor: Paula Forest
Food Stylists: Janet Pittman, Sharon Stilwell
Contributing Photographers: Mike Dieter, Scott Little

The photograph on page 91 is used by permission of the Department of Interior
and the National Park Service.

Our seal assures you that every recipe in
Recipes from Prizewinning Cooks has been tested in the
Better Homes and Gardens® Test Kitchen.
This means that each recipe is practical and reliable,
and meets our high standards of taste appeal.

On the front cover:
Rolled Roast with Spinach-Mushroom Stuffing (see recipe, page 27),
Italian Cheese Twists (see recipe, page 112), Italian Vegetable Toss (see recipe, page 151).

CONTENTS

THIS IS A SPECIAL COOKBOOK— SPECIAL BECAUSE THE PAGES ARE BRIMMING WITH RECIPES FROM CONTEST-WINNING COOKS. THEY'RE THE KINDS OF RECIPES YOU'LL ENJOY SERVING YOUR FAMILY OR GUESTS AT POTLUCKS AND SPECIAL OCCASIONS. YOU'RE SURE TO FIND SEVERAL RECIPES TO ADD TO YOUR REPERTOIRE OF "THE BEST I EVER COOKED."

ALL-OCCASION SNACKS AND BEVERAGES

WHATEVER THE OCCASION—AN AFTER-SCHOOL SNACK, A COCKTAIL PARTY, OR THE BETWEEN-MEAL MUNCHIES—QUIET YOUR GROWLING STOMACH OR RELIEVE YOUR PARCHED THROAT WITH ONE OF THESE EASY SNACK IDEAS, MAKE-AHEAD APPETIZERS, OR REFRESHING DRINKS.

So-Good Health Bars

2 tablespoons butter *or* margarine, softened
2 tablespoons brown sugar
1 tablespoon honey
1 tablespoon molasses
1 cup quick-cooking rolled oats
2 tablespoons whole wheat flour
⅔ cup snipped mixed dried fruit
1 tablespoon butter *or* margarine

1 slightly beaten egg
½ cup chopped walnuts
¼ cup packed brown sugar
¼ cup whole wheat flour
2 tablespoons toasted wheat germ
2 tablespoons unprocessed wheat bran
¾ teaspoon ground cinnamon
¼ teaspoon ground cloves

> 66 *They're great anytime. I enjoy them with milk for breakfast, in brown bag lunches, and as a midnight snack.* 99

For crust, in a mixing bowl stir together the 2 tablespoons butter or margarine, the 2 tablespoons brown sugar, honey, and molasses. Stir in oats and the 2 tablespoons whole wheat flour. Press into a greased 8x8x2-inch baking pan. Bake in a 350° oven for 5 minutes.

Meanwhile, combine dried fruit, the 1 tablespoon butter or margarine, and ½ cup *boiling water*. Let stand for 5 minutes. Stir in egg, nuts, the ¼ cup brown sugar, the ¼ cup whole wheat flour, wheat germ, wheat bran, cinnamon, cloves, and ½ teaspoon *salt*. Spread fruit mixture over crust. Bake in a 350° oven for 25 to 30 minutes more. Cool completely. Cut into bars. Makes about 20.

Russell Haymen, Lake Worth, Florida

Honey-Granola Bars

1 cup granola
1 cup quick-cooking rolled oats
½ cup all-purpose flour
½ cup flaked coconut
½ cup chopped almonds
½ cup raisins *or* semisweet chocolate pieces

¼ cup toasted wheat germ
¼ cup packed brown sugar
1 slightly beaten egg
½ cup honey
¼ cup butter *or* margarine, melted
1 teaspoon vanilla

Sandra kept two goals in mind as she developed this easy snackin' recipe—"It's gotta be tasty and chewy." We think she achieved both.

Combine granola, oats, flour, coconut, almonds, raisins, wheat germ, and brown sugar. Combine egg, honey, butter, and vanilla; add to granola mixture, stirring till well coated. Spread into a greased 12x7½x2-inch baking pan. Bake in a 325° oven for 30 to 35 minutes or till browned on edges. Cool. Cut into bars. Makes about 24.

Sandra C. Abbott, Potomac, Maryland

Shrimp-Oyster Cocktail

12 fresh *or* frozen medium shrimp, cooked and shelled, *or* one 6-ounce package frozen cooked shrimp
12 shucked oysters, halved
1 cup cocktail sauce
1 medium avocado, seeded, peeled, and chopped
1 small tomato, seeded and chopped (½ cup)
1 small onion, finely chopped

¼ cup lime juice
2 tablespoons snipped parsley
1 jalapeño pepper, seeded and chopped
½ teaspoon bottled hot pepper sauce
1 clove garlic, minced
Leaf lettuce
Assorted crackers
Lemon wedges

Cut shrimp into bite-size pieces, if necessary. In a large mixing bowl combine shrimp, oysters, cocktail sauce, avocado, tomato, onion, lime juice, parsley, jalapeño pepper, hot pepper sauce, and garlic. Cover and chill for several hours, stirring occasionally.

Serve in individual lettuce-lined dishes with crackers and lemon wedges. Makes 4 to 6 servings.

Anthony Lamar Bierly, Winona, Minnesota

Hot and Spicy Cranberry Dip

Challenged by a friend to re-create a recipe enjoyed at a party, Mrs. Greene kept experimenting till she came up with just the right flavor combination for this great make-ahead dip.

1 16-ounce can jellied cranberry sauce
3 tablespoons prepared horseradish
2 tablespoons honey
1 tablespoon Worcestershire sauce

1 tablespoon lemon juice
½ teaspoon ground red pepper
1 clove garlic, minced
Orange pieces
Pineapple tidbits
Vienna sausages, sliced

In a medium saucepan combine cranberry sauce, horseradish, honey, Worcestershire sauce, lemon juice, red pepper, and garlic. Bring to boiling. Reduce heat and simmer, covered, for 5 minutes. Serve warm with orange pieces, pineapple, and sausages. Makes 1½ cups dip.

Mrs. Paul Greene, Galesburg, Illinois

Pâté Maison Frank

4 slices bacon
1 pound boneless pork
8 ounces boneless veal
4 ounces prosciutto *or* fully
cooked ham
⅓ cup all-purpose flour
8 ounces chicken livers,
halved
¼ cup butter *or* margarine
2 eggs
½ cup brandy
1 large onion, cut up

1 medium carrot, cut up
4 cloves garlic
1 tablespoon paprika
1 teaspoon salt
1 teaspoon dried rosemary,
crushed
½ teaspoon ground allspice
½ teaspoon pepper
2 bay leaves
French bread
Assorted crackers

Take Frank's suggestion and serve his sophisticated pâté as a first-course appetizer with French bread, olives, and crisp raw vegetables.

In a skillet partially cook bacon. Drain bacon on paper towels and set aside. Discard drippings.

Using the coarse plate of a food grinder or a food processor, grind together pork, veal, and prosciutto or ham. (If using a food processor, grind *half* of the meat at a time.) Transfer meat mixture to a large mixing bowl and stir in flour. Set aside.

In the skillet cook chicken livers in butter or margarine till pink. In a blender container or food processor bowl combine livers, eggs, brandy, onion, carrot, garlic, paprika, salt, rosemary, allspice, and pepper. Cover and blend or process till smooth. Stir liver mixture into meat mixture.

Line the bottom and sides of a 9x5x3-inch loaf pan with the partially cooked bacon slices. Spoon the meat mixture into the pan. Top with bay leaves. Fold the ends of the bacon slices over the meat mixture. Cover the pan tightly with foil and place on a baking sheet. Bake in a 350° oven for 1½ hours.

Remove foil and drain off fat, but do not remove pâté from the pan. Place the pan on a wire rack. To compact the pâté, place several pieces of heavy-duty foil directly on pâté. Place 2 unopened 1-pound food cans or a brick on the foil. Cool to room temperature. Refrigerate overnight, leaving the weight atop the pâté.

To serve, remove weight, foil, and bay leaves. Unmold pâté onto a serving platter. Serve thinly sliced pâté with French bread or crackers. Makes 20 servings.

Frank Malone, Houston, Texas

Miniature Tex-Mex Egg Rolls

½ pound ground beef
¼ cup chopped onion
2 tablespoons chopped green pepper
½ of a 16-ounce can refried beans
¼ cup shredded cheddar cheese (1 ounce)

1 tablespoon catsup
1½ teaspoons chili powder
¼ teaspoon ground cumin
48 wonton skins
Cooking oil for deep-fat frying
Taco sauce

Nancy keeps her freezer stocked with these tasty egg rolls because they're so easy to reheat when she's in a hurry. When someone in her Mexican-food-loving clan wants a snack, she just pops them into a 350° oven, loosely covered, for 10 to 12 minutes or till heated through.

For filling, in a large skillet cook ground beef, onion, and green pepper till meat is brown and vegetables are tender. Drain off fat. Stir beans, cheese, catsup, chili powder, and cumin into meat mixture.

Position a wonton skin with 1 point toward you. Spoon a generous teaspoon of filling across the center of the skin. Fold bottom point of skin over filling. Tuck point under filling. Fold side corners over, forming an envelope shape. Roll up skin toward remaining corner. Moisten point; press to seal. Repeat with remaining filling and skins.

Fry egg rolls, a few at a time, in deep hot oil (375°) about 1 minute on each side or till golden. Use a slotted spoon to remove egg rolls. Drain on paper towels. Serve warm with taco sauce. Makes 48.

Nancy A. Crha, Oshkosh, Wisconsin

No-Rise Cheese Crescents

To stave off the after-school hunger pangs of her daughter, Karlis came up with these biscuitlike rolls. They're a great alternative to cookies.

1⅓ cups packaged biscuit mix
¼ cup apple juice
1 3-ounce package cream cheese, softened
1 tablespoon toasted wheat germ

¼ cup shredded cheddar cheese (1 ounce)
1 tablespoon butter *or* margarine, melted
1½ teaspoons toasted sesame seed

In a medium mixing bowl combine biscuit mix and apple juice, stirring till mixture clings together. Turn dough out onto a lightly floured surface and knead 10 to 12 strokes. Roll dough into a 10-inch circle. Spread cream cheese over *half* of the dough, then sprinkle with wheat germ. Fold over other half of dough. Roll to ¼-inch thickness, retaining the half-circle shape. Sprinkle with cheddar cheese, pressing lightly into dough. Cut dough into 12 wedges.

To shape, begin at wide end of wedge and roll toward point. Place, point down, on a greased baking sheet. Brush with butter or margarine. Sprinkle with sesame seed. Bake in a 425° oven for 10 to 12 minutes. Makes 12.

Karlis Hennrich, Austin, Texas

Quick Chicken Spread

Shape this no-bake spread into a ball, heart, log, or any design to fit your mood or the occasion.

2 cups chopped cooked chicken
½ cup sliced celery
3 tablespoons mayonnaise *or* salad dressing
2 tablespoons dry sherry
1 teaspoon lemon juice
¼ teaspoon salt
¼ teaspooon ground nutmeg
Dash pepper
3 sprigs parsley
½ cup finely chopped almonds, toasted
Assorted crackers *or* party rye bread

In a medium mixing bowl combine chicken, celery, mayonnaise or salad dressing, sherry, lemon juice, salt, nutmeg, pepper, and parsley. Transfer *half* of the chicken mixture to a blender container. Cover and blend till nearly smooth. Repeat with remaining chicken mixture. (*Or*, process the chicken mixture, all at once, in a food processor bowl.) Cover and chill for several hours or overnight.

Before serving, shape chicken mixture into a ball, then roll in nuts. Serve with crackers or rye bread. Makes 1 ball (about 2 cups).

Mrs. Lynn Blayney, Charlotte, North Carolina

Layered Taco Bean Dip

Helen put some of her favorite Tex-Mex ingredients to good use in this easy, creamy dip.

2 10½-ounce cans bean dip
1 1¼-ounce envelope taco seasoning mix
6 green onions, finely chopped
1 cup mayonnaise *or* salad dressing
1 cup dairy sour cream
½ cup sliced, pitted ripe olives
Corn chips *or* tortilla chips

In a medium mixing bowl stir together bean dip and taco seasoning mix. Spread mixture on a 10-inch tray or pie plate. Sprinkle with onions. Stir together mayonnaise or salad dressing and sour cream, then spread over onions. Top with olives. Cover and chill for several hours. Serve with chips. Makes 2½ cups.

Helen Meikle, Brookings, Oregon

Fiesta Appetizer Pie

This reminder from Sally— spread the sour cream completely over the avocado layer so the avocado doesn't darken while the pie is chilling.

3 small avocados, peeled, seeded, and cut up
1 tablespoon lemon juice
1 8-ounce carton dairy sour cream
1 8-ounce bottle taco sauce

2 green onions, finely chopped
1 cup shredded Monterey Jack cheese (4 ounces)
Tortilla chips

In a mixing bowl mash the avocados with the lemon juice. Spread mixture evenly in the bottom of a 9-inch pie plate. Spread sour cream evenly over avocado mixture. Spoon taco sauce over sour cream layer. Sprinkle green onions over taco sauce. Top with cheese. Cover and chill for several hours. Serve with chips. Makes about 4 cups.

Sally M. Flanzer, Little Rock, Arkansas

Lemon-Nut Wafer Canapés

1½ cups all-purpose flour
½ teaspoon salt
½ cup shortening
1 slightly beaten egg
½ teaspoon finely shredded lemon peel
2 tablespoons lemon juice
1 tablespoon milk

¼ cup finely chopped pecans
1 8-ounce package cream cheese, softened
3 tablespoons cocktail sauce
¼ teaspoon seasoned salt
Quartered cucumber slices, halved radish slices, and olive slices

For wafer dough, in a medium mixing bowl stir together flour and salt. Cut in shortening till combined. Add egg, lemon peel, lemon juice, and milk. Mix well. Stir in pecans. Shape dough into ¾-inch balls. Place on an ungreased baking sheet. Flatten slightly with the bottom of a floured glass. Bake in a 375° oven for 10 to 15 minutes. Cool on a wire rack.

In a mixer bowl beat cream cheese till fluffy. Beat in cocktail sauce and seasoned salt. Cover and chill.

To serve, pipe about *1 teaspoon* cheese mixture onto each wafer. Garnish each with a slice of cucumber, radish, or olive. Makes 36.

Mrs. Andrew Petersen, Marietta, Georgia

MARY MARGARET BARROW, FREDONIA, ALA.

In Fredonia, Alabama (population 150 families), Mary Margaret and Joseph Barrow have a simple life-style that many big-city dwellers would envy. Living in a comfortable wood frame house situated on West Point Lake under tall pine trees, the Barrows have retired to do what they love best—boating, traveling in their RV, and being active in church, community, and camping clubs. It also means looking after two kittens, a rabbit, and a duck, and tending to the tiger lilies, wild persimmons, grapes, azaleas, and blueberries.

Whatever you've heard about the charm and hospitality found

south of the Mason-Dixon line is certainly true for the Barrows. Yes, Mary cooks grits and makes great biscuits, but her cooking goes beyond those clichés. "I think I've been interested in cooking practically all of my life," says Mary, in her soft Alabama drawl. "When I was young, I lived on my grandmother's farm during the summers and spent many hours watching her cook. Everything was made from scratch on a wood-burning stove."

Today, Mary seems to have done a superb job of combining her grandmother's cooking philosophy with her own. A retired dietitian, she's interested both in nutrition and trying unusual recipes. But unlike her ancestors, Mary doesn't spend hours in the kitchen. She's an efficient planner and relies on make-ahead specialties for the entertaining and club activities that she and Joe enjoy.

When it's necessary, she will send out for some part of the

menu, like the exceptional fried chicken from Ms. Mac's restaurant down the road. And two appliances—a food processor and a microwave—are her time- and effort-saving mainstays. "We got the microwave accidentally," confesses Mary. "The ovens we wanted for this house were out of production, so they loaned me a microwave to cook with till the ovens came. And I kept it."

(continued)

MARY MARGARET BARROW, FREDONIA, ALA.

Potlucks with her local Home-maker's Club at the Fredonia Community Church are an opportunity for Mary and her friends to try out new recipes and catch up on local news. But the biggest event of the year is the Community Club's annual barbecue fund-raiser. Part of the menu consists of Brunswick

> *At our club suppers, everyone expects me to bring something special, so I try not to disappoint them.*

Even their motor home is equipped with a mini-microwave, to meet the challenge of cooking during cross-country or weekend camping trips with their club, the Valley Vagabonds. Joe says, "Since my wife's on vacation, too, we try to eat light with one big meal a day." The families often share mealtime chores, deciding ahead on the contributions they'll make. For the other meals, Mary makes up menus, then tailors her shopping list to them. "I prefer to do most of the cooking ahead at home; then I warm it in the microwave in our camper," says Mary.

Stew for 1,800, and if you're interested, you'd better buy your ticket early. According to Joe, the recipe for the stew is a "secret formula" and takes two days to make properly, even with the men helping out. "They cook chicken first, till it's real tender," Joe relates. "Then the meat is ground, along with ham and corn. Brown sugar, vinegar, hot sauce, and tomatoes are added." The ladies do a lot of tasting and last-minute seasoning just before the crowds appear. The result is a deliciously hearty stew made for biscuits and corn bread. It's the epitome of all things Southern—just like the Barrows.

MARY MARGARET BARROW, FREDONIA, ALA.

Mary had never submitted a recipe to *Better Homes & Gardens®* until she decided to share her Nut-and-Raisin Spread. It was an instant hit with the food editors.

This healthful snack spread, a result of Mary's adventurous experimentation with ingredients on hand, is a favorite with her friends and family. And it's evidence of Mary's reliance on her food processor, a Christmas gift she received one year from her daughters. "I use my food processor just about every day," Mary admits. Besides this recipe, she finds it exceptionally handy for chopping vegetables that go into salads and casseroles.

Nut-and-Raisin Spread

For a pretty presentation, halve an orange with a scalloped cutter. Then hollow out the halves and use them as colorful containers for this spread.

1 medium orange, quartered and seeded
1 cup pecans
1 15-ounce carton (2½ cups) raisins
¾ cup mayonnaise *or* salad dressing
Sliced apples *or* pears

In food processor bowl* combine quartered orange and nuts. Cover and process with on/off turns till finely chopped. Add *half* of the raisins and all of the mayonnaise or salad dressing. Cover and process till raisins are chopped. Add remaining raisins. Cover and process till chopped. Transfer spread mixture to a covered container. Store, tightly covered, in the refrigerator up to 2 weeks. *Or,* seal, label, and freeze up to 2 months. To serve, spread on sliced apples or pears. Makes 3½ cups.
*Note: If you don't have a food processor, run all the ingredients *except* mayonnaise or salad dressing through the fine plate of a food grinder. Stir in mayonnaise or salad dressing.

Cheese and Spinach Puffs

1 10-ounce package frozen chopped spinach
½ cup chopped onion
2 slightly beaten eggs
½ cup grated Parmesan cheese
½ cup shredded cheddar cheese (2 ounces)
½ cup blue cheese salad dressing
¼ cup butter *or* margarine, melted
⅛ teaspoon garlic powder
1 8½-ounce package corn muffin mix

Your guests are bound to give these morsels a four-star rating.

In a saucepan cook spinach and onion according to spinach package directions. Drain well, pressing out excess liquid. In a medium mixing bowl, stir together eggs, cheeses, salad dressing, butter or margarine, and garlic powder. Stir in muffin mix and spinach mixture till combined. Cover and chill thoroughly. Shape spinach mixture into 1-inch balls. Cover and chill till serving time. (*Or,* place balls in a freezer container. Seal, label, and freeze.)

Before serving, place balls on a baking sheet. Bake chilled balls in a 350° oven for 10 to 12 minutes or till light brown. (Bake frozen balls for 12 to 15 minutes.) Serve warm. Makes about 60.

Elaine W. Sanders, Blackstone, Virginia

Apricot Burritos

1 cup water
1 6-ounce package dried apricots, snipped
¼ cup sugar
¼ cup packed brown sugar
¼ teaspoon ground cinnamon
¼ teaspoon ground nutmeg
20 to 25 6-inch flour tortillas
Cooking oil

In a small saucepan combine water, apricots, sugar, brown sugar, cinnamon, and nutmeg. Bring to boiling. Reduce heat and simmer, uncovered, for 10 to 15 minutes or till fruit is tender and mixture is thickened, stirring occasionally. Cool.

To assemble, spoon about *1 tablespoon* of the apricot mixture along one edge of *each* tortilla. Roll tortilla up. Keep tortillas covered with a damp towel before and after filling.

In a heavy 12-inch skillet heat about ¾ inch cooking oil to 350°. Place 5 tortillas, seam side down, in hot oil. Cook about 2 minutes or till tortillas are golden, turning once. Drain tortillas on paper towels. Repeat with remaining tortillas. Serve warm or cool. Makes 20 to 25.

Mrs. LaVerne Bowman, Patterson, California

Dreamy Coconut Shake

½ pint coconut ice cream
1 8¼-ounce can crushed
  pineapple
¾ cup light cream *or* milk
½ of a 6-ounce can (⅓ cup)
  frozen tangerine *or*
  orange juice concentrate

1 small banana, cut into
  chunks
3 or 4 ice cubes
  Toasted coconut (optional)

Mrs. Ross gets rave reviews when she serves this top-notch tropical shake on warm summer days.

In a blender container combine ice cream, *undrained* pineapple, light cream or milk, frozen concentrate, and banana. Cover and blend till combined. With blender running, add ice cubes, one at a time, through hole in lid, blending till mixture is thick and foamy. Serve immediately in chilled glasses. Garnish with toasted coconut, if desired. Makes 4 (8-ounce) servings.

Mrs. L. K. Ross, Sonora, California

Cranberry-Cinnamon Punch

This festive punch was first served at the December wedding of Judith's sister. It's been one of their favorite holiday traditions ever since.

2 cups fresh cranberries
8 cups water
½ cup sugar
¼ cup red cinnamon candies
3 whole cloves
½ cup orange juice
2 tablespoons lemon juice
Orange *or* lemon slices, quartered

In a large saucepan combine cranberries with *3 cups* of water. Bring to boiling. Reduce heat and simmer, uncovered, about 5 minutes or till cranberry skins pop. Remove from heat. Cool. Press cranberries through a food mill or sieve. Strain the cranberry juice through several layers of cheesecloth to remove small seeds.

In a 4½-quart Dutch oven combine cranberry juice, remaining water, sugar, candies, and cloves. Bring to boiling. Reduce heat and boil gently for 5 minutes, stirring to dissolve candies. Remove cloves, then stir in orange juice and lemon juice. Serve hot or cold. Garnish with orange or lemon slices. Makes about 10 (6-ounce) servings.

Judith Janzen, Salem, Oregon

Rhubarb-and-Lemon Punch

Irene's mother didn't want any of her flourishing rhubarb crop going to waste, so she devised this tart and refreshing thirst quencher.

1 small lemon
6 cups fresh *or* frozen chopped rhubarb
4 cups water
2 cups unsweetened pineapple juice
1 0.67-ounce envelope low-calorie lemonade soft drink mix
Ice cubes

Using a lemon zester or vegetable peeler, remove the yellow portion of the peel from the lemon. Cut peel into thin slices.

In a large saucepan combine rhubarb, water, and lemon peel. Bring mixture to boiling. Reduce heat and simmer, uncovered, for 10 minutes. Carefully strain rhubarb mixture, *one-third* at a time, through a sieve, pressing with a spoon to remove liquid. Discard the pulp. Stir pineapple juice and lemonade mix into the rhubarb liquid. Cover and chill. Serve over ice. (*Or,* freeze and serve as a slush.) Makes 12 (4-ounce) servings.

Irene Thearle, Neenah, Wisconsin

Cantaloupe Frost

Take the edge off a sultry summer night by sipping on one of these frothy fruit coolers.

2 cups cubed cantaloupe
  or honeydew melon
  (½ of a medium melon)
2 cups cold milk

¼ teaspoon ground ginger
1 pint orange sherbet
  Orange peel curls
  (optional)

Freeze melon cubes till firm. In a blender container combine frozen melon cubes, milk, and ginger. Cover and blend till slushy. With blender running, add sherbet, a spoonful at a time, through hole in lid, blending till thoroughly combined. Stop machine to scrape down sides as necessary. Serve immediately in chilled glasses. Garnish with orange peel curls, if desired. Makes 6 (8-ounce) servings.

Patricia Drake, Leverett, Massachusetts

Apple-Raisin Shake

Janet takes advantage of her state's abundant apple crop when she cooks, as evidenced by the applesauce in this extra-thick shake.

1 cup milk
¼ cup raisins
1 cup vanilla ice cream

1 cup applesauce, chilled
  Apple slices (optional)

In a blender container combine milk and raisins. Cover and blend till nearly smooth. Add ice cream and applesauce. Cover and blend till combined. Serve immediately in chilled glasses. Garnish with apple slices, if desired. Makes 3 (8-ounce) servings.

Janet L. Keeth, Wapato, Washington

COMPANY-SPECIAL ENTRÉES

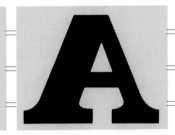

A SPECIAL OCCASION WARRANTS A SPECIAL MEAL—ONE THAT GOES A STEP BEYOND THE EVERYDAY. IT CAN BE AS SIMPLE AS TAKING A LITTLE EXTRA TIME TO ROLL UP A YUMMY STUFFING IN A ROAST . . . OR MAYBE IT'S INTRODUCING YOUR GUESTS TO ORIENTAL FOOD AT A STIR-FRIED DINNER. BEFORE YOU PREPARE THAT MEMORABLE MEAL, GLANCE THROUGH THIS CHAPTER AND BE INSPIRED BY THESE AWARD-WINNING MAIN DISHES.

Cantonese Beef Stir-Fry

To help satisfy her "yen" for stir-fried Chinese foods, Carol came up with this palate-pleaser.

1 pound boneless beef sirloin	1 tablespoon cornstarch
¼ cup soy sauce	3 tablespoons cooking oil
2 tablespoons cream sherry	4 cups broccoli flowerets
2 tablespoons hoisin sauce	3 medium carrots, thinly
2 teaspoons sugar	bias sliced
¾ teaspoon chili paste	2 cups fresh pea pods
¾ teaspoon sesame oil	½ cup sliced green onion
⅛ teaspoon whole aniseed	½ cup cashews
½ cup water	Hot cooked rice

Partially freeze beef. Thinly slice across the grain into bite-size strips. For marinade, in a mixing bowl stir together soy sauce, sherry, hoisin sauce, sugar, chili paste, sesame oil, and aniseed. Add beef, stirring to coat well. Cover and marinate in refrigerator for 2 to 3 hours, stirring occasionally. Drain well, reserving marinade. Stir together water and cornstarch, then stir into reserved marinade. Set aside.

Preheat a wok or large skillet over high heat. Add cooking oil. (Add more oil as necessary during cooking.) Stir-fry broccoli and carrots in hot oil for 4 minutes. Add pea pods and green onion. Stir-fry for 2 minutes more. Remove vegetables from wok.

Add *half* of the beef to the hot wok or skillet. Stir-fry for 2 to 3 minutes or till done. Remove beef. Stir-fry remaining beef for 2 to 3 minutes. Return all beef to wok. Push from center of wok or skillet.

Stir marinade, then add to center of wok or skillet. Cook and stir till thickened and bubbly, then cook and stir 1 minute more. Return vegetables to wok or skillet. Stir ingredients together to coat with sauce. Cook and stir for 1 minute. Stir in cashews. Serve immediately over rice. Makes 6 servings.

Carol Happley, Jordan, Minnesota

Rolled Roast with Spinach-Mushroom Stuffing

Like most of us when we entertain, Sharon hates to be stuck in the kitchen with last-minute preparations. With that in mind, she came up with this impressive main dish that can be prepared up to 24 hours in advance.

1 2-pound beef eye of round roast
2 cups loosely packed fresh spinach leaves
8 ounces fresh mushrooms
1 slightly beaten egg
2 tablespoons butter *or* margarine

2 tablespoons grated Parmesan cheese
½ teaspoon garlic salt
Sliced mushrooms (optional)
Spinach leaves (optional)
Creamy Yogurt Sauce

To butterfly roast, make a single lengthwise cut down the center of the meat, cutting to within ½ inch of the other side. Make 2 more cuts, 1 on each side of the first cut, cutting through the thickest portions of the meat to within ½ inch of the other side. Cover with clear plastic wrap. Pound with a meat mallet to ½- to ¾-inch thickness.

For stuffing, finely chop spinach and mushrooms. Steam chopped vegetables for 4 minutes. Drain well, pressing out liquid. Stir in egg, butter or margarine, Parmesan cheese, and garlic salt. Spread stuffing over roast. Roll roast up, jelly-roll style, starting from one of the short sides. Tie with string to secure. Cover and chill up to 24 hours.

Insert a meat thermometer near center of roast. Roast in a 325° oven about 1¼ hours or till thermometer registers 140°. (*Or,* in a covered grill arrange preheated coals around a drip pan. Test for *medium-hot* coals above pan. Place roast on rack over drip pan but not over coals. Lower grill hood. Grill for 1 to 1¼ hours or till meat thermometer registers 140°.) Cover with foil and let stand 10 minutes.

To serve, transfer roast to a serving platter. Slice meat thinly. Garnish with sliced mushrooms and spinach leaves, if desired. Serve with Creamy Yogurt Sauce. Makes 8 servings.

Creamy Yogurt Sauce: Combine ½ cup plain *yogurt,* 4 teaspoons *all-purpose flour,* ½ teaspoon instant *beef bouillon granules,* and ⅛ teaspoon *white pepper or* freshly ground *black pepper.* Cover and chill till serving time. Before serving, stir ½ cup *light cream* into yogurt mixture. Cook and stir till thickened and bubbly, then cook and stir 1 minute more. Sprinkle sauce with a little *paprika* before serving. Makes about 1 cup.

Sharon Stilwell, Des Moines, Iowa

Rolled Roast with Spinach-Mushroom Stuffing, Creamy Yogurt Sauce, Orange-Almond Pilaf (see recipe, page 140)

Garden Steak Rolls

1½ pounds boneless beef round steak
3 slices bacon
1 9-ounce package frozen whole green beans, thawed, *or* 2 cups fresh green beans
3 small carrots, cut into julienne strips
Garlic powder
1 10¼-ounce can beef gravy
Mashed potatoes (optional)

Cut meat into 6 portions. Pound each portion to ¼-inch thickness. Cut bacon in half crosswise. In a 10-inch skillet cook bacon just till done. Drain on paper towels, reserving drippings in skillet. Place 1 piece of bacon and several green beans and carrot strips on each meat portion. Sprinkle with salt, pepper, and garlic powder. Roll up each meat portion jelly-roll style. Secure with wooden toothpicks.

Brown meat rolls on all sides in hot drippings. Drain off fat. Pour gravy over meat rolls. Cover and simmer for 40 minutes. Uncover and cook for 10 to 15 minutes more or till gravy is thickened and meat is tender. Remove toothpicks from rolls. Serve with mashed potatoes, if desired. Makes 6 servings.

Pamela Biagini, South Lake Tahoe, California

Stuffed Steak

Steamed broccoli and fluted mushrooms make attractive accompaniments for this special-occasion entrée.

1 beef top loin steak, cut 1½ to 2 inches thick (about 1 pound)
2 tablespoons chopped onion
2 tablespoons chopped mushrooms
2 teaspoons butter *or* margarine
½ cup diced fully cooked ham
2 teaspoons fine dry bread crumbs
2 teaspoons snipped parsley
2 teaspoons cooking oil
Dash pepper
½ slice Swiss cheese (½ ounce)

Cut a deep slit horizontally in steak to form a pocket. Set aside. For stuffing, cook onion and mushrooms in butter or margarine till tender but not brown. Stir in ham, bread crumbs, parsley, oil, and pepper. Cook and stir for 2 minutes more. Place cheese in meat pocket, then spoon stuffing into pocket. Secure pocket with skewers.

Place steak on an unheated rack in a broiler pan. Broil 3 to 4 inches from heat to desired doneness, turning once (allow 18 to 20 minutes total time for medium). Makes 2 to 3 servings.

Lori Anderson Engebretson, St. Cloud, Minnesota

Meatballs in Rosé-Tomato Sauce

1 beaten egg
2 small apples, peeled and shredded (1 cup)
¼ cup finely chopped onion
¼ cup fine dry seasoned bread crumbs
⅛ teaspoon garlic powder
1 pound lean ground beef
1 tablespoon cooking oil

½ cup chopped onion
¾ cup rosé wine
¾ cup water
1 6-ounce can tomato paste
¼ teaspoon dried rosemary, crushed
¼ teaspoon dried basil, crushed
Hot cooked noodles

Mama mia! A little garlic bread and a vegetable vinaigrette salad round out this award-winning Italian entrée.

Combine egg, apple, the ¼ cup onion, bread crumbs, garlic powder, ¾ teaspoon *salt,* and ⅛ teaspoon *pepper.* Add ground beef and mix well. Shape into 1½-inch meatballs. Brown meatballs, *half* at a time, in hot oil. Remove from skillet and set aside. Reserve drippings in pan.

Cook the ½ cup onion in drippings till tender but not brown. Drain off fat. Stir in wine, water, tomato paste, rosemary, and basil. Return meatballs to skillet. Bring to boiling. Reduce heat and simmer, covered, for 15 to 20 minutes or till meatballs are done. Serve over hot cooked noodles. Makes 4 servings.

Mrs. Irene Shanahan, Sound Beach, New York

Poor Boy Fillets

5 slices bacon
1 pound lean ground beef
Lemon pepper
¼ cup grated Parmesan cheese
1 2-ounce can mushroom stems and pieces, drained

3 tablespoons finely chopped pimiento-stuffed olives
2 tablespoons finely chopped onion
2 tablespoons finely chopped green pepper

66 Guests love the fillets, and they're a great way to dress up ground beef. 99

Partially cook bacon. Drain on paper towels. On a piece of waxed paper pat ground beef into a 12x7½-inch rectangle. Sprinkle with lemon pepper and Parmesan cheese. Combine mushrooms, olives, onion, and green pepper. Spread evenly over meat. Use waxed paper to start rolling up meat jelly-roll style, beginning with one of the short sides. Carefully cut meat into five 1½-inch-thick slices. Wrap partially cooked bacon strips around each meat slice. Secure bacon strips with wooden toothpicks.

Place meat on an unheated rack in a broiler pan. Broil 4 inches from heat to desired doneness, turning once (allow about 11 minutes total time for medium). Remove toothpicks before serving. Serves 5.

John Darby, Tulsa, Oklahoma

Mustard Beef and Mushrooms

> 66 *I got the inspiration for this entrée from one of my guests who loves stroganoff.* 99

1 3-pound boneless beef eye of round
2 tablespoons butter *or* margarine
½ cup thinly sliced green onion
1 tablespoon butter *or* margarine
2¼ cups sliced fresh mushrooms
¼ cup water
¼ cup light cream *or* milk
½ teaspoon instant beef bouillon granules
1 tablespoon all-purpose flour
1 tablespoon prepared mustard *or* Dijon-style mustard
Dash pepper
½ cup plain yogurt
Parslied Rice

Cut a 1-pound piece of meat off the roast. Seal, label, and freeze remaining roast for another use. Cut the 1-pound portion of meat into eight ¼-inch-thick slices. In a 12-inch skillet brown meat quickly on both sides in the 2 tablespoons butter or margarine for 1 to 1½ minutes per side. Remove meat from skillet. Keep warm.

For sauce, cook green onion in the 1 tablespoon butter or margarine just till tender. Stir in mushrooms and cook 2 minutes more. Stir in water, cream or milk, and bouillon granules. Cook and stir till granules are dissolved. Stir flour, mustard, and pepper into yogurt. Slowly add yogurt mixture to skillet, stirring constantly. Cook and stir till thickened and bubbly, then cook and stir 1 minute more. Serve meat and sauce with Parslied Rice. Makes 4 servings.

Parslied Rice: In a saucepan combine 1⅓ cups cold *water*, ⅔ cup long grain *rice*, 2 teaspoons *butter or margarine*, and ¾ teaspoon *salt*. Cover with a tight-fitting lid. Bring to boiling. Reduce heat and simmer, covered, for 15 minutes. Do not lift cover. Remove from heat. Let stand, covered, for 10 minutes. Stir in ¼ cup snipped *parsley*. If desired, press *one-fourth* of the rice mixture into a 1-cup mold. Invert onto a baking sheet. Repeat with remaining rice, making 4 rice molds. Cover and keep warm till ready to serve.

Pat Teberg, Des Moines, Iowa

> **❝** *I decided I had to find something to make other than Eggplant Parmesan. I experimented using what I had from the garden. The results turned out to be delicious.* **❞**

Italian Eggplant Beef Stew

1½ pounds beef stew meat, cut into 1-inch cubes
2 tablespoons cooking oil
3 medium tomatoes, peeled and cut into wedges
1 cup chopped onion
1 teaspoon chili powder
¼ teaspoon dried parsley flakes
¼ teaspoon dried oregano, crushed
1 clove garlic, minced

1 cup beef broth
1 large potato, peeled and cubed (1 cup)
1 cup dry white wine
2 cups coarsely chopped peeled eggplant
1 cup chopped green pepper
¾ cup sliced fresh mushrooms
½ cup seeded and coarsely chopped jalapeño pepper
¼ cup grated Parmesan cheese

In a Dutch oven brown *half* of the beef at a time in hot oil. Drain off fat. Return all meat to Dutch oven. Add tomatoes, onion, chili powder, parsley flakes, oregano, garlic, ½ teaspoon *salt*, and ¼ teaspoon *pepper*. Stir in broth. Bring to boiling. Reduce heat and simmer, covered, for 45 minutes. Stir in potato and wine. Simmer, covered, for 10 minutes more. Stir in eggplant, green pepper, mushrooms, and jalapeño pepper. Simmer, covered, for 15 to 20 minutes more or till meat and vegetables are tender. Stir in cheese and heat through. Makes 6 to 8 servings.

Arthur Signorella, D.D.S., Du Bois, Pennsylvania

Grilled Lamb Burgers

Nancy's effort to improve upon a dish she had tasted at a restaurant resulted in this moist and flavorful burger.

¼ cup bulgur
½ cup snipped parsley
2 tablespoons finely chopped onion
1 tablespoon dry red wine
½ teaspoon snipped fresh mint *or* ⅛ teaspoon dried mint, crushed
¼ teaspoon ground allspice
1 small clove garlic, minced
1 pound ground lamb
 Lettuce leaves (optional)
2 large pita bread rounds, halved crosswise
 Chopped cucumber
 Plain yogurt

Soak bulgur in warm water for 1 hour. Drain well. In a medium mixing bowl combine bulgur with parsley, onion, wine, mint, allspice, garlic, and ½ teaspoon *salt.* Add lamb and mix well.

Shape meat mixture into four ¾-inch-thick patties. Grill patties, on an uncovered grill, directly over *medium-hot* coals to desired doneness, turning once (allow 10 to 12 minutes total for medium).

Serve burgers in lettuce-lined pita halves with cucumber and yogurt. Makes 4 servings.

Nancy Drake, Sylvania, Ohio

Spicy Fruited Lamb

Restrain yourself from peeking into that slow cooker 'cause even the quickest glance cools the food several degrees.

4 lamb shanks, halved crosswise
¼ cup all-purpose flour
2 tablespoons cooking oil
½ cup dried apricots
½ cup dried, pitted prunes, halved
½ cup light raisins
¼ cup sugar
¼ cup dry red wine
2 tablespoons vinegar
2 tablespoons lemon juice
1 tablespoon honey
½ teaspoon ground allspice
½ teaspoon ground cinnamon
1 tablespoon cornstarch
1 tablespoon cold water
 Hot cooked rice

Sprinkle shanks with a little salt and pepper, then coat with flour. In a Dutch oven brown shanks on all sides in hot oil. Drain well. In a 4-quart electric crockery cooker combine apricots, prunes, raisins, sugar, wine, vinegar, lemon juice, honey, allspice, and cinnamon. Place shanks on top of fruit mixture. Cover cooker. Cook on low-heat setting for 9 to 10 hours. Remove shanks and keep warm.

For sauce, strain cooking juices, reserving fruit. Skim fat from juices. Measure juices. Add enough water to make 1¼ cups liquid. Transfer to a saucepan. Combine cornstarch and water. Stir into saucepan. Cook and stir till thickened and bubbly, then cook and stir 2 minutes more. Stir in reserved fruit. Serve over rice. Serves 4 to 6.

Theodora Wesselmann, Columbia, Missouri

Cod Potato Salad In Green Mayonnaise

Serve a loaf of crusty French bread with this refreshing whole-meal salad.

1 pound fresh *or* frozen cod fillets
3½ cups sliced, peeled, cooked potatoes
2 hard-cooked eggs, chopped
4 *or* 5 anchovy fillets
1 cup mayonnaise *or* salad dressing
⅓ cup snipped parsley
3 tablespoons snipped chives *or* sliced green onion
6 pitted green olives
1 tablespoon milk
½ teaspoon dry mustard

Thaw fish, if frozen. Measure thickness of fish. In a 10-inch skillet bring *water* (about 1 to 2 inches deep) just to boiling. Add fillets. Return just to boiling. Reduce heat and simmer, covered, till fish flakes easily (allow 4 to 6 minutes per ½-inch thickness of fish). Remove from skillet; pat dry. Coarsely break up fish with a fork.

Combine potatoes and eggs. Set aside. For dressing, pat anchovies dry. In a blender container or food processor bowl place anchovies, mayonnaise, parsley, chives, olives, milk, and mustard. Cover and blend or process till smooth. Fold dressing into potato mixture. Add fish, stirring gently. Cover and chill at least 3 hours. Serves 6.

Mrs. Gloria McAdams, New York, New York

Coconut Fish Fillets

1 pound fresh *or* frozen sole fillets *or* other fish fillets
1 beaten egg
⅓ cup cornflake crumbs
⅓ cup flaked coconut
2 tablespoons cooking oil
¼ cup butter *or* margarine, melted
2 tablespoons lemon juice
1 tablespoon snipped parsley
1 teaspoon sugar
Lemon twists (optional)
Green onion brushes (optional)

Thaw fish, if frozen. In a shallow dish combine egg and ¼ teaspoon *salt.* In another shallow dish combine cornflake crumbs and coconut. Pat fillets dry with paper towels. Dip fillets into the egg mixture, coating both sides. Coat both sides of fillets with crumb mixture.

In a large skillet heat oil. Arrange fillets in a single layer in skillet. Fry fillets in hot oil about 3 minutes on each side or till fish flakes easily when tested with a fork. Transfer to a serving platter.

Meanwhile, combine melted butter or margarine, lemon juice, parsley, and sugar. Pour over fillets. Garnish with lemon twists and green onion brushes, if desired. Makes 4 servings.

Carol A. Schlotterbeck, Longwood, Florida

Italian-Style Seafood Creole

½ cup cubed peeled eggplant
½ cup thinly sliced zucchini
½ cup sliced fresh mushrooms
½ cup chopped onion
½ of a medium green pepper, sliced
¼ cup chopped celery
2 tablespoons cooking oil
1 16-ounce can tomatoes, cut up
½ cup dry red wine
1 tablespoon soy sauce
1 teaspoon Italian seasoning
1 teaspoon dried oregano, crushed

¼ teaspoon ground sage
¼ teaspoon garlic powder
⅛ teaspoon pepper
½ cup peeled and deveined shrimp, cut up
2 tablespoons capers, drained
1 6½-ounce can tuna, drained
¼ cup pimiento-stuffed olives, halved
Hot cooked rice (optional)

> ❝ *Italian seasonings make most dishes taste very good, so I thought I'd try adding them to fish.* ❞

In a large saucepan cook eggplant, zucchini, mushrooms, onion, green pepper, and celery in hot oil till tender. Stir in *undrained* tomatoes, wine, soy sauce, Italian seasoning, oregano, sage, garlic powder, and pepper. Simmer, uncovered, for 30 minutes. Stir in shrimp and capers. Simmer, uncovered, for 8 minutes. Stir in tuna and olives and heat through. Serve in bowls with rice, if desired. Makes 4 servings.

John LaSusa, Elk Grove, Illinois

Easy Fish Florentine

1 pound fresh *or* individually frozen fish fillets
1 12-ounce package frozen spinach soufflé, thawed
⅓ cup crushed rich round crackers (about 8 crackers)

2 tablespoons toasted wheat germ
2 tablespoons grated Parmesan cheese
Lemon wedges (optional)

A package of frozen spinach soufflé makes this main dish surprisingly simple to prepare.

Thaw fish, if frozen. Arrange fillets in a single layer in a 12x7½x2-inch baking dish. Spoon thawed soufflé over fish. In a small mixing bowl stir together crushed crackers, wheat germ, and Parmesan cheese. Sprinkle over all.
    Bake, uncovered, in a 400° oven for 15 to 20 minutes or till fish flakes easily when tested with a fork. Garnish with lemon wedges, if desired. Makes 4 servings.

Daphne Doerr, Glendale, Arizona

Sausage Oriental Stir-Fry

1 cup water
¼ cup soy sauce
2 tablespoons cornstarch
2 tablespoons cooking oil
1 pound hot Italian sausage links, cut into 1-inch pieces
8 ounces fresh mushrooms, sliced
1 cup thinly sliced daikon
1 medium green pepper, cut into ¾-inch pieces
3 green onions, sliced
4 cups torn Swiss chard
2 cups fresh bean sprouts *or* one 16-ounce can bean sprouts, drained
1⅓ cups fresh pea pods

> 66 *This recipe is for those who like highly seasoned foods. It packs a spicy wallop.* 99

For sauce, combine water and soy sauce. Stir in cornstarch. Set aside. Preheat a wok or large skillet over high heat. Add cooking oil. (Add more oil as necessary.) Stir-fry sausage in hot oil for 10 minutes. Add mushrooms, daikon, green pepper, and green onions. Stir-fry for 5 minutes. Add Swiss chard, bean sprouts, and pea pods. Stir-fry for 3 minutes more or till sausage is cooked and vegetables are crisp-tender. Push sausage and vegetables from center of wok. Stir sauce; add to wok or skillet. Cook and stir till thickened and bubbly, then cook and stir 2 minutes more. Stir to coat with sauce. Serves 4.

Bob Lane, Hoosick Falls, New York

Country Ribs with Waldorf Gravy

3½ to 4 pounds pork country-style ribs, trimmed of excess fat
1 tablespoon cooking oil
¾ cup chopped onion
1 10¾-ounce can condensed cream of celery soup
½ of a 6-ounce can (⅓ cup) frozen apple juice concentrate, thawed
½ teaspoon poultry seasoning
¼ teaspoon ground cinnamon
1 bay leaf
1 cup chopped apple
½ cup chopped celery
½ cup raisins
¼ cup evaporated milk
¼ cup chopped walnuts
Hot cooked rice

In a large skillet brown ribs on all sides in hot oil. Remove ribs from skillet and drain, reserving 1 tablespoon drippings. Cook onion in drippings till tender but not brown. Stir in soup, apple juice concentrate, poultry seasoning, cinnamon, and bay leaf. Return ribs to skillet. Simmer, covered, for 45 minutes.

Stir in apple, celery, and raisins. Simmer, uncovered, for 15 minutes more. Stir in evaporated milk and heat through. Stir in walnuts. Remove bay leaf. Serve with hot cooked rice. Makes 6 to 8 servings.

F. Hill, Long Beach, California

Five-Spice Pork Roast

Pick up five-spice powder in an Oriental food store or a large supermarket.

1 4-pound pork shoulder roast
1½ teaspoons five-spice powder
2 tablespoons cooking oil
¼ cup chopped onion
1 to 2 tablespoons sesame seed
1 clove garlic, minced
1 cup apple juice *or* cider
½ cup dry white wine
3 tablespoons soy sauce
2 tablespoons cold water
4 teaspoons cornstarch

Rub roast with five-spice powder. In a 4-quart Dutch oven brown meat in hot oil. Remove meat from Dutch oven and add onion, sesame seed, and garlic. Cook and stir for 2 to 3 minutes or till sesame seed is golden. Stir in apple juice or cider, wine, and soy sauce. Return roast to Dutch oven. Bring mixture to boiling. Reduce heat and simmer, covered, for 2½ to 3 hours or till meat is tender. Transfer meat to a serving platter and keep warm.

Skim fat from pan juices. Add water, if necessary, to measure 1½ cups liquid. Return juices to Dutch oven. Stir together cold water and cornstarch. Stir into juices in Dutch oven. Cook and stir till thickened and bubbly, then cook and stir 2 minutes more. Spoon over roast. Makes 8 servings.

Ms. Carley Lindsay, Iowa City, Iowa

Grilled Seeded Roast

Inspired by an herbed roast she had purchased while traveling through Pennsylvania, Anne experimented with various seed combinations till she hit on the flavor she was after.

1 3½-pound boneless pork top loin roast
3 tablespoons soy sauce
2 tablespoons aniseed
2 tablespoons fennel seed
2 tablespoons caraway seed
2 tablespoons dillseed

Trim any excess fat from roast. Rub soy sauce over surface with your fingers. In a 15x10x1-inch baking pan combine aniseed, fennel, caraway, and dillseed. Roll meat in seeds to coat evenly. If necessary, press the seeds onto the surface of the roast to make them stick. Wrap meat in foil. Refrigerate for 1 to 2 hours or overnight.

Remove foil. Insert meat thermometer near center of roast. In a covered grill arrange preheated coals around a drip pan. Test for *medium* heat above pan. Place roast on rack over drip pan but not over coals. Lower grill hood. Grill for 2 to 2½ hours or till thermometer registers 170°. Makes 12 to 14 servings.

Anne Torda, Bedford, Texas

JOHN F. CARAFOLI, SAGAMORE BEACH, MASS.

About 60 easy miles from Boston is the picturesque town of Cape Cod. Nestled at the west end of the Cape, with its own white picket fences, rambling homes, and restful oceanfront, lies the village of Sagamore Beach. It's here that John Carafoli, a writer, bed-and-breakfast inn owner, and cook extraordinaire, lives his fascinating life. The area has been the inspiration for John's artistic endeavors, his healthy life-style, and his undeniable enthusiasm about food.

> 66 *Food to me is like design work—I think of it in terms of colors, textures, shapes, and forms.* 99

"I've been cooking since I was twelve," says John, in his unmistakable Massachusetts accent. "I used to go over to our Italian neighbors," John relates, "and they would be cooking tortellinis, chicken cacciatore, or some other Northern Italian dish, and I'd come home and make them too."

This "cooking by observation and instinct," as John calls it, has kept his "fingers in the pot" ever since. So has his professional designer's eye. Being a graphic designer at one time has complemented John's culinary interests perfectly. "I prepare food in much the same way that I approached my design work," admits John. "I think of both in terms of colors, textures, shapes, and forms." What comes from John's kitchen can only be described as mouthwateringly colorful.

John's fun-loving attitude toward cooking epitomizes a *laissez faire* philosophy. "People take food too seriously,"

comments John. Worrying about choosing exactly the right wine, or following recipe proportions to the letter is, to his way of thinking, a pretty distasteful approach. "As a boy, when I wanted to make something, I'd ask my neighbor Rosina how much of this or that to use.

(continued)

JOHN F. CARAFOLI, SAGAMORE BEACH, MASS.

She'd say, 'not too much and not too little!' " From that bit of wisdom, John learned to create new recipes from his mistakes—like the time he poured some questionable pancake batter into muffin tins, producing a surprisingly delicious hot bread.

Living on the East Coast, John discovered a seafood paradise, and now it's an important part of his culinary repertoire. He comes up with impressive catches of lobster (from his own pots used to trap the live crustaceans), mussels plucked from rocks in the Cape Cod canal, and clams (also called quahogs) that require waders and good timing for harvest.

John is just as devoted to the kitchen preparations as he is to his fishing technique. For him, the succulence of lobster steamed in beer is oceans apart from that boiled in water. "Water takes out the flavor. Using beer makes all the difference," John insists. Freshly harvested mussels, soaked in flour and water for several hours to rid them of sand, are likely to be prepared the same way and served up with melted butter. Not surprisingly, John is known around these parts for his seafood feasts, often consisting of a traditional New England lobster boil or a gregarious clambake on the sand.

The second floor of John's classic colonial house is open as cozy bed-and-breakfast quarters. Guests delight in the hearty morning repasts prepared by John and served on the second floor porch in full view of the ocean. A typical menu includes freshly squeezed orange juice, warm banana-nut or bran muffins, and plump strawberries drizzled with Vermont maple syrup. It's enough to make any guest consider the possibility of staying on indefinitely!

JOHN F. CARAFOLI, SAGAMORE BEACH, MASS.

A Carafoli family tradition at the Christmas holidays has always been an Italian-American dinner. John annually produces an impressive ethnic spread during the holidays for his family and friends. One of his favorite entrées is a roasted capon stuffed with shrimp, scallops, and hazelnuts.

Seafood Stuffing

Quahogs (CO-hogs) are the East Coast variety of hard-shelled clams.

6 to 8 fresh *or* frozen quahog clams in shells, rinsed
2 cups chopped onion
½ cup dry white wine
¼ cup snipped parsley
½ teaspoon dried thyme, crushed
½ pound fresh *or* frozen peeled and deveined shrimp
½ pound fresh *or* frozen scallops
¼ cup butter *or* margarine

1 cup chopped celery
¼ cup snipped chives
½ teaspoon dried oregano, crushed
¼ to ½ teaspoon ground red pepper
5 cups dry bread cubes
½ cup chopped hazelnuts (filberts), toasted
½ cup grated Parmesan cheese
1 beaten egg
1 tablespoon lemon juice

In a large saucepan combine clams, *1 cup* chopped onion, wine, *1 teaspoon* parsley, thyme, and dash *pepper*. Simmer about 5 minutes or till clams open. (Discard any clams that don't open.) Cool. Remove clams from shells, discarding shells. Coarsely chop clams. Set aside. Strain cooking liquid and reserve.

Meanwhile, thaw shrimp and scallops, if frozen. Coarsely chop shrimp and scallops. Cook in *2 tablespoons* butter or margarine for 2 minutes or till nearly done. Remove from heat. Set aside. Cook remaining chopped onion and celery in remaining butter or margarine till tender but not brown. Stir in chives, oregano, red pepper, and remaining parsley. Remove from heat.

In a large mixing bowl combine bread cubes, nuts, cheese, egg, lemon juice, onion mixture, and chopped clams, shrimp, and scallops. Add enough reserved cooking liquid to moisten mixture (½ to ⅔ cup). Use to stuff one 6- to 8-pound capon. Makes 10 to 12 servings.

Pork with Papaya

1 pound boneless pork
1 large papaya, seeded, peeled, and cut lengthwise into ¼-inch-thick slices
3 tablespoons soy sauce
1 tablespoon cornstarch
2 slices bacon
3 cloves garlic, minced
1 tablespoon cooking oil (optional)
3 green onions, thinly bias sliced
1 large tomato, seeded and chopped
Hot cooked rice

When he was stationed near Hawaii, Louis found himself without zucchini for a recipe. He substituted papaya and ended up with this tasty Polynesian-style meal. (Pictured at left.)

Partially freeze pork. Thinly slice into bite-size strips. Set aside. Halve papaya slices crosswise. Set aside. For sauce, stir together soy sauce, cornstarch, and 1 cup *water*. Set aside.

In a wok or large skillet cook bacon till crisp. Drain on paper towels. Reserve drippings in wok or skillet. Crumble bacon. Set aside.

Stir-fry garlic in hot drippings for 15 seconds. (If necessary, add cooking oil to the wok or skillet.) Add green onions and stir-fry about 1½ minutes or till tender. Remove from the wok or skillet.

Add *half* of the pork to the wok. Stir-fry about 3 minutes or till no longer pink. Remove pork. Stir-fry remaining pork about 3 minutes. Return all pork to the wok. Push from center of the wok or skillet.

Stir sauce. Add sauce to the center of the wok. Cook and stir till thickened and bubbly, then cook and stir 2 minutes more. Add papaya and tomato. Stir together to coat with sauce. Cover and cook for 1 minute. Stir in reserved bacon. Serve immediately with rice. Garnish with green onion fans, if desired. Makes 4 servings.

Louis Severino, West Haven, Connecticut

Pork Chops Dijon

4 pork loin chops, cut ¾ inch thick
2 tablespoons Italian salad dressing
2 tablespoons Dijon-style mustard
¼ teaspoon freshly ground black pepper
1 small onion, sliced and separated into rings

Look no further for a quick-and-easy supper idea. These tasty chops cook in 30 minutes or less.

Trim excess fat from chops. In a small bowl combine salad dressing, mustard, and pepper. Brush mixture on both sides of chops.

In a 12-inch skillet cook chops, covered, over medium-low heat for 20 minutes. Turn chops and add onion. Cover and cook for 5 to 10 minutes more or till meat is tender. To serve, place chops on a platter. Top with onions and pan juices. Makes 4 servings.

Jane M. Christensen, Okemos, Michigan

Pork-Spinach Pie

1 9-inch frozen unbaked deep-dish pastry shell
1½ cups shredded Monterey Jack *or* Swiss cheese (6 ounces)
½ pound bulk pork sausage
½ cup herb-seasoned stuffing mix
½ of a 10-ounce package frozen chopped spinach, thawed and well drained
3 beaten eggs
1½ cups light cream *or* milk

For timesaving convenience, Barbara makes this hearty, quichelike pie with a frozen pastry shell. If you prefer, use a homemade pastry shell instead.

Place frozen pastry shell on a baking sheet. Do not prick. Bake in a 400° oven for 5 minutes. Remove from oven. Reduce the oven temperature to 325°. Sprinkle cheese in bottom of pastry shell. Set aside. Meanwhile, in a skillet cook sausage till brown. Drain off fat. Stir in stuffing mix and spinach. Spoon sausage mixture over cheese. In a medium mixing bowl combine eggs and light cream or milk. Carefully pour egg mixture over sausage mixture.

Bake, uncovered, in a 325° oven for 50 to 55 minutes or till a knife inserted near center comes out clean. Let stand 10 minutes before serving. Makes 6 servings.

Barbara Stewart, Yuba City, California

Heritage Ham Pastries

2 beaten eggs
2 tablespoons milk
1 cup finely chopped celery
1 cup peeled and shredded butternut squash
½ cup fine dry bread crumbs
½ cup finely chopped onion
1 teaspoon prepared horseradish
1 teaspoon soy sauce
1 pound ground fully cooked ham
6 frozen patty shells, thawed Milk

During the summer, Pat substitutes shredded carrot for the winter squash.

In a medium mixing bowl combine eggs and milk. Stir in celery, squash, bread crumbs, onion, horseradish, soy sauce, and ¼ teaspoon *pepper*. Add ham and mix well. Shape mixture into six ¾-inch-thick patties. Place patties in a well-greased shallow baking pan.

On a lightly floured surface, roll each patty shell into a 5-inch circle. Drape *1* rolled-out pastry shell over *each* ham patty, tucking under slighty. Brush lightly with milk. Preheat oven to 450°.

Place pastries in oven. Reduce oven temperature to 400°. Bake for 25 to 30 minutes or till golden brown. Serve immediately. Serves 6.

Pat Nelson, Moncks Corner, South Carolina

Ham Linguine Florentine

½ cup slivered almonds
1½ cups sliced fresh mushrooms (4 ounces)
¾ cup chopped onion
3 tablespoons butter *or* margarine
3 tablespoons cooking oil
3 tablespoons all-purpose flour
¾ teaspoon dried thyme, crushed
1 14½-ounce can beef broth
¾ cup light cream *or* milk
¾ pound fully cooked ham, cut into julienne strips (1½ cups)
½ cup snipped parsley
3 tablespoons Dijon-style mustard
6 ounces linguine, cooked
8 ounces fresh spinach, coarsely chopped

This colorful entrée emerged from Mrs. O'Donoghue's high school classroom recipe exchange. Her students raved about this tasty dish.

In a heavy 12-inch skillet brown almonds over medium heat about 5 minutes or till golden, stirring constantly. Remove from skillet. Set aside. In same skillet cook mushrooms and onion in butter and oil till onions are tender but not brown. Stir in flour and thyme. Add beef broth and cream all at once. Cook and stir over medium heat till thickened and bubbly, then cook and stir 1 minute more. Stir in ¼ *cup* of the almonds, ham, parsley, and mustard. Stir in linguine.

To serve, place chopped spinach on a platter. Top with hot linguine mixture. Sprinkle with remaining almonds. Makes 6 servings.

Mrs. Paul O'Donoghue, Bay Village, Ohio

Brunch Enchiladas

12 ounces ground fully cooked ham (2 cups)
½ cup sliced green onion
½ cup chopped green pepper
2½ cups shredded cheddar cheese (10 ounces)
8 7-inch flour tortillas
4 beaten eggs
2 cups light cream *or* milk
1 tablespoon all-purpose flour
¼ teaspoon garlic powder
Few drops bottled hot pepper sauce

Combine ham, onion, and green pepper. Place ⅓ *cup* of the ham mixture and *3 tablespoons* shredded cheese onto each tortilla, then roll up. Carefully place filled tortillas, seam side down, in a greased 12x7½x2-inch baking dish. Combine eggs, cream or milk, flour, garlic powder, and hot pepper sauce. Pour egg mixture over tortillas. Cover and refrigerate several hours or overnight.

Bake, uncovered, in a 350° oven for 45 to 50 minutes or till set. Sprinkle with remaining cheese. Bake about 3 minutes more or till cheese melts. Let stand 10 minutes. Makes 8 servings.

Sue Lewallen, Tualatin, Oregon

ROXANNE CHAN, ALBANY, CALIF.

On a scenic hilltop above Albany, California, Roxanne and Bock Chan enjoy a 360-degree view of the Berkeley hills, San Francisco Bay, downtown Oakland, and the Golden Gate bridge. Several years ago, they moved from the East to design and build their dream house (in conjunction with the School of Architecture at the University of California at Berkeley) on a hillside lot. It's an ultramodern structure that seems like a tree house built around a circular staircase. Filled with plants, Oriental art, and light, "the house that Roxie and Bock built" is a cozy window on their world.

During the process of building and furnishing their new home, Roxanne had to shelve her cooking hobby. But when her "ideal" kitchen and dining room were finished, and the garden was planted, Roxanne's creative instincts took over. "Moving to California opened up a whole new variety of fresh produce and ethnic ingredients that I'd never known before," exclaims Roxanne. "Food became my passion, from growing most of my own vegetables, fruits, and herbs to creating recipes with our produce."

To say that Roxanne's green thumb has put their small sloping lot to good use is an understatement. Sweet cherry, plum, and peach trees shelter neat rows of greens: cabbage, lettuce, chard, Belgian endive, and salad savoy. The rest is devoted to vegetables such as baby carrots, yellow squash, peas, tomatoes, leeks, green beans, and artichokes. Rhubarb, strawberries, and blackberries add their sweet aroma, and out back are neat rows of flowering, ready-to-be-savored fresh herbs.

> ❝ *Moving to California opened up a whole new variety of fresh produce and ethnic ingredients that I'd never known before.* ❞

Having a veritable produce market outside their door is wonderful inspiration for Roxanne's recipes. So is her husband's Oriental heritage and his enthusiasm for the light, fresh style that characterizes Chinese cooking. Roxanne confesses, "I didn't know how to cook before I was married." But with Bock's encouragement, she now entertains every week. "From small intimate dinners for four to open house buffets for thirty-five," says Roxanne proudly.

(continued)

ROXANNE CHAN, ALBANY, CALIF.

❝ *My favorite way to entertain is with a multi-course dinner, which provides a whole evening's entertainment.* ❞

Once each month, the Chans meet with their wine-tasting group—several couples who take a long lunch break to sample wine and Roxie's latest cooking efforts. Pairing food with particular wines is a special challenge for Roxanne. She cautions, "You can easily overpower a food with wine or vice versa."

Roxanne's cooking approach is definitely "hands-on." She explains, "I feel it's important to interact with the food, so the only two appliances I use are a hand mixer and a blender." In creating recipes, she looks for textural contrasts, interesting color plays, and emphasizes that "it must be a taste treat."

Interestingly, Roxanne chooses not to drive a car, so all of her grocery shopping is done, as she puts it, "on foot with my trusty backpack, or with the help of public transportation. Exercise is very important to me, and a real necessity if you love to eat!"

ROXANNE CHAN, ALBANY, CALIF.

"After a few years of cooking from cookbooks, my husband encouraged me to begin creating my own recipes," says Roxanne. She turns to her cookbook collection and food magazines for inspiration. But it isn't until she is asked for a recipe, or decides to enter a cooking contest like *Better Homes and Gardens®* magazine's monthly recipe competition, that Roxanne actually puts her recipes down on paper. She does keep a file of ideas—divided into fruit, vegetables, and meat suggestions—then simply creates new dishes from what's on hand. This winning recipe, Turkey Slices with Curried Cream Sauce, is Roxanne's delicious answer to holiday leftovers. But with fresh turkey parts available year-round, you won't have to wait for the holiday bird to try it.

Turkey Slices with Curried Cream Sauce

Homegrown zucchini and yellow squash, along with a hearty red wine and fresh fruit, complete Roxanne's simple post-holiday menu that's special enough for company.

- 6 slices turkey breast meat, cut ½ inch thick (about ¾ pound)
- 2 tablespoons butter *or* margarine
- 2 tablespoons all-purpose flour
- ½ teaspoon curry powder
- 1 cup chicken broth
- ¼ cup milk
- 1 small banana, diced (½ cup)
- ¼ cup chopped pitted dates
- ¼ cup chopped cashews
- ½ teaspoon finely shredded lemon peel
- 3 cups hot cooked rice *or* bulgur

Wrap turkey slices in foil. Place in a shallow baking pan. Heat in a 350° oven for 20 minutes. Meanwhile, for sauce, in a medium saucepan melt butter or margarine. Stir in flour and curry powder. Add chicken broth and milk all at once. Cook and stir till thickened and bubbly, then cook and stir 1 minute more. Stir in banana, dates, cashews, and lemon peel. Arrange turkey slices over rice or bulgur. Serve some sauce atop turkey. Pass remaining sauce. Serves 6.

Japanese Chicken Salad

Alexandra's main-dish salad recipe originated with a Japanese family member. She "Americanized" it by calling for ingredients that are more readily available in the states.

¼ cup salad oil
¼ cup vinegar
1 tablespoon sesame seed
2 teaspoons sugar
1 teaspoon sesame oil
8 cups torn mixed greens
4 cups chopped cooked chicken

6 radishes, sliced
3 green onions, sliced
2 hard-cooked eggs, chopped
2 ounces rice sticks
Cooking oil for deep-fat frying

For dressing, in a screw-top jar combine salad oil, vinegar, sesame seed, sugar, sesame oil, 1 teaspoon *salt*, and ½ teaspoon *pepper*. Cover and shake well. Chill thoroughly. For salad, in a salad bowl combine greens, chicken, radishes, onion, and eggs. Toss lightly.

Fry rice sticks, a few at a time, in deep hot oil (375°) about 5 seconds or just till sticks puff and rise to the top. Drain well.

Immediately arrange rice sticks on individual salad plates. Serve salad atop rice sticks. Shake dressing again just before serving. Drizzle salads with dressing. Makes 8 servings.

Alexandra Garinger, Guthrie, Oklahoma

Sausage-Stuffed Turkey Thighs

If you prefer dark meat over white meat (as the Smiths' daughter does), this thrifty poultry dish is for you!

2 fresh *or* frozen turkey thighs
½ pound bulk pork sausage
½ cup chopped onion
1 cup soft bread crumbs, toasted
1 4-ounce can chopped mushrooms, drained
½ cup chopped apple

½ cup chopped walnuts
2 tablespoons snipped parsley
¼ teaspoon dried sage, crushed
¼ teaspoon dried thyme, crushed
1 beaten egg

Thaw thighs, if frozen. For stuffing, in a skillet cook sausage and onion till meat is brown and onion is tender. Drain off fat. Stir in bread crumbs, mushrooms, apple, nuts, parsley, sage, thyme, ⅛ teaspoon *salt*, and ⅛ teaspoon *pepper*. Stir in egg.

Debone thighs. Pound thighs to ½-inch thickness. With skin side down, spoon *half* of the stuffing onto the center of *each* thigh. Roll up, jelly-roll style, starting at the narrow end. Secure with string. Place rolls in a shallow baking pan. Bake, covered, in a 350° oven for 1 hour. Uncover and bake for 45 to 60 minutes more or till tender. Makes 6 to 8 servings.

Mrs. Lester H. Smith, Decatur, Alabama

Manhattan-Style Chicken

The flavor of this colorful grilled chicken is reminiscent of Manhattan clam chowder.

1 6½-ounce can minced clams
1 8-ounce bottle (1 cup) clam juice
1 cup catsup
1 small onion, finely chopped (¼ cup)
2 tablespoons cooking oil
1 tablespoon Worcestershire sauce
½ teaspoon finely shredded lemon peel (optional)
1 tablespoon lemon juice
1 clove garlic, minced
2 tablespoons snipped parsley
1 2½- to 3-pound broiler-fryer chicken, cut up

Drain clams, reserving liquid. Set clams aside. For sauce, in a medium saucepan combine reserved clam liquid; clam juice; catsup; onion; oil; Worcestershire sauce; lemon peel, if desired; lemon juice; and garlic. Bring mixture to boiling. Reduce heat and simmer, uncovered, for 30 to 35 minutes or to desired consistency. Remove saucepan from heat. Stir in clams and parsley.

Grill chicken pieces with bone side up, on an uncovered grill, directly over *medium* coals for 20 minutes. Turn and grill 10 to 20 minutes more or till tender, brushing often with sauce during last 10 minutes of grilling. Heat any remaining sauce and pass with chicken. Makes 6 servings.

Roxanne E. Chan, Albany, California

Skillet Chicken Risotto

1 2½- to 3-pound broiler-fryer chicken, cut up
2 tablespoons cooking oil
1 cup chopped onion
¾ cup long grain rice
1½ teaspoons poultry seasoning
8 ounces fresh mushrooms, sliced (3 cups)

4 medium carrots, bias-sliced ½ inch thick (2 cups)
2 cups water
Paprika
Cherry tomatoes, halved (optional)
Celery leaves (optional)

Top honors for a skillet supper go to Diane's tasty one-dish meal.

In a 12-inch skillet brown chicken pieces on all sides in hot oil about 15 minutes. Remove chicken. Drain fat, reserving 2 tablespoons in skillet. Stir onion, rice, poultry seasoning, and 1 teaspoon *salt* into skillet. Cook and stir till rice is lightly browned. Stir in mushrooms, carrots, and water. Place chicken atop rice mixture. Sprinkle with paprika. Simmer, covered, for 30 to 35 minutes or till chicken and rice are tender. Garnish with halved cherry tomatoes and celery leaves, if desired. Makes 4 servings.

Diane P. Stevens, Bloomington, Indiana

Chutney Chicken

1 cup chopped apple
½ cup tomato sauce
¼ cup raisins
¼ cup packed brown sugar
2 tablespoons chopped onion
2 tablespoons vinegar
1 tablespoon diced mixed
   candied fruits and peels
   (optional)

1 tablespoon lemon juice
¼ teaspoon ground ginger
⅛ teaspoon ground cinnamon
   Dash ground cloves
1 2½- to 3-pound broiler-
   fryer chicken, cut up
1 teaspoon paprika
   Hot cooked rice
1 tablespoon cornstarch

For chutney, in a small saucepan combine apple; tomato sauce; raisins; brown sugar; onion; vinegar; candied fruits and peels, if desired; lemon juice; ginger; cinnamon; cloves; and ¼ teaspoon *salt*. Bring to boiling. Reduce heat and simmer, uncovered, for 15 minutes.

Meanwhile, place chicken in a 13x9x2-inch baking dish. Sprinkle with paprika. Bake, uncovered, in a 350° oven for 30 minutes. Drain off fat. Turn chicken pieces. Pour chutney over chicken. Cover and bake for 30 minutes more. Arrange chicken over rice. Keep warm.

For sauce, skim fat from chutney. Transfer to a saucepan. Stir together cornstarch and ¼ cup cold *water*. Stir into chutney. Cook and stir till thickened and bubbly, then cook and stir 1 minute more. Serve sauce with chicken and rice. Makes 6 servings.

Mary Deschner, Ponca City, Oklahoma

Curry Chicken Delight

4 whole large chicken
   breasts (about 4 pounds
   total), skinned, halved
   lengthwise, and boned
⅓ cup all-purpose flour
4 slices bacon

¼ cup honey
2 tablespoons prepared
   mustard
½ teaspoon salt
½ teaspoon curry powder

66 This recipe is easy to prepare and can be made ahead if you're entertaining. I simply heat it before serving. 99

Rinse chicken; pat dry. Coat chicken pieces with flour. Set aside.

In a large skillet cook bacon till crisp. Drain bacon on paper towels, reserving drippings in skillet. Crumble bacon and set aside. In same skillet, brown chicken on all sides in hot drippings about 10 minutes. Transfer chicken to an 8x8x2-inch baking dish. Bake, uncovered, in a 350° oven for 30 minutes.

Meanwhile, combine honey, mustard, salt, and curry powder. Drizzle honey mixture over chicken in baking dish. Bake, uncovered, for 15 minutes more. Top chicken with crumbled bacon. Serves 8.

Larry Kovalcin, Fort Lauderdale, Florida

Herbed Chicken À la Française

2 whole medium chicken breasts (about 1½ pounds total), skinned, halved lengthwise, and boned
2 green onions, sliced
½ teaspoon dried tarragon, crushed
1 tablespoon butter or margarine
⅓ cup dry white wine or chicken broth
1 egg white
½ cup mayonnaise or salad dressing
1 tablespoon grated Parmesan cheese
1 tablespoon snipped parsley

66 Teaching me how to cook three meals a day for myself was probably the smartest thing my mother ever did. 99

Arrange chicken breast halves in a 12x7½x2-inch baking dish. Sprinkle green onion and tarragon atop chicken. Dot with butter or margarine. Season with salt and pepper. Add wine to baking dish.

Bake, uncovered, in a 350° oven for 30 minutes. Remove from oven. In a mixer bowl beat egg white till stiff peaks form. Fold mayonnaise or salad dressing into stiffly beaten egg white. Spoon egg white mixture over chicken breasts. Sprinkle with Parmesan cheese.

Return to oven and bake, uncovered, for 12 to 15 minutes more or till lightly browned. Sprinkle chicken breasts with parsley. Serves 4.

Mike Gauvin, Ypsilanti, Michigan

Chicken à la Maria

¾ cup fine dry Italian-seasoned bread crumbs
¼ cup grated Parmesan cheese
6 whole large chicken breasts (about 6 pounds total), skinned, halved lengthwise, and boned
½ cup sliced green onions
2 tablespoons butter or margarine
2 tablespoons all-purpose flour
1 cup milk
1 10-ounce package frozen chopped spinach, thawed and well drained
1 4-ounce package sliced fully cooked ham, chopped

Serve this elegant winner at large family gatherings, or halve it for a smaller get-together.

In a pie plate or shallow bowl combine bread crumbs and cheese. Coat chicken with crumb mixture. Arrange chicken in a 13x9x2-inch baking dish. Set remaining crumb mixture aside.

Cook onion in butter or margarine till tender. Stir in flour. Add milk all at once. Cook and stir till thickened and bubbly, then cook and stir 1 minute more. Stir in spinach and ham. Spoon spinach mixture over chicken. Sprinkle with remaining crumb mixture. Baked, uncovered, in a 350° oven for 40 to 45 minutes or till tender. Serves 12.

Mrs. John Coder, Timonium, Maryland

Herbed Chicken Stir-Fry

2 whole medium chicken breasts (about 1½ pounds total), skinned and boned
¾ cup cold water
2 tablespoons all-purpose flour
2 teaspoons instant chicken bouillon granules
1 teaspoon seasoned salt
½ teaspoon dried basil, crushed

¼ teaspoon dried oregano, crushed
2 tablespoons cooking oil
1 clove garlic, minced
¼ cup chopped onion
3 medium zucchini, thinly bias sliced
3 tomatoes, cut into wedges
Hot cooked rice *or* pasta (optional)

By stir-frying the minced garlic first, its distinctive flavor seasons the oil that's used to cook the remaining ingredients.

Cut chicken into 1-inch pieces. For sauce, stir together water, flour, bouillon granules, salt, basil, and oregano. Set aside.

Preheat a wok or large skillet over high heat. Add cooking oil. (Add more oil as necessary during cooking.) Stir-fry garlic in hot oil for 15 seconds. Add onion and zucchini. Stir-fry 3 to 4 minutes or till vegetables are crisp-tender. Remove vegetables from wok or skillet.

Add *half* of the chicken to the hot wok or skillet. Stir-fry about 3 minutes or till done. Remove chicken. Stir-fry remaining chicken about 3 minutes or till done. Return all chicken to the wok. Push chicken from the center of the wok.

Stir sauce, then add to the center of the wok. Cook and stir till thickened and bubbly, then cook and stir 2 minutes more. Return vegetables to the wok or skillet. Stir ingredients together to coat with sauce. Add tomatoes. Cover and cook for 1 minute. Serve immediately with rice or pasta, if desired. Makes 4 servings.

Deborah S. Harris, Burlington, New Jersey

Shrimp, Spinach, And Cheese Soufflé

1 4½-ounce can shrimp
¼ cup butter *or* margarine
¼ cup all-purpose flour
¾ cup milk
½ cup grated Parmesan cheese
¼ cup dry white wine
1 cup finely chopped fresh spinach
5 egg yolks
5 egg whites

Finding herself with leftover shrimp and spinach after a party, Diane improvised on a basic soufflé and ended up with this eye-catching main dish. (Pictured at right.)

Attach a foil collar to a 1½-quart soufflé dish. Set aside. Rinse and drain shrimp, reserving 2 shrimp. Finely chop remaining shrimp.

Melt butter. Stir in flour. Add milk all at once. Cook and stir till thickened and bubbly, then cook and stir 1 minute more. Remove from heat. Stir in cheese and wine. Fold in spinach and shrimp.

In a mixer bowl beat egg yolks till thick and lemon colored. *Slowly* stir in spinach mixture. Wash beaters thoroughly. In a large mixer bowl beat egg whites till stiff peaks form (tips stand straight). Fold spinach mixture into the beaten egg whites.

Spoon mixture into prepared soufflé dish. Bake in a 325° oven for 50 to 55 minutes or till a knife inserted near center comes out clean. Gently peel off collar. Garnish with reserved shrimp. Serve immediately. Makes 4 servings.

Diane Shabino, Kalamazoo, Michigan

Tex-Mex Cheese Strata

4 cups nacho-cheese-flavored tortilla chips, broken
2 cups shredded Monterey Jack cheese (8 ounces)
½ cup finely chopped onion
1 tablespoon butter *or* margarine
6 beaten eggs
2½ cups milk
1 4-ounce can diced green chili peppers, drained
3 tablespoons catsup
¼ teaspoon bottled hot pepper sauce

Linda hit on a winner with this peppy, make-ahead, Mexican-style entrée.

Sprinkle broken tortilla chips evenly over the bottom of a greased 12x7½x2-inch baking dish. Sprinkle with cheese. Set dish aside.

In a small saucepan cook onion in butter or margarine till tender but not brown. In a medium mixing bowl use a rotary beater to combine eggs, milk, chili peppers, catsup, hot pepper sauce, and cooked onion. Pour egg mixture over cheese in prepared dish. Cover and refrigerate several hours or overnight.

Bake, uncoverd, in a 325° oven for 50 to 55 minutes or till eggs are set and lightly browned. Garnish with additional tortilla chips and tomato slices, if desired. Makes 6 servings.

Mrs. Linda Allison, Manassas, Virginia

Sicilian Frittata

2 potatoes, peeled and sliced (1½ cups)
2 tablespoons olive oil *or* cooking oil
½ cup chopped onion
¼ cup finely chopped green pepper
2 cloves garlic, minced
2 cups fresh *or* frozen chopped broccoli, thawed

6 eggs
¼ cup grated Parmesan cheese
¼ cup water
½ teaspoon dried basil, crushed
½ cup shredded Monterey Jack cheese (2 ounces)

Anita's open-face omelet features a winning blend of olive oil, onion, garlic, Parmesan cheese, and basil.

In a 10-inch skillet cook potatoes, uncovered, in hot oil about 10 minutes or till just tender, turning occasionally. Add onion, green pepper, and garlic. Cook till onion is tender but not brown. Add broccoli. Reduce heat and cook, covered, for 5 minutes.

In a large mixing bowl beat together eggs, Parmesan cheese, water, basil, ¼ teaspoon *salt,* and ⅛ teaspoon *pepper.* Pour egg mixture over vegetables in skillet. Cook, covered, over medium-low heat for 10 to 15 minutes or till eggs are set. Sprinkle with Monterey Jack cheese. Remove from heat. Cover. Let stand 5 minutes. Serves 4 to 6.

Mrs. Anita M. Evans, Orinda, California

Winter Squash Quiche

Anne likes to use pureed butternut, banana, or buttercup squash. They add rich flavor and warm color to this prize-winning quiche.

4 slices bacon	¼ teaspoon salt
2 tablespoons chopped onion	⅛ teaspoon ground nutmeg
3 beaten eggs	⅛ teaspoon pepper
1½ cups milk	Pastry Shell
1 cup mashed, cooked winter squash	1 cup shredded Swiss cheese (4 ounces)

In a small skillet cook bacon till crisp. Drain bacon on paper towels, reserving 1 tablespoon drippings in skillet. Crumble bacon and set aside. Cook onion in reserved drippings till tender but not brown. Remove from heat. In a medium mixing bowl combine eggs, milk, squash, salt, nutmeg, pepper, and cooked onion.

Prepare Pastry Shell. Sprinkle cheese and crumbled bacon into the *hot* baked pastry shell. Carefully pour egg mixture into pastry shell.

Bake in a 325° oven for 40 to 50 minutes or till a knife inserted near center comes out clean. Let quiche stand 10 minutes before serving. Makes 6 servings.

Pastry Shell: In a medium mixing bowl stir together 1¼ cups *all-purpose flour* and ½ teaspoon *salt.* Cut in ⅓ cup *shortening or lard* till pieces are the size of small peas. Sprinkle 1 tablespoon *cold water* over part of the mixture. Gently toss with a fork. Push to side of bowl. Repeat with 2 to 3 tablespoons additional water till all is moistened. Form dough into a ball.

On a lightly floured surface flatten dough with hands. Roll dough from center to edge, forming a circle about 12 inches in diameter. Wrap pastry around a rolling pin. Unroll onto a 9-inch pie plate. Ease pastry into pie plate, being careful not to stretch pastry. Trim to ½ inch beyond edge of pie plate. Fold under extra pastry. Flute edge.

Line the unpricked pastry shell with a double thickness of heavy-duty foil. Bake in a 450° oven for 5 minutes. Remove foil and bake about 5 minutes more or till pastry is nearly done. Remove pastry from oven. Reduce oven temperature to 325°.

Anne Westbrook, Athol, Massachusetts

FAMILY-PLEASING MAIN DISHES

HOME-STYLE COOKING—A RELAXED WAY OF COOKING THAT TURNS EVERYDAY INGREDIENTS INTO DOWNRIGHT GOOD FOOD—IS WHAT THIS CHAPTER IS ALL ABOUT. YOU'LL RECOGNIZE SOME OF THE CASSEROLES, SANDWICHES, SOUPS, AND STEWS AS ANOTHER COOK'S VARIATION ON LONG-STANDING FAVORITES FROM YOUR FAMILY'S RECIPE FILE. OTHERS ARE DESTINED TO BECOME DELICIOUS NEW ADDITIONS TO YOUR RECIPE COLLECTION.

Citrus Flank Steak

1 1¼- to 1½-pound beef
  flank steak
½ cup low-calorie Italian
  salad dressing
⅓ cup soy sauce
⅓ cup dry red *or* white wine
3 tablespoons sliced green
  onion

½ teaspoon dry mustard
⅛ teaspoon lemon pepper
3 lemon slices, cut ⅛ inch
  thick
1 clove garlic, minced

Because of her interest in health and weight-watching, Julie tries to cook with only the leanest red meats. Versatile flank steak is one of her favorite cuts.

Place meat in a shallow baking dish. For marinade, combine salad dressing, soy sauce, wine, onion, mustard, lemon pepper, lemon slices, and garlic. Pour marinade over meat. Cover and marinate in refrigerator for 8 hours or overnight, turning occasionally.

Drain meat, reserving marinade. Place meat on an unheated rack in a broiler pan. Broil 3 inches from heat for 5 to 6 minutes. Brush with marinade. Turn and broil for 5 to 6 minutes more. Brush with marinade just before serving. Makes 4 servings.

Julie Lamb, Southfield, Michigan

Sweet-and-Sour Brisket

1 16-ounce can stewed
  tomatoes, cut up
1 8-ounce can sauerkraut
1 cup applesauce
2 tablespoons brown sugar

1 2½- to 3½-pound fresh
  beef brisket
2 tablespoons cold water
2 tablespoons cornstarch

Joan's first-place recipe in the "Budget Roasts" category stars economical beef brisket.

In a 10-inch skillet combine *undrained* tomatoes, *undrained* sauerkraut, applesauce, and brown sugar. Bring to boiling. Reduce heat and add brisket, spooning some of the tomato mixture over the meat. Simmer, covered, for 2½ to 3 hours or till meat is tender, spooning tomato mixture over meat occasionally. Transfer meat to a serving platter and keep warm.

For sauce, skim fat from pan juices. Combine water and cornstarch, then stir into tomato mixture. Cook and stir till thickened and bubbly, then cook and stir 2 minutes more. Spoon some sauce over meat. Pass remaining sauce. Makes 6 to 8 servings.

Joan Tunnicliff, Omaha, Nebraska

BBQ Beef Salad Sandwiches

1 3-pound boneless beef eye of round roast
1 8-ounce carton plain yogurt
¼ cup finely chopped green onion

½ teaspoon dried dillweed
1 teaspoon pepper
½ teaspoon garlic powder
4 Sandwich Rounds
    Marinated Vegetable Toss

> **❝** *Like many people today, I lead a hectic life. Consequently, I prefer make-ahead cooking. This dinner requires only a half hour of final preparation.* **❞**

Cut two 1-inch-thick slices of meat (8 ounces each) off roast. Seal, label, and freeze remaining meat for another use. In a small bowl combine yogurt, onion, and dillweed. Cover and chill 3 to 24 hours.

Combine pepper and garlic powder. Sprinkle *one-fourth* of the pepper mixture onto one side of *each* beef slice. Rub and press into surface of meat. Rub remaining pepper mixture onto other side of *each* beef slice. Let stand 30 minutes. Grill over *medium-hot* coals to desired doneness, turning once. (Allow 15 to 20 minutes total time for medium.) *Or,* broil 3 inches from heat. (Allow 12 to 14 minutes total time for medium.) Cover and chill beef for 3 to 24 hours.

To serve, thinly slice beef into bite-size strips. For each sandwich, spread some yogurt mixture on inside of a Sandwich Round. Place some sliced beef and Marinated Vegetable Toss on half of the round. Fold over. Pass remaining yogurt mixture. Serves 4.

Sandwich Rounds: In a large mixing bowl combine yeast from one 13¾-ounce package *hot roll mix* and 1 cup warm *water* (110° to 115°); stir till dissolved. Stir in flour from roll mix. Turn out onto a floured surface. Knead 1 to 2 minutes. Cover and let rest 15 minutes. Divide dough into 8 portions. With lightly floured hands roll each portion into a smooth ball. Cover and let rest 10 minutes. On a floured surface flatten 1 ball of dough without creasing dough. Lightly roll dough into a 7-inch round, *turning dough over once.* Do not stretch or crease dough. Place on a baking sheet. Repeat with another piece of dough. Bake, 2 at a time, in a 450° oven for 4 minutes or till softly set. Turn over and bake for 3 to 4 minutes more. Place in a paper bag at once to soften. Repeat with remaining dough. Wrap individually in moisture- and vaporproof wrap. Label and freeze. To use, let thaw 1 hour. Makes 8.

Marinated Vegetable Toss: Combine 1 pint fresh *mushrooms,* chopped; 2 large *tomatoes,* chopped; and ½ cup sliced *green onion.* In a screw-top jar combine ½ cup *salad oil;* ½ cup dry *white wine;* 2 tablespoons *vinegar;* 2 teaspoons *sugar;* 1 teaspoon dried *basil,* crushed; and ½ teaspoon *salt.* Cover and shake well. Pour over and toss with vegetables. Cover and chill for 3 to 24 hours, stirring occasionally. Before serving, drain vegetables well. In a bowl toss vegetables with 8 ounces fresh *spinach,* torn. Serve with BBQ Beef Salad Sandwiches. Makes 4 to 6 servings.

Sharyl Heiken, Des Moines, Iowa

BBQ Beef Salad Sandwiches, Strawberry-Rice Fluff (see recipe, page 185)

Shredded-Beef Sandwiches

1 3-pound beef chuck pot roast
⅓ cup vinegar
1 large onion, cut up
3 bay leaves
½ teaspoon salt

¼ teaspoon ground cloves
⅛ teaspoon garlic powder
Spinach *or* lettuce leaves (optional)
8 to 10 French-style rolls, split

Trim excess fat from roast. Cut roast, as necessary, to fit into a 3½- or 4-quart electric slow crockery cooker. Place meat in cooker. Combine vinegar, onion, bay leaves, salt, cloves, and garlic powder. Pour over meat. Cover cooker. Cook on low-heat setting for 11 to 12 hours or till meat is very tender.

Remove meat from crockery cooker. Use two forks to shred meat, discarding bones and fat. Line rolls with spinach or lettuce leaves, if desired. Place shredded meat on rolls. Strain meat juices. Skim fat from juices. Serve juices with sandwiches for dipping. Serves 8 to 10.

Mrs. Jim Lanz, Sartell, Minnesota

Rice Pilaf Salad

2 cups chopped cooked beef
1¼ cups cooked brown rice
1 cup canned garbanzo beans
1 8-ounce can red kidney beans, drained
1 apple, cored and chopped
1 small green pepper, chopped
½ cup sliced celery
¼ cup sliced, pitted ripe olives

¼ cup sliced green onion
¼ cup snipped parsley
Zippy Dressing
Spinach leaves
1 apple, cored and sliced
2 hard-cooked eggs, sliced
Alfalfa sprouts
½ cup sunflower nuts

In a large mixing bowl combine beef, rice, beans, chopped apple, green pepper, celery, olives, green onion, and parsley. Pour Zippy Dressing over all. Toss gently to coat. Cover and chill.

To serve, arrange on a spinach-lined platter with apple slices, egg slices, and sprouts. Sprinkle nuts atop. Makes 6 servings.

Zippy Dressing: In a screw-top jar combine ⅓ cup *wine vinegar;* 2 teaspoons *dry mustard;* 1 teaspoon *sugar;* 1 teaspoon *salt;* 1 teaspoon *lemon juice;* ½ teaspoon *paprika;* 2 small cloves *garlic,* minced; and dash *ground red pepper.* Cover and shake well.

Yael Efron, Ames, Iowa

Stir-Fried Gazpacho Salad

Spicy seasonings turn this Oriental-style main dish into a winning entrée.

1 pound beef top round steak
2 tablespoons cooking oil
8 ounces fresh mushrooms, sliced (3 cups)
1 medium green pepper, cut into thin strips (1 cup)
1 medium onion, sliced and separated into rings
1 small cucumber, seeded and chopped (½ cup)

1 clove garlic, minced
1 teaspoon Italian seasoning
1 teaspoon seasoned salt
⅛ teaspoon ground red pepper
1 large tomato, cut into wedges
8 ounces fresh spinach, torn (6 cups)

Partially freeze beef. Thinly slice across the grain into bite-size strips. Preheat a wok or large skillet over high heat. Add oil. (Add more oil as necessary during cooking.) Stir-fry mushrooms, green pepper, onion, cucumber, garlic, Italian seasoning, seasoned salt, and red pepper in hot oil about 3 minutes or till vegetables are crisp-tender. Remove vegetables from the wok or skillet.

Add *half* of the beef to the hot wok or skillet. Stir-fry for 2 to 3 minutes or till done. Remove beef. Stir-fry remaining beef for 2 to 3 minutes or till done. Return all beef, vegetables, and tomato to the wok or skillet. Cover and cook about 1 minute or till heated through. Transfer beef-vegetable mixture to a bowl. Keep warm.

Add spinach leaves to the wok or skillet. Cover and cook about 1 minute or till slightly wilted. To serve, arrange wilted spinach leaves on 4 serving plates. Spoon beef-vegetable mixture atop. Serves 4.

Trish Kondziela, Buffalo, New York

Beef Stir-Fry with Mushrooms

1 pound beef top round steak
⅓ cup water
¼ cup soy sauce
2 tablespoons dry red wine
4 teaspoons cornstarch
1 tablespoon molasses *or* honey

1 tablespoon cooking oil
8 ounces fresh mushrooms, sliced (3 cups)
5 green onions, bias-sliced into 1-inch lengths (1 cup)
Hot cooked rice

> **❝** *I use recipes much as an artist uses a sketch. I start with the basic recipe idea and decide generally what ingredients to include. As I cook, I add or subtract ingredients to suit my tastes.* **❞**

Partially freeze beef. Thinly slice across the grain into bite-size strips. Set aside. For marinade, in a medium mixing bowl combine water, soy sauce, wine, cornstarch, and molasses or honey. Add beef, stirring to coat well. Cover and marinate at room temperature for 30 minutes or in the refrigerator for 2 hours, stirring occasionally. Drain well, reserving marinade. Set aside.

Preheat a wok or large skillet over high heat. Add oil. (Add more oil as necessary during cooking.) Stir-fry mushrooms and green onions in hot oil about 2 minutes or till crisp-tender. Remove vegetables from the wok or skillet.

Add *half* of the beef to the hot wok or skillet. Stir-fry for 2 to 3 minutes or till done. Remove beef. Stir-fry the remaining beef for 2 to 3 minutes or till done. Return all beef to the wok. Push from the center of the wok or skillet.

Stir marinade. Add to the center of the wok or skillet. Cook and stir till thickened and bubbly, then cook and stir for 1 minute more. Return vegetables to the wok or skillet. Stir ingredients together to coat with sauce. Cook and stir for 1 minute. Serve immediately over hot cooked rice. Makes 4 servings.

Alethea Sparks, Des Moines, Iowa

Beef Stir-Fry with Mushrooms, Steamed Ginger Buns (see recipe, page 132), Sugar-Almond Wafers (see recipe, page 185)

Beef and Cabbage Taco Casserole

1½ cups peeled and shredded
  potatoes (2 medium)
½ cup shredded cheddar
  cheese (2 ounces)
⅛ teaspoon onion salt
1 pound lean ground beef
1½ cups shredded cabbage
1 4-ounce can diced green
  chili peppers, drained
½ cup taco sauce
⅛ teaspoon onion salt
1 cup shredded cheddar
  cheese (4 ounces)
Taco sauce (optional)

Tired of using your ground beef the same old way? So was Mrs. Marx till she came up with this mildly spicy, south-of-the-border-style casserole.

Toss together potatoes, the ½ cup cheese, onion salt, and ¼ teaspoon *pepper*. Press into the bottom and up the sides of a greased 1-quart shallow baking dish. Bake in a 350° oven for 20 minutes.

Meanwhile, in a large skillet brown ground beef. Drain well and set aside. In the same skillet cook and stir cabbage over high heat for 2 to 3 minutes. Remove from heat and stir in ground beef, chili peppers, the ½ cup taco sauce, onion salt, and ¼ teaspoon *pepper*. Mound beef mixture into the partially baked potato crust. Bake for 20 minutes. Remove from oven and top with the 1 cup cheese. Return to oven and bake for 2 to 3 minutes more or till cheese is melted.

Let stand 10 minutes before serving. Serve with additional taco sauce, if desired. Makes 4 to 5 servings.

Mrs. Donald Marx, West Bend, Wisconsin

Reuben Meat Loaf

1 beaten egg
¼ cup Russian salad dressing
1 cup soft rye bread crumbs
½ cup chopped onion
¼ cup sweet pickle relish
1 tablespoon Worcestershire
  sauce
1½ pounds lean ground beef
  or pork
1 8-ounce can sauerkraut,
  drained and finely
  snipped
1 cup shredded Swiss cheese
  (4 ounces)

Bake some potatoes along with the meat loaf for an easy and energy-wise meal.

In a large mixing bowl combine egg and salad dressing. Stir in bread crumbs, onion, relish, Worcestershire sauce, ½ teaspoon *salt*, and ¼ teaspoon *pepper*. Add ground meat and mix well.

On a sheet of waxed paper, pat meat mixture into a 12x8-inch rectangle. Top with sauerkraut and ¾ *cup* of the cheese. Using waxed paper to lift rectangle, roll up meat from short side. Pinch edges together to seal.

Place roll, seam side down, in a 13x9x2-inch baking pan. Bake in a 350° oven for 50 minutes. Sprinkle remaining cheese atop. Bake 2 to 3 minutes more or till cheese is melted. Makes 8 servings.

Nickie Cartwright, Sunrise Beach, Missouri

Rancho Meatball Bake

1	16-ounce can tomatoes
1	15¾-ounce can barbecue beans
1	beaten egg
⅔	cup instant mashed potato flakes
½	of a 1¼-ounce envelope (¼ cup) *regular* onion soup mix
2	tablespoons catsup
2	teaspoons Worcestershire sauce
1	pound lean ground beef
½	cup all-purpose flour
1½	teaspoons baking powder
¼	teaspoon chili powder
¼	cup milk
2	tablespoons cooking oil

Cut up tomatoes. Combine *undrained* tomatoes and beans. Transfer to a 10x6x2-inch baking dish. Combine egg, potato flakes, soup mix, catsup, Worcestershire sauce, and ⅛ teaspoon *pepper.* Add beef and mix well. Shape beef mixture into 18 meatballs. Arrange meatballs atop bean mixture. Bake, covered, in a 375° oven for 35 minutes.

Meanwhile, for dumplings, stir together flour, baking powder, chili powder, and ¼ teaspoon *salt.* Add milk and oil, mixing well. Drop batter by spoonfuls to form 6 dumplings among the meatballs. Return to oven and bake, uncovered, for 20 minutes more. Serves 6.

Jennifer Such, Northridge, California

Lasagna in a Bun

¾	pound ground beef
1	8-ounce can tomato sauce
½	of a 1¼-ounce envelope (¼ cup) *regular* onion soup mix
¼	teaspoon dried oregano, crushed
¼	teaspoon dried basil, crushed
1	beaten egg
¾	cup ricotta *or* cream-style cottage cheese, drained
½	cup shredded mozzarella cheese (2 ounces)
8	hard rolls

Agnes credits her Grandma with this Italian-style meal-in-a-bun.

Cook ground beef till brown. Drain off fat. Stir in tomato sauce, soup mix, oregano, and basil. Cook, covered, over low heat for 5 minutes. Uncover and cook for 10 to 15 minutes more, stirring frequently.

Meanwhile, combine egg and cheeses. Cut a thin slice off the top of *each* roll. Remove soft bread in center of the bottom half of *each* roll, leaving a ½-inch shell. Spoon *half* of the meat mixture into bottom shells. Spoon egg-cheese mixture over meat. Spoon remaining meat mixture atop egg-cheese mixture. Replace roll tops. Wrap sandwiches individually in foil. Bake in a 400° oven 20 to 25 minutes. Serves 8.

Agnes B. Kleinhenz, Willoughby Hills, Ohio

Althea's budget-stretching one-dish meal goes together fast.

Corned Beef Stew

½ cup chopped onion
¼ cup chopped celery
¼ cup chopped green pepper
1 tablespoon cooking oil
2 cups water
2 medium potatoes, peeled and cubed (2 cups)
1 16-ounce can stewed tomatoes

1 medium zucchini, coarsely chopped
1 tablespoon catsup
1 tablespoon Worcestershire sauce
1 teaspoon instant beef bouillon granules
1 12-ounce can corned beef, cut into cubes

In a Dutch oven cook onion, celery, and green pepper in hot oil till tender but not brown. Stir in water, potatoes, *undrained* tomatoes, zucchini, catsup, Worcestershire sauce, and bouillon granules. Bring to boiling. Reduce heat and simmer, covered, about 15 minutes or till vegetables are tender. Stir in corned beef. Cook for 1 to 2 minutes more or till heated through. Serve immediately. Makes 4 servings.

Althea Taconi, Biloxi, Mississippi

Mediterranean Stew

3 medium potatoes, peeled and cut into 1-inch cubes (3 cups)
4 medium carrots, cut into 1-inch pieces (2 cups)
2 medium onions, cut into chunks
1 pound beef stew meat, cut into 1-inch cubes
1 8-ounce can tomato sauce
1 cup dry red wine
2 tablespoons wine vinegar
1 tablespoon brown sugar
1 teaspoon salt
¼ teaspoon ground cumin
⅛ teaspoon garlic powder
⅛ teaspoon pepper
¼ cup raisins
½ teaspoon whole cloves
1 inch stick cinnamon
1 bay leaf

By adding cinnamon, cloves, raisins, and wine, Linda transformed a basic beef stew into a pleasantly spicy Mediterranean-style meal.

In a 3½- or 4-quart electric slow crockery cooker place potatoes, carrots, onions, and stew meat. In a medium bowl combine tomato sauce, wine, vinegar, brown sugar, salt, cumin, garlic powder, and pepper. Stir in raisins, cloves, stick cinnamon, and bay leaf. Pour tomato sauce mixture over meat in cooker. Cover the cooker. Cook on high-heat setting for 5 to 6 hours, or on low-heat setting for 10 to 12 hours, or till tender. Remove cloves, stick cinnamon, and bay leaf before serving. Makes 5 or 6 servings.

Linda Becker, Roseburg, Oregon

Sesame Chipped Beef In Yogurt Sauce

2 tablespoons butter *or* margarine
2 tablespoons all-purpose flour
¼ teaspoon seasoned salt
1 cup milk
½ cup plain yogurt
1 3-ounce package sliced dried beef, cut into thin strips
¼ cup thinly sliced green onion
2 tablespoons toasted sesame seed
English muffins, toast points, *or* corn bread squares

Faith turned an old favorite— chipped beef—into a new low-cost dish for two.

In a 1-quart saucepan melt butter or margarine. Stir in flour and salt. Add milk all at once. Cook and stir till thickened and bubbly, then cook and stir 1 minute more. Gradually stir hot mixture into yogurt, stirring constantly. Return mixture to saucepan. Stir in dried beef, green onion, and sesame seed. Cook and stir till heated through. Serve over muffins, toast points, or corn bread squares. Serves 2.

Faith Clark, Macomb, Illinois

Sausage-Vegetable Skillet

½ cup brown rice
½ cup bulgur
8 ounces fully cooked smoked sausage links, thinly sliced
1 large green pepper, chopped
1 medium onion, thinly sliced and separated into rings
1 medium zucchini, thinly sliced
1 medium carrot, shredded
1 tablespoon cornstarch
1 tablespoon soy sauce
1 tablespoon honey
1 tablespoon dry sherry (optional)
1 teaspoon instant chicken bouillon granules
¼ teaspoon ground ginger
¼ teaspoon curry powder

Pictured at right.

Combine *uncooked* rice, 2¼ cups *water*, and ½ teaspoon *salt*. Bring to boiling. Reduce heat and simmer, covered, for 25 minutes. Stir in bulgur. Simmer, covered, for 15 to 20 minutes more or till done.

In a large skillet brown sausage. Add green pepper, onion, zucchini, and carrot. Cook and stir for 5 minutes. In a small bowl combine cornstarch; soy sauce; honey; sherry, if desired; bouillon granules; ginger; curry powder; and ¾ cup *cold water*. Add to skillet. Cook and stir till mixture is thickened and bubbly, then cook and stir for 2 minutes more. Serve sausage mixture over rice mixture. Serves 3.

Lois Jean Beer, Houston, Texas

Breakfast Pizza

1 pound bulk pork sausage
1 package (8) refrigerated crescent rolls
1 cup frozen loose-pack hash brown potatoes, thawed
1 cup shredded sharp cheddar cheese
5 beaten eggs
¼ cup milk
2 tablespoons grated Parmesan cheese

> **❝ I guess I've startled more than a few of my guests when I've mentioned we're having pizza for breakfast. ❞**

In a medium skillet cook and stir sausage till no longer pink. Drain well. Separate crescent dough into 8 triangles. Place dough in an ungreased 12-inch pizza pan, with points toward the center. Press over bottom and up sides to form a crust; seal perforations. Spoon sausage over crust. Sprinkle with potatoes. Top with cheddar cheese.

In a bowl stir together eggs, milk, and ⅛ teaspoon *pepper*. Carefully pour over mixture in crust. Sprinkle Parmesan cheese atop. Bake in a 375° oven about 25 minutes or till set. Makes 6 to 8 servings.

Roger Heisler, Reno, Nevada

Easy Sausage Dinner

By changing the fruits and spices in a magazine recipe, Kayleen tailored a recipe that was more suited to her family's tastes.

1 pound fully cooked Polish sausage, cut into ¼-inch-thick slices
1 large onion, thinly sliced
1 green pepper, cut into 1-inch squares
2 tablespoons cooking oil
1 16-ounce can sliced peaches
2 tablespoons sweet pickle relish
¼ cup cold water
1 tablespoon cornstarch
2 teaspoons prepared mustard
½ teaspoon instant chicken bouillon granules
2 cups hot cooked brown rice

Cook sausage, onion, and green pepper in hot oil for 5 minutes or till onion is tender. Drain. Stir in *undrained* peaches and pickle relish. Bring to boiling. Reduce heat and simmer, covered, for 5 minutes.

In a small bowl stir water into cornstarch. Stir in mustard, bouillon granules, and dash *pepper*. Stir into sausage mixture. Cook and stir till mixture is thickened and bubbly, then cook and stir for 2 minutes more. Serve over hot cooked rice. Makes 4 servings.

Kayleen L. Sloboden, Puyallup, Washington

Maple-Sauced Chops

If you'd rather use thinner chops, grill ½-inch pork loin chops, on an uncovered grill, directly over medium-hot coals for 5 minutes. Turn and grill for 5 to 7 minutes more or till no longer pink, brushing often with sauce during the last 5 minutes of grilling.

1 cup catsup
1 cup maple-flavored syrup
¾ cup dry white wine
¼ cup water
1 teaspoon instant beef bouillon granules
1 teaspoon dried thyme, crushed
1 teaspoon dried basil, crushed
1 teaspoon grated gingerroot *or* ¼ teaspoon ground ginger
½ teaspoon chili powder
½ teaspoon dry mustard
⅛ teaspoon ground cloves
2 cloves garlic, minced
1 bay leaf
4 pork loin chops, cut 1½ inches thick

For sauce, in a medium saucepan stir together catsup, maple-flavored syrup, wine, water, bouillon granules, thyme, basil, gingerroot, chili powder, mustard, cloves, garlic, bay leaf, ½ teaspoon *salt,* and ¼ teaspoon *pepper*. Bring mixture to boiling. Reduce heat and simmer, uncovered, about 30 minutes or till mixture is reduced to about 2 cups, stirring often. Remove bay leaf.

Grill chops on an uncovered grill directly over *medium* coals for 25 minutes. Turn chops and grill for 20 to 25 minutes more or till no longer pink, brushing often with sauce during the last 10 minutes of grilling. Pass any remaining sauce with the chops. Makes 4 servings.

Barbara Hope, New Haven, Connecticut

Split Pea-Bratwurst Stew

1 11½-ounce can condensed
  split pea soup
1 10-ounce package frozen
  whole kernel corn
1 10-ounce package frozen
  peas and carrots
1½ cups chopped, peeled
  potatoes (2 medium)

½ pound smoked bratwurst
  links, thinly sliced
1 cup chopped tomato
½ cup chopped celery
¼ cup chopped green pepper
1½ teaspoons dried dillweed
1½ teaspoons onion powder
1½ teaspoons chili powder

To move her menu plan beyond the usual, Tyanna improvised with foods she had on hand and came up with this savory stew.

In a Dutch oven combine soup, corn, peas and carrots, potatoes, bratwurst, tomato, celery, green pepper, dillweed, onion powder, chili powder, and 1¼ cups *water*. Cook, covered, about 10 minutes or till vegetables are thawed and mixture boils. Reduce heat and simmer, covered, about 25 minutes or till vegetables are tender. Serves 6.

Tyanna J. LaFrance, Aurora, Colorado

Salami 'n' Cheese Vegetablewiches

1¼ cups sliced cauliflower
  flowerets
½ cup frozen cut green beans
1 cup shredded Monterey
  Jack cheese (4 ounces)
4 ounces salami, cut up
1 medium green pepper, cut
  into julienne strips
⅔ cup shredded carrot
⅓ cup shredded dill pickle
¼ cup sliced green onion
¼ cup sliced radishes

6 individual French
  bread rolls
3 tablespoons butter *or*
  margarine, softened
3 tablespoons mayonnaise *or*
  salad dressing
1½ teaspoons prepared
  mustard
Leaf lettuce
3 tomato slices
⅓ cup creamy Italian
  salad dressing

Use a fork to lightly scrape and remove the bread from the bottom halves of the rolls.

Cook cauliflower and green beans, covered, in a small amount of boiling water for 3 to 5 minutes or till crisp-tender. Drain and chill. Combine chilled vegetables, cheese, salami, green pepper, carrot, pickle, onion, and radishes. Toss to mix well.

Cut a thin slice off tops of rolls. Remove bread from bottom halves, leaving ¼-inch shells. Stir together butter, mayonnaise, and mustard. Spread some of the mayonnaise mixture into *each* bottom shell. Line bottom shells with lettuce leaves. Divide vegetable mixture among bottom shells. Halve tomato slices and place atop the vegetable mixture. Drizzle about *1 tablespoon* Italian salad dressing over each. Replace bread tops. Makes 6 servings.

Mrs. Amelia Shearouse, Orlando, Florida

Barbecue-Style Pork Steaks

Barbecue in your crockery cooker? Alice did—with award-winning results!

4 pork shoulder steaks, cut
   ½ inch thick
1 tablespoon cooking oil
1 large onion, thinly sliced
   and separated into rings
1 large green pepper, thinly
   sliced

2 tomatoes, sliced
1 tablespoon quick-cooking
   tapioca
½ cup bottled barbecue sauce
¼ cup dry red wine
½ teaspoon ground cumin

Cut pork steaks in half crosswise. Trim excess fat. In a large skillet brown steaks on both sides in hot oil. Drain steaks on paper towels.

In a 3½- or 4-quart electric slow crockery cooker arrange the onion, green pepper, and tomatoes. Sprinkle tapioca over vegetables. Place pork steaks atop vegetables and tapioca. In a small bowl stir together barbecue sauce, wine, and cumin. Pour over meat and vegetables in the crockery cooker. Cover and cook on low-heat setting for 6 to 8 hours or till meat and vegetables are tender. To serve, transfer meat and vegetables to a serving platter. Makes 4 to 6 servings.

Alice Lewis, Boulder, Colorado

Pork Ribs with Apple Butter Sauce

If you'd like, precook the ribs and make the apple butter sauce a day ahead. Just keep them in the refrigerator till you're ready to grill.

4 pounds country-style pork ribs
1 14-ounce jar apple butter
¼ cup vinegar
3 tablespoons lemon juice
2 teaspoons prepared horseradish
1 teaspoon prepared mustard
½ teaspoon celery seed
½ teaspoon sugar
½ teaspoon garlic powder
Dash ground red pepper
Dash ground cumin

Place ribs in a large Dutch oven. Add enough water to cover. Bring to boiling. Reduce heat and simmer, covered, for 45 to 60 minutes or till meat is tender. Drain well. Sprinkle ribs with salt and pepper.

For sauce, stir together apple butter, vinegar, lemon juice, horseradish, mustard, celery seed, sugar, garlic powder, red pepper, cumin, ½ cup *water*, ½ teaspoon *salt*, and ⅛ teaspoon *pepper*. Bring to boiling. Reduce heat and simmer, uncovered, about 25 minutes or till mixture is reduced to about 2 cups, stirring often.

Place the ribs in a rib rack, if desired. Grill the ribs, on an uncovered grill, directly over *slow* coals about 45 minutes or till heated through, turning every 15 minutes. Brush ribs often with sauce during the last 15 minutes of grilling. Makes 4 to 6 servings.

Helen P. Ogren, Olympia, Washington

Tortilla Roll-Ups

Lee Ann wrapped Italian seasonings, sausage, and spaghetti sauce in Mexican tortillas for a two-in-one international dining experience.

1½ pounds bulk Italian sausage
2 cups cream-style cottage cheese
2 tablespoons all-purpose flour
3 cups spaghetti sauce
1 teaspoon dried oregano, crushed
1 teaspoon dried basil, crushed
¼ teaspoon garlic powder
10 large flour tortillas
1½ cups shredded mozzarella cheese (6 ounces)

Cook and stir sausage till no longer pink. Drain well. Stir in *undrained* cottage cheese and flour. Set aside. Combine spaghetti sauce, oregano, basil, and garlic powder. Stir ½ *cup* of the spaghetti sauce mixture into the sausage mixture. Spoon about ⅓ *cup* of the sausage mixture onto *each* tortilla. Roll up. Place tortillas, seam side down, in a 13x9x2-inch baking pan. Pour remaining spaghetti sauce mixture atop. Bake, covered, in a 375° oven for 35 to 40 minutes or till heated through. Uncover. Sprinkle mozzarella cheese atop. Bake about 3 minutes more or till cheese is melted. Serves 8 to 10.

Lee Ann Zimmerley, Rochester, Minnesota

Fiesta Ham Pie

½ cup chopped onion
⅓ cup chopped green pepper
2 tablespoons cooking oil
2 tablespoons all-purpose flour
½ of a 1¼-ounce package (2 tablespoons) taco seasoning mix
3 cups fully cooked ham, cut into bite-size strips (1 pound)

1 8-ounce can whole kernel corn
1 8-ounce can tomato sauce
1 cup water
½ cup sliced, pitted ripe olives
1 8½-ounce package corn muffin mix
¾ cup shredded cheddar cheese (3 ounces)

In a large saucepan cook onion and green pepper in hot oil till onion is tender but not brown. Stir in flour and taco seasoning mix. Add ham, *undrained* corn, tomato sauce, water, and olives. Bring mixture to boiling, stirring constantly. Remove from heat and set aside.

Prepare corn muffin mix according to package directions. Stir in ½ *cup* of the cheese. Pour ham mixture into a 9x9x2-inch baking pan. Top with spoonfuls of corn muffin batter. Bake in a 375° oven for 25 minutes. Sprinkle remaining ¼ cup cheese atop. Bake about 5 minutes more or till cheese is melted. Let stand 5 minutes before serving. Makes 8 servings.

Mrs. Maxine Docken, Browns Valley, California

Ham and Fruit Sandwiches

For an informal lunch or supper, arrange the makings for this fresh-tasting sandwich on a tray and let each person help himself.

1½ cups diced fully cooked ham
1 medium apple, cored and chopped (1 cup)
1 8¼-ounce can crushed pineapple, drained
½ cup thinly sliced celery

½ cup mayonnaise *or* salad dressing
8 slices raisin bread, toasted and buttered
4 slices Muenster cheese, halved diagonally
Apple slices

In a medium mixing bowl stir together the ham, apple, pineapple, celery, and mayonnaise or salad dressing. Spread *each* toast slice with about ⅓ *cup* of the ham mixture. Top each with cheese and apple slices. Makes 4 servings.

Mrs. Barbara C. Gossage, Springfield, Virginia

Vegetable-Ham Roll

2 tablespoons chopped onion
2 tablespoons butter *or* margarine
1 tablespoon all-purpose flour
¼ cup milk

1 beaten egg
1 6½-ounce can chunk-style ham, drained and broken up
Pastry
Vegetable Sauce

Wrapped in flaky pastry and smothered in a vegetable sauce, canned chunk ham takes on an elegant appearance.

For filling, in a small saucepan cook onion in butter or margarine till tender but not brown. Stir in flour and a dash *pepper*. Add milk all at once. Cook and stir till bubbly. Reserve 1 tablespoon of the beaten egg. Gradually stir filling into remaining beaten egg. Stir in ham.

Prepare pastry. Spread filling lengthwise down the center of the pastry rectangle, leaving about 2 inches along each side. Fold one pastry edge over filling. Brush with some of the reserved egg. Fold remaining pastry edge over filling and pastry. Seal.

Place roll, seam side down, on a greased baking sheet. Brush top with remaining reserved egg. Bake in a 400° oven for 35 to 40 minutes or till pastry is golden brown. Serve with Vegetable Sauce. Makes 4 to 6 servings.

Pastry: In a medium mixing bowl stir together 1 cup *all-purpose flour* and ½ teaspoon *salt.* Cut in ⅓ cup *shortening* till pieces are the size of small peas. Sprinkle 1 tablespoon *cold water* over part of the flour mixture and toss with a fork. Push to side of bowl. Repeat with 2 to 3 tablespoons more *water* till all is moistened. Form dough into a ball. On a floured surface roll dough into a 12x7-inch rectangle.

Vegetable Sauce: Drain one 8-ounce can *mixed vegetables,* reserving liquid. Add enough *milk* to reserved liquid to make 1 cup. In a small saucepan, melt 2 tablespoons *butter or margarine.* Stir in 2 tablespoons *all-purpose flour.* Add milk mixture all at once. Cook and stir till thickened and bubbly. Stir in ½ cup shredded *American cheese* till melted. Stir in vegetables. Heat through.

Mrs. Elmo Stutlien, Blair, Wisconsin

Orange Chicken Delight

Lois put some zing into her potluck chicken-and-noodle dish when she added an appealing orange sauce. (Pictured at left.)

4 cups wide egg noodles
1½ cups chicken broth
½ cup frozen orange juice concentrate, thawed

2 tablespoons cornstarch
½ teaspoon fines herbes
2 cups cubed cooked chicken
½ cup sliced almonds, toasted

Cook noodles according to package directions. Drain. Set aside. In a large saucepan stir together the chicken broth, orange juice concentrate, cornstarch, and fines herbes. Cook and stir till thickened and bubbly, then cook and stir for 2 minutes more. Carefully stir in cooked noodles and chicken. Transfer mixture to a 2-quart casserole. Bake, uncovered, in a 350° oven for 15 to 20 minutes or till heated through. Sprinkle with almonds. Makes 6 servings.

Lois Sorenson, Bonney Lake, Washington

Chicken Cannelloni

¾ cup thinly sliced celery
½ cup thinly sliced carrot
½ cup sliced fresh mushrooms
1 small onion, sliced
1 clove garlic, minced
1 tablespoon cooking oil
1 8-ounce can tomato sauce
1 7½-ounce can tomatoes, cut up
1 teaspoon Italian seasoning
¾ teaspoon sugar

3 whole medium chicken breasts (about 2¼ pounds), skinned, boned, and halved lengthwise
½ cup ricotta cheese
3 tablespoons grated Parmesan cheese
1 tablespoon sliced green onion
½ teaspoon Italian seasoning
2 ounces mozzarella cheese

For sauce, cook celery, carrot, mushrooms, onion, and garlic in hot oil till onion is tender. Stir in tomato sauce, *undrained* tomatoes, the 1 teaspoon Italian seasoning, and sugar. Bring to boiling. Reduce heat and simmer, uncovered, for 20 minutes.

Place each chicken piece, boned side up, between two pieces of clear plastic wrap. Working from center to edges, lightly pound the chicken with the fine-toothed or flat side of a meat mallet to ¼-inch thickness. Remove plastic wrap. Stir together ricotta cheese, Parmesan cheese, onion, the ½ teaspoon Italian seasoning, and dash *pepper*. Place about *1½ tablespoons* cheese mixture onto *each* chicken piece. Roll up. Place rolls, seam side down, in an 8x8x2-inch baking dish. Pour sauce atop. Bake, covered, in a 375° oven about 25 minutes or till tender. Cut mozzarella into thin strips. Place atop. Bake about 3 minutes more or till cheese is melted. Makes 6 servings.

Laura de Ghitaldi-Boessevain, Boulder, Colorado

Chicken and Wheat Berry Bake

Wheat berries are unpolished whole wheat kernels. Look for them in large supermarkets or in health food shops.

½ cup chopped onion
2 tablespoons cooking oil
½ cup wheat berries
2 to 3 teaspoons curry powder

3 cups chicken broth
1 cup brown rice
1 16-ounce package frozen mixed vegetables
2 cups cubed cooked chicken

In a large saucepan cook onion in hot oil till tender but not brown. Add wheat berries and curry powder. Cook and stir for 1 minute more. Stir in chicken broth. Bring mixture to boiling. Reduce heat and cook, covered, for 15 minutes. Add the rice. Cook, covered, for 35 minutes more. Stir in the vegetables and chicken.

Transfer mixture to a 2-quart casserole. Bake, covered, in a 350° oven for 30 to 35 minutes. Uncover and bake for 5 minutes more or till vegetables are tender. Makes 6 servings.

JoLoyce Kaia, Hana, Hawaii

Chicken-Rice Pockets

For serving ease, Stephanie suggests making the filling for this superb sandwich several hours ahead. Store it in the refrigerator till you're ready to eat.

⅓ cup long grain rice
½ teaspoon instant chicken bouillon granules
1½ cups cubed cooked chicken
2 *or* 3 small tomatoes, seeded and chopped
1 avocado, seeded, peeled, and chopped
1 cup frozen chopped broccoli, cooked and drained
½ cup shredded cheddar cheese (2 ounces)
¼ cup sliced, pitted ripe olives
1 hard-cooked egg, chopped
½ cup mayonnaise *or* salad dressing
1 tablespoon Dijon-style mustard
2 teaspoons honey
¼ teaspoon celery salt
⅛ teaspoon pepper
4 *or* 5 large pita bread rounds, halved crosswise

In a small saucepan bring ⅔ cup *water* to boiling. Stir in the *uncooked* rice and bouillon granules. Reduce heat and simmer, covered, for 20 minutes or till rice is tender and water is absorbed.

Meanwhile, in a large mixing bowl, combine chicken, tomatoes, avocado, broccoli, cheese, olives, and egg. Add cooked rice. For dressing, in a small mixing bowl stir together mayonnaise or salad dressing, mustard, honey, celery salt, and pepper. Pour dressing over chicken mixture. Toss to coat well. Cover and chill well. To serve, spoon about ½ *cup* of the chicken mixture into *each* pita bread half. Makes 8 to 10 servings.

Stephanie T. Stitt, Berea, Ohio

Oriental Chicken-Salad Sandwich

Donna's partiality to Asian seasonings such as rice wine vinegar and sesame oil is deliciously reflected in her pita creation.

2 cups finely chopped cooked chicken
1 cup fresh *or* canned bean sprouts
3 green onions, sliced (about ⅓ cup)
2 tablespoons soy sauce
2 tablespoons rice wine vinegar *or* white wine vinegar
2 teaspoons sesame oil
2 large pita bread rounds, halved crosswise
4 lettuce leaves

In a large bowl combine chicken, sprouts, and green onions. Set aside. For dressing, in a screw-top jar combine soy sauce, rice wine vinegar or white wine vinegar, and sesame oil. Cover. Shake well. Pour dressing over chicken mixture. Toss to coat well. Cover and chill.

To serve, line *each* pita half with a lettuce leaf. Spoon about ½ *cup* of the chicken mixture into *each* pita half. Makes 4 servings.

Donna Holohan, Worcester, Massachusetts

Hot and Spicy Chicken Pie

When you're in the mood for something a little hot 'n' spicy, try Shirley's winning Tex-Mex chicken-vegetable pie. (Pictured at right.)

3 whole medium chicken breasts (about 2¼ pounds), skinned, boned, and cut into bite-size pieces
1 cup frozen whole kernel corn
½ cup sliced celery
½ cup chicken broth
1 medium onion, cut into thin wedges
½ cup salsa
4 teaspoons cornstarch
1 8½-ounce package corn bread mix
2 4-ounce cans diced green chili peppers, drained
1½ cups shredded cheddar cheese (6 ounces)
Hot peppers (optional)

In a medium saucepan combine chicken, corn, celery, broth, and onion. Bring mixture to boiling. Reduce heat and simmer, uncovered, for 10 to 15 minutes or till vegetables are crisp-tender. Add salsa. Stir 2 tablespoons cold *water* into cornstarch and stir into chicken mixture. Cook and stir till mixture is thickened and bubbly, then cook and stir for 2 minutes more. Transfer chicken mixture to a 10x6x2-inch baking dish. Sprinkle with chili peppers and cheese. Prepare corn bread mix according to package directions. Spoon corn bread batter atop chicken mixture. Bake in a 425° oven about 20 minutes or till golden. Garnish with hot peppers, if desired. Makes 4 to 6 servings.

Shirley C. Marbach, Lancaster, California

Raspberry Chicken

Using readily available ingredients instead of the more expensive berry vinegars, Sally created a recipe full of flavor and sophistication.

2 whole large chicken breasts (about 2 pounds), skinned, boned, and halved lengthwise
2 tablespoons butter *or* margarine
¼ cup finely chopped onion
3 tablespoons raspberry jelly
3 tablespoons wine vinegar
¼ cup whipping cream

Sprinkle chicken lightly with salt. In a 10-inch skillet melt butter or margarine. Add chicken pieces. Cook over medium heat for 5 minutes. Turn chicken and add onion to skillet. Cook about 5 minutes more or till chicken is no longer pink and onion is tender. Remove chicken from skillet and keep warm.

For sauce, add jelly and wine vinegar to skillet. Cook and stir, scraping up bits of chicken from the bottom of the pan. Bring mixture to boiling. Boil about 1 minute or till slightly reduced. Stir in cream. Heat just to boiling. Pour sauce over chicken. Makes 4 servings.

Sally Vog, Springfield, Oregon

JACQUELINE McCOMAS, FRAZER, PA.

This culinary yarn begins 40 miles outside historic Philadelphia, in small-town Frazer. That's where Jacqueline McComas shares an apartment with her two daughters, Chantel and Cari.

Frazer has its own historic atmosphere, being close to Valley Forge National Park, a carefully restored site of Washington's encampment. In the summertime, the park provides an ideal spot for Jackie to picnic with friends who line up to devour her latest cooking masterpieces.

But this story really begins with Jacqueline, whose mother encouraged her to experiment in the kitchen as a small child. "Mother is the best cook," says Jackie. "She makes terrific meat loaf, stuffings, and gravies. To this day I can't make a pot roast like she can." But Jackie developed her own specialties, and her talents were officially recognized when she was in junior high. "My first real prize in cooking was a cookbook I received for winning the home economics award," she says.

That was the beginning of a long career of winning national and local contests for her recipe inventions. "I've won everything from two dollars to $500 and a silver tray, but I've enjoyed all the contests very much," admits Jackie. Some of the competi-tions have been tests of more than just culinary skill. "The night before I was to enter the Maryland Oyster contest, I was involved in a car accident. A friend of mine drove me to the contest, but when I arrived, I was assigned an oven that refused to work. I wound up sharing other contestants' ovens. But," laughs Jackie, "I won first prize!"

At one point, Jackie also found time to dabble in the food business. "For two years," she says, "I worked at a garden and gourmet center, assisting cooks at the cooking school. On weekends, I demonstrated various appliances. I developed my own recipes to go with the demonstrations." Since it was also a garden center, Jackie incorporated fresh herbs into the recipes. That first-hand experience in the food business led Jackie to catering small dinners and parties for friends.

(continued)

JACQUELINE McCOMAS, FRAZER, PA.

> **66** *As a single parent with two teenage daughters, I often need to put a meal together in just a few minutes.* **99**

Now with a six-day-a-week secretarial job and a couple of teenagers at home, Jackie focuses on quick and easy suppers that fit in with their busy schedules. "Putting a meal together in a few minutes is important to me," she admits. "I like to save as much time as possible." That philosophy has prompted her to develop some ingenious shortcuts. Like the time she needed to make individual pastry cups for a recipe contest entry. She opted for round bread slices cut with a biscuit cutter and rolled to fit muffin cups. Besides saving ten minutes preparation time, she won the contest.

Not surprisingly, Jackie's daughters now wield a pretty mean spatula themselves. "I think my children have learned to cook simply by osmosis," says Jackie. Chantel, the oldest, is fond of vegetarian dishes and has begun winning prizes, too. "And Cari, a more traditional cook, makes a wonderful apple pie," says her proud mother.

The girls, along with Jackie's bosses, are also good critics, cheerleaders, and willing taste-testers. It's not unusual for Jackie to head off to work armed with a barrage of new recipe creations to try out on her willing judges. Proof enough that when Jackie cooks, it's no contest.

JACQUELINE McCOMAS, FRAZER, PA.

Chicken Crumb Pie is just one of the many entries for which Jackie has won prizes in *Better Homes and Gardens*® magazine's contests. A delicious example of her quick and easy philosophy, this pie bakes up in just about a half hour. "There's no need to roll out the crust, because I just press the dough into the pan," says Jackie.

Chicken Crumb Pie

When fresh basil is in season, Jackie likes to top the finished pie with a sprig.

¾ cup all-purpose flour
1 teaspoon dried basil, crushed, *or* 1 tablespoon snipped fresh basil
¼ cup butter *or* margarine
2 tablespoons milk
1 whole large chicken breast (about 1 pound), skinned, boned, and cut into strips
2 tablespoons all-purpose flour
⅓ cup chopped onion
⅓ cup chopped celery
½ cup chopped sweet red *or* green pepper
3 tablespoons butter *or* margarine
½ of a 3-ounce package cream cheese, cubed
¼ cup dairy sour cream
¼ cup milk
⅛ teaspoon pepper
Crumb Topper
Sweet red *or* green pepper strips (optional)
Celery leaves (optional)

For crust, in a bowl stir together the ¾ cup flour and basil. Cut in the ¼ cup butter or margarine till pieces are the size of small peas. Stir in the 2 tablespoons milk till mixture is moistened. Press mixture evenly over the bottom and up the sides of a shallow casserole dish or a 7-inch pie plate. Bake in a 350° oven for 12 minutes.

Meanwhile, coat chicken strips with the 2 tablespoons flour. In a large skillet cook onion, celery, and red and green pepper in the 3 tablespoons butter or margarine till onion is tender but not brown. Add chicken strips. Cook and stir for 2 to 3 minutes or till chicken is no longer pink. Stir in cream cheese, sour cream, the ¼ cup milk, and pepper. Spoon chicken mixture into baked crust.

Bake, uncovered, in a 350° oven about 15 minutes or till heated through. Sprinkle with Crumb Topper. Bake for 5 minutes more. Garnish with sweet red or green pepper strips and celery leaves, if desired. Makes 3 servings.

Crumb Topper: In a small mixing bowl combine ¼ cup seasoned *fine dry bread crumbs,* 1 tablespoon grated *Parmesan cheese,* and 1 tablespoon melted *butter or margarine.* Stir to mix well.

Turkey Chili With Pasta

2 pounds ground raw turkey
1 large onion, chopped
3 cloves garlic, minced
1 tablespoon cooking oil (optional)
2 16-ounce cans tomatoes, cut up
¼ cup unsweetened cocoa powder
2 tablespoons chili powder
1 teaspoon crushed red pepper

1 teaspoon dried oregano, crushed
1 teaspoon ground cumin
1 16-ounce can dark red kidney beans
4 cups hot cooked vermicelli (8 ounces)
1 cup shredded cheddar cheese (4 ounces)
½ cup oyster crackers

This is Cincinnati-style chili, served over hot vermicelli. The ground turkey makes Jane's version special.

In a Dutch oven cook and stir ground turkey, onion, and garlic till turkey is no longer pink and onion is tender (add oil if necessary). Stir in *undrained* tomatoes, cocoa powder, chili powder, red pepper, oregano, cumin, and 1 teaspoon *salt*. Bring to boiling. Reduce heat and simmer, covered, for 1 hour, stirring often. Stir in *undrained* kidney beans and ½ cup *water*. Return to boiling. Reduce heat and simmer, covered, for 30 minutes more. Serve over vermicelli. Sprinkle with cheddar cheese. Top with oyster crackers. Serves 8.

Jane Hufford Downes, Toledo, Ohio

Turkey-Apple Burgers

1 tablespoon dried minced onion
2 tablespoons brandy *or* apple juice
1 slightly beaten egg
1½ cups soft rye bread crumbs (2 slices)

1 large apple, cored and coarsely shredded (1⅓ cups)
1 pound turkey breakfast sausage
Lettuce leaves

Mickey prefers turkey breakfast sausage over its pork counterpart because it's lower in fat and calories. She saves additional calories by serving the burgers on lettuce leaves instead of hamburger buns.

In a bowl combine onion and brandy or apple juice. Stir in egg, bread crumbs, and apple. Add turkey sausage. Mix well. Shape mixture into four ½-inch-thick patties. Place patties in a greased shallow baking pan. Bake in a 350° oven for 16 to 18 minutes or till no longer pink. (*Or*, grill patties, on an uncovered grill, directly over *medium-hot* coals for 10 to 12 minutes or till well done.) Serve burgers on lettuce leaves with tomato slices and onion slices, if desired. Serves 4.

Mickey Strang, Ridgecrest, California

Ratatouille Casserole

2½ cups herb-seasoned croutons, crushed
1 large onion, coarsely chopped (1 cup)
1 clove garlic, minced
2 tablespoons cooking oil
1 small eggplant, peeled and cut into ½-inch pieces
1 cup thinly sliced zucchini
1 green pepper, cut into ½-inch pieces (¾ cup)
2 tomatoes, seeded and chopped
1 cup sliced fresh mushrooms
3 cups cubed cooked turkey
1 teaspoon Italian seasoning
2 cups shredded Swiss cheese (8 ounces)

Kayleen delightfully disguised leftover turkey in this attractive and economical Italian-seasoned casserole.

Spread crushed croutons evenly in the bottom of a 12x7½x2-inch baking dish. Set aside. In a large skillet cook onion and garlic in hot oil till onion is tender but not brown. Add eggplant, zucchini, and green pepper. Cook and stir for 5 minutes. Add tomatoes and mushrooms. Cook for 1 minute. Stir in turkey and Italian seasoning. Cook for 1 minute more.

Sprinkle ½ *cup* cheese over croutons. Top with *half* of the turkey mixture and *1 cup* of the cheese. Spread remaining turkey mixture atop. Bake, covered, in a 350° oven for 30 minutes. Top with remaining ½ cup cheese. Bake, uncovered, for 10 minutes more. Let stand for 5 minutes. Makes 10 servings.

Kayleen L. Sloboden, Puyallup, Washington

Turkey Red Reuben

1 tablespoon mayonnaise *or* salad dressing
2 slices rye bread
2 ounces thinly sliced cooked turkey breast
⅓ cup sweet-sour red cabbage, drained
1½ ounces sliced Monterey Jack cheese

Fairah revised the classic Reuben sandwich by using sliced turkey and sweet-sour cabbage to decrease the fat and sodium.

For sandwich, spread *half* of the mayonnaise or salad dressing on *each* slice of bread. Place sliced turkey on *1* slice of bread, then top with drained cabbage. Place sliced cheese atop the cabbage. Top with remaining bread slice. Chill till serving time. Makes 1 serving.

Fairah Randall, Seattle, Washington

The cornmeal topper makes a hearty addition to Anne's full-flavored vegetable soup.

Tamale-Lentil Soup

3½ cups water
½ cup dry lentils
1 cup frozen whole kernel corn
1 cup frozen cut green beans
1 cup sliced zucchini *or* yellow summer squash
1 cup sliced celery
1 cup sliced carrot
1 8-ounce can stewed tomatoes
1 7¾-ounce can semi-condensed tomato soup

½ cup chopped onion
½ cup chopped green pepper
1 clove garlic, minced
¾ teaspoon salt
¾ teaspoon chili powder
¼ teaspoon ground cumin
⅛ teaspoon pepper
Tamale Topper
½ cup shredded cheddar cheese (2 ounces)

In a 4½-quart Dutch oven combine *1½ cups* of water and lentils. Bring to boiling. Reduce heat and simmer, covered, for 20 minutes or till lentils are softened. Drain. Add remaining 2 cups water, corn, green beans, zucchini or summer squash, celery, carrot, tomatoes, soup, onion, green pepper, garlic, salt, chili powder, cumin, and pepper. Return to boiling. Reduce heat and simmer, covered, about 20 minutes or till vegetables are crisp-tender. Drop Tamale Topper by tablespoonfuls atop the lentil mixture. Simmer, covered, about 20 minutes more or till a toothpick inserted in the Topper comes out clean (do not lift cover while cooking). Top with cheese. Serves 4.

Tamale Topper: In a medium saucepan combine ¾ cup *cornmeal* and ½ teaspoon *salt.* Stir in 1¼ cups *milk.* Cook and stir till mixture is thickened and bubbly. Gradually stir hot cornmeal mixture into 1 beaten *egg.* Stir in ½ cup shredded *cheddar cheese.*

Anne Glenn, Eugene, Oregon

Chili-Polenta Deep-Dish Pie

¾ cup cornmeal
¾ cup cold water
½ teaspoon salt
1 16-ounce can dark red kidney beans, drained
1 15-ounce can chili with beans
1 7½-ounce can chili with beans
¼ cup dried minced onion
1 teaspoon paprika
¼ teaspoon curry powder
Corn chips (optional)
Green pepper rings (optional)
Cherry tomatoes (optional)

In a saucepan bring 2 cups *water* to boiling. Meanwhile, in a small bowl combine cornmeal, cold water, and salt. Gradually stir cornmeal mixture into boiling water in saucepan, stirring constantly. Cook till mixture is thick, stirring frequently. Cook, covered, over low heat for 10 minutes. Cool slightly. Pour mixture into a greased 2-quart casserole, pushing mixture up the sides to form a shell. Cover surface with waxed paper and chill about 1 hour or till set.

Meanwhile, combine kidney beans, chili with beans, onion, paprika, and curry powder. Spoon bean mixture into cornmeal shell. Bake, covered, in a 400° oven for 30 minutes. Uncover and bake about 20 minutes more or till heated through. Garnish with corn chips, green pepper rings, and cherry tomatoes, if desired. Makes 4 servings.

Mrs. Roger Nacker, Madison, Wisconsin

Peanut Butter-Cream Cheese Sandwiches

Two all-American taste treats team up for a double-decker delight.

1 8-ounce package cream cheese, softened
1 tablespoon Worcestershire sauce
1⅓ cups chopped celery
½ cup shredded carrot
3 tablespoons toasted sesame seed
⅛ teaspoon dried oregano, crushed
Milk (optional)
16 slices whole wheat bread
Shredded lettuce
Peanut butter

In a mixer bowl beat together cream cheese and Worcestershire sauce till fluffy. Stir in celery, carrot, sesame seed, and oregano. Cover. Chill well. (If necessary, stir in a little milk to make mixture spreadable.)

Spread ¼ *cup* of the cream cheese mixture on *1 slice* of bread. Top with some shredded lettuce. On *another* slice of bread spread some peanut butter. Place bread, peanut butter side down, atop lettuce. Repeat to make remaining sandwiches. Makes 8 sandwiches.

Gloria E. Rodebough, Lima, Ohio

Velvety Garbanzo Soup

Pictured at right.

1½ cups dry garbanzo beans
1 cup chopped onion
1 clove garlic, minced
1 tablespoon cooking oil

6 cups water
2 tablespoons soy sauce
¾ teaspoon salt
¼ cup snipped parsley
¼ cup chopped peanuts

In a medium mixing bowl combine dry garbanzo beans with enough water to cover. Cover and refrigerate overnight. Drain.

In a Dutch oven or large saucepan cook onion and garlic in hot oil till onion is tender but not brown. Add drained garbanzo beans, the 6 cups water, soy sauce, and salt. Bring to boiling. Reduce heat and simmer, covered, about 3 hours or till beans are tender.

Transfer *half* of the bean mixture to a blender container or food processor bowl. Cover and blend or process till smooth. Repeat with remaining bean mixture. Return all of the bean mixture to the Dutch oven or large saucepan. Heat through. Sprinkle with parsley. Top each serving with peanuts. Makes 4 servings.

Mrs. Debbie Hess, Glenside, Pennsylvania

Teriyaki Tofu-Bean Salad

If you need to store tofu for a few days, drain and rinse it. Place the tofu in a container and cover with cold water. Tightly seal the container and refrigerate. Drain the tofu and change the water daily.

1 16-ounce package fresh bean curd (tofu), cubed (3 cups)
1 15-ounce can garbanzo beans, drained
2 cups sliced fresh mushrooms
1 small green pepper, cut into bite-size pieces
1 small tomato, seeded and chopped
⅓ cup sliced green onion

¼ cup snipped parsley
1 clove garlic, minced
¼ cup red wine vinegar
¼ cup olive oil *or* cooking oil
2 tablespoons Dijon-style mustard
1 teaspoon soy sauce
½ teaspoon salt
½ teaspoon ground ginger
Leaf lettuce
Sesame seed (optional)

In a large mixing bowl combine bean curd, garbanzo beans, mushrooms, green pepper, tomato, green onion, and parsley. For dressing, in a screw-top jar combine garlic, vinegar, olive oil or cooking oil, mustard, soy sauce, salt, and ginger. Cover and shake well. Pour dressing over bean curd mixture. Toss to mix well. Cover and chill for several hours or overnight. To serve, use a slotted spoon to arrange bean curd mixture atop lettuce. Sprinkle with sesame seed, if desired. Makes 4 or 5 servings.

Katherine S. Hartman, Brandon, Florida

Cheesy Rice Balls

3 cups cooked rice, chilled	½ cup finely crushed
3 slightly beaten eggs	saltine crackers
⅓ cup all-purpose flour	Cooking oil
¼ teaspoon salt	Vegetable Sauce
¼ teaspoon pepper	
3 ounces American cheese,	
cut into ½-inch cubes	

Attractively round out this meatless meal by garnishing the serving platter with cooked broccoli spears.

In a medium mixing bowl combine rice, eggs, flour, salt, and pepper. Stir to mix well. For *each* rice ball, with wet hands, shape about *2 tablespoons* of the rice mixture around *1* cheese cube (reserve extra cheese cubes for use in the Vegetable Sauce). Roll rice balls in the crushed crackers.

In an 8-inch skillet heat ½ inch of cooking oil to 365°. Fry rice balls, 4 or 5 at a time, in hot oil for 2½ to 3 minutes or till golden, turning once. Drain rice balls on paper towels. Keep warm. Prepare Vegetable Sauce. To serve, place rice balls on a serving platter. Pour Vegetable Sauce over rice balls. Makes 4 servings.

Vegetable Sauce: In a small saucepan cook 2 tablespoons chopped *green pepper*, 2 tablespoons chopped *onion*, and 2 tablespoons shredded *carrot* in 2 tablespoons *butter or margarine* till onion is tender but not brown. Stir in 2 tablespoons *all-purpose flour* and dash *pepper*. Add 1¼ cups *milk* all at once. Cook and stir till mixture is thickened and bubbly, then cook and stir for 1 minute more. Add any reserved cheese cubes, stirring till cheese is melted.

Mrs. Deanna Powers, Rapid City, South Dakota

Brunch Scrambled Eggs

Robin added chopped spinach and feta cheese to ordinary scrambled eggs for an out-of-the-ordinary entrée.

1 10-ounce package frozen chopped spinach, thawed
12 eggs
½ cup milk
¼ teaspoon salt
2 tablespoons butter *or* margarine
1 cup shredded Colby *or* cheddar cheese
1 cup crumbled feta cheese

Drain spinach well, pressing out excess liquid. Set aside. In a medium bowl beat together eggs, milk, salt, and ⅛ teaspoon *pepper*. In a skillet melt butter or margarine over medium heat. Pour in egg mixture. Cook, without stirring, till mixture begins to set on the bottom and around edges. Using a spatula, lift partially cooked eggs so uncoooked portion flows underneath. Stir in spinach, Colby or cheddar cheese, and *half* of the feta cheese. Cook and stir for 2 to 3 minutes or till eggs are cooked, but still glossy and moist. Transfer to a serving platter. Sprinkle with remaining feta cheese. Serves 6.

Robin Cronin, Royal Oak, Michigan

Peppy Avocado-Stuffed Eggs

Olivia crossed a deviled egg recipe with an egg casserole recipe to come up with this sure-fire winner.

4 hard-cooked eggs
  Lemon juice
1 avocado, seeded, peeled, and halved lengthwise
2 teaspoons prepared horseradish mustard
1 teaspoon lemon juice
1 tablespoon finely chopped onion
2 tablespoons butter *or* margarine
2 tablespoons all-purpose flour
1 teaspoon instant chicken bouillon granules
1 teaspoon dried parsley flakes
½ cup milk
¼ cup chopped fully cooked ham

Peel eggs and halve lengthwise. Remove yolks and put in a small bowl. Set egg whites aside. Rub lemon juice over cut edges of *1* avocado half. Store for another use. Mash remaining avocado half and combine with egg yolks, mustard, the 1 teaspoon lemon juice, and 1 teaspoon *salt*. Mix well. Fill egg whites with avocado mixture. Arrange in 2 individual casseroles. For sauce, cook onion in butter or margarine till tender. Stir in flour, bouillon, and parsley. Add milk and ½ cup *water* all at once. Cook and stir till thickened and bubbly, then cook and stir for 1 minute more. Pour *half* of the sauce over *each* casserole. Top with ham. Bake, uncovered, in a 325° oven about 15 minutes or till heated through. Makes 2 servings.

Olivia H. Heiman, Hemphill, Texas

Cheesy Vegetable Stew

1 46-ounce can (5¾ cups) tomato juice
1 cup chopped carrot
1 cup shredded cabbage
1 cup frozen cut green beans
1 cup chopped zucchini
2 tablespoons sliced green onion
1 teaspoon dried basil, crushed
½ teaspoon garlic powder
½ teaspoon crushed red pepper
1 7¼-ounce package macaroni and cheese dinner mix
4 ounces Monterey Jack cheese, cut into julienne strips

You'd never guess that this satisfying vegetable stew is based on a macaroni 'n' cheese dinner mix. (Pictured at left.)

In a 4½-quart Dutch oven combine tomato juice, carrot, cabbage, green beans, zucchini, green onion, basil, garlic powder, red pepper, and 2 cups *water*. Stir in the cheese sauce mix from the dinner mix. Bring mixture to boiling. Reduce heat and simmer, covered, for 15 minutes. Stir in the macaroni from the dinner mix. Simmer, covered, for 10 to 15 minutes more or till macaroni and vegetables are tender. Sprinkle Monterey Jack cheese over each serving. Makes 4 servings.

Carol Haseley, Wichita, Kansas

Vegetable-Style Rarebit

½ cup finely chopped cabbage
½ cup finely chopped carrot
½ cup finely chopped green pepper
½ cup finely chopped celery
½ cup finely chopped onion
½ cup finely chopped radishes
6 slices whole wheat bread, toasted
3 cups shredded cheddar cheese (12 ounces)
¼ cup beer *or* water
Dash white pepper
Dash ground red pepper
Alfalfa sprouts

❝ This recipe has been in my family for years. It probably originated from some thrifty soul who had an abundance of fresh garden vegetables. ❞

In a medium mixing bowl combine cabbage, carrot, green pepper, celery, onion, and radishes. Place toasted bread slices on a baking sheet. Top *each* slice with ½ *cup* of the vegetable mixture.

For cheese sauce, in a saucepan combine cheese, beer or water, white pepper, and red pepper. Cook and stir till the cheese is melted.

Spoon *equal* portions of the cheese sauce over *each* toasted bread slice. Broil sandwiches 4 inches from heat about 5 minutes or till cheese is light brown and bubbly. Transfer sandwiches to serving plates. Top *each* sandwich with alfalfa sprouts. Makes 6 servings.

Sunny Luteman, Troutville, Virginia

Pastry-Wrapped Salmon Ring

1   15½-ounce can pink
    salmon
2   beaten eggs
1½ cups soft bread crumbs
    (2 slices)
½   cup finely chopped celery
2   tablespoons finely chopped
    green pepper
2   tablespoons finely chopped
    onion

1   tablespoon lemon juice
1   8-ounce package (8)
    refrigerated crescent
    rolls
    Tomato wedges (optional)
    Celery leaves (optional)
    Dairy sour cream
    Snipped chives

*Refrigerated crescent rolls are the
quick 'n' easy pastry wrap for
Kathryn's eye-catching specialty.*

Generously grease a 4½-cup metal ring mold (8-inch diameter). Set aside. In a medium mixing bowl drain and flake salmon, removing and discarding skin and bones. Stir in eggs, bread crumbs, celery, green pepper, onion, and lemon juice.

Separate crescent roll dough into triangles. Arrange dough triangles in the prepared ring mold, alternating the points and wide ends of the triangles so dough drapes over the center and outer edges of the mold. Pat the dough lightly to seal the perforations and completely line the mold.

Spoon the salmon mixture evenly into the dough-lined mold. Fold the ends of dough over the salmon mixture to cover. Press to seal the edges. Bake in a 375° oven about 30 minutes or till pastry is golden. Loosen the edges. Invert salmon ring onto a serving platter. Garnish platter with tomato wedges and celery leaves, if desired. Serve salmon ring with sour cream and chives. Makes 4 to 6 servings.

Kathryn Hillen, Bartlesville, Oklahoma

Corn Bread Fish Bake

1 pound fresh *or* frozen
   fish fillets
1½ cups cornmeal
¾ teaspoon baking soda
½ teaspoon salt
¼ cup finely chopped onion
2 tablespoons chopped
   canned green chili
   peppers

1 cup buttermilk
2 eggs
¼ cup shortening, melted
¼ cup butter *or* margarine,
   melted
2 tablespoons prepared
   mustard
   Paprika

Thaw fish, if frozen. Cut fillets into 4x1-inch strips. Set aside. In a large mixing bowl stir together cornmeal, baking soda, and salt. Add onion and chili peppers. In a small mixing bowl beat together buttermilk and eggs. Stir buttermilk mixture and melted shortening into cornmeal mixture. Spread cornmeal mixture evenly in a greased 12x7½x2-inch baking dish.

Place fish strips in rows atop the cornmeal mixture. Lightly press fish strips into cornmeal mixture. In a small mixing bowl stir together the melted butter or margarine and mustard. Spread mustard mixture over fish strips. Sprinkle with paprika. Bake in a 450° oven about 20 minutes or till cornmeal mixture is golden. Serves 4.

A. M. Berry, Oklahoma City, Oklahoma

Tuna and Zucchini Cakes

½ cup chopped onion
1 tablespoon butter *or*
   margarine
1 cup shredded zucchini
1 6½-ounce can tuna,
   drained and flaked

¾ cup fine dry seasoned
   bread crumbs
2 slightly beaten eggs
⅓ cup snipped parsley
⅛ teaspoon pepper
2 tablespoons cooking oil

Serve fresh steamed vegetables with this dressed-up fish patty.

In a small saucepan cook the onion in butter or margarine till tender but not brown. Remove from heat. Stir in zucchini, tuna, ½ *cup* of the bread crumbs, eggs, parsley, and pepper. Mix well.

Shape tuna mixture into six ½-inch-thick patties. Coat patties with remaining ¼ cup bread crumbs. In a medium skillet heat cooking oil. Cook the patties in hot oil over medium heat about 3 minutes on each side or till golden brown. Makes 3 servings.

Mabel Pellettier, Rockville, Maryland

FAVORITE BREAD, RICE, AND PASTA RECIPES

ARE YOU THE TYPE WHO SAVORS THE AROMA OF WARM-FROM-THE-OVEN YEAST BREADS, INVITING COFFEE CAKES, OR PIPING-HOT MUFFINS SMOTHERED WITH BUTTER? WE PACKED THIS CHAPTER FULL OF THE BEST-OF-THE-BEST BREAD RECIPES, PLUS A FEW ENTICING RICE AND PASTA DISHES. ONE OF THEM IS BOUND TO INSPIRE YOU TO ROLL UP YOUR SLEEVES AND START BAKING.

Tropical Java Bread

This fruit-filled quick bread will be easier to slice if it's wrapped in foil and stored overnight.

1 17-ounce package date quick bread mix
¾ cup orange juice
½ cup mashed banana
1 slightly beaten egg
2 teaspoons instant coffee crystals
½ cup flaked coconut
¼ cup raisins (optional)
Cream cheese (optional)

Grease an 8x4x2-inch loaf pan. Set aside. In a large mixing bowl stir together date quick bread mix, orange juice, banana, egg, and coffee crystals. Mix well. Stir in coconut and raisins, if desired. Transfer batter to prepared pan. Bake in a 350° oven for 55 to 60 minutes or till a wooden toothpick inserted near center comes out clean. Cool in pan for 10 minutes. Remove loaf from pan. Cool completely on a wire rack. Wrap and store overnight before slicing. If desired, serve with cream cheese. Makes 1 loaf.

Mrs. Joseph A. A. Graf, Kentwood, Michigan

Nutty Corn Bread

Bulgur, precooked cracked wheat kernels, is available in health foods stores or in the specialty section of your grocery store.

1 8½-ounce package corn muffin mix
½ cup quick-cooking rolled oats
¼ cup bulgur
2 slightly beaten eggs
½ cup milk
½ cup chopped pecans
1 tablespoon maple-flavored syrup
Maple-flavored syrup
Butter *or* margarine

Grease a 9x9x2-inch baking pan. Set aside. In a medium mixing bowl stir together corn muffin mix, rolled oats, and bulgur. Add eggs and milk. Stir just till dry ingredients are moistened. Stir in the pecans. Spread batter evenly in the prepared pan. Drizzle the 1 tablespoon maple-flavored syrup over the top.

Bake in a 400° oven about 20 minutes or till golden. Cut into squares. Serve warm with additional maple-flavored syrup and butter or margarine. Makes 9 servings.

Ann Wilson, LaPorte, Indiana

Cranberry Ripple Cake

Pictured at right.

2 cups all-purpose flour
1 teaspoon baking powder
1 teaspoon baking soda
½ cup butter *or* margarine
1 cup sugar
½ teaspoon almond extract

2 eggs
1 8-ounce carton dairy sour cream
1 8-ounce can whole cranberry sauce
½ cup chopped pecans

Grease and flour a 10-inch tube pan. Set aside. Stir together flour, baking powder, soda, and ¼ teaspoon *salt*. In a large mixer bowl beat butter or margarine with an electric mixer on medium speed for 30 seconds. Add sugar and almond extract. Beat till fluffy. Add eggs and beat well. Add flour mixture and sour cream alternately to beaten mixture, beating on low speed after each addition till smooth.

Spread *half* of the batter into the prepared pan. Spoon ½ *cup* of the cranberry sauce over batter. Spoon remaining batter over sauce, spreading out batter as much as possible. Dot with the remaining cranberry sauce. Sprinkle pecans atop. Bake in a 350° oven for 40 to 50 minutes or till done. Cool in the pan for 10 minutes. Remove from pan. Cool completely on wire rack. Makes 1 ring.

Mrs. Billie Taylor, Afton, Virginia

Crispy Apricot Cake

A favorite kids' cereal is the key to this quick and crunchy topping.

¼ cup butter *or* margarine, softened
3 tablespoons sugar
½ teaspoon ground cinnamon
2 cups crisp rice cereal
1½ cups all-purpose flour

2 teaspoons baking powder
1 16-ounce can peeled whole apricots
¼ cup butter *or* margarine
¾ cup sugar
1 egg

Grease a 9x9x2-inch baking pan. Set aside. Combine the softened butter, 3 tablespoons sugar, and cinnamon. Stir in cereal. Set aside.

In a small mixing bowl stir together flour, baking powder, and ¼ teaspoon *salt*. Drain apricots, reserving ½ *cup* syrup. Mash apricots. In a medium mixer bowl beat ¼ cup butter or margarine with an electric mixer on medium speed for 30 seconds. Add the ¾ cup sugar and beat till combined. Add egg. Beat till light and fluffy. Add flour mixture and reserved apricot syrup alternately to beaten mixture, beating on low speed after each addition just till combined. Transfer batter to prepared pan. Dot with *three-fourths* of the apricots. Sprinkle cereal mixture atop. Dot with remaining apricots. Bake in a 350° oven about 45 minutes or till done. Serve warm. Makes 1.

Mrs. Addis Bush, Coolidge, Arizona

Italian Cheese Twists

Frozen bread dough gets a cheesy touch in these fast and fabulous soft herbed breadsticks.

3 tablespoons butter *or* margarine, softened
¼ teaspoon dried basil, crushed
¼ teaspoon dried oregano, crushed
¼ teaspoon dried marjoram, crushed

¼ teaspoon garlic powder
1 16-ounce loaf frozen bread dough, thawed
¾ cup shredded mozzarella cheese (3 ounces)
1 slightly beaten egg
1 teaspoon water
2 tablespoons sesame seed

In a small mixing bowl stir together butter or margarine, basil, oregano, marjoram, and garlic powder. Set aside.

On a lightly floured surface roll bread dough into a 12-inch square. Spread butter mixture evenly over dough. Sprinkle with cheese. Fold dough into thirds. With a sharp knife, cut dough crosswise into twenty-four ½-inch-wide strips. Twist each strip twice and pinch ends to seal. Place twists about 2 inches apart on a greased baking sheet. Cover. Let rise in a warm place till almost double (about 30 minutes).

In a small bowl stir together egg and water. Brush some of the egg mixture over each twist. Sprinkle with sesame seed. Bake in a 375° oven for 10 to 12 minutes or till golden. Makes 24 twists.

Crystal Garrard, Lebec, California

Date-Nut Ring

Covering this quick bread with foil during the last 15 minutes of baking prevents overbrowning.

1½ cups water
1 cup chopped pitted dates
1 cup cooking oil
3 slightly beaten eggs
1 teaspoon vanilla

3 cups all-purpose flour
1½ cups sugar
1 teaspoon baking soda
½ teaspoon salt
1 cup chopped walnuts

Grease a 10-inch tube pan. Set aside. In a 3-quart saucepan bring water to boiling. Remove from heat. Stir in dates. Let stand for 15 minutes. Stir in oil, eggs, and vanilla. Mix well.

In a large mixing bowl stir together flour, sugar, soda, and salt. Add flour mixture to date mixture in saucepan. Stir to mix well. Stir in nuts. Transfer mixture to prepared pan. Bake in a 350° oven for 50 to 60 minutes or till a wooden toothpick inserted near center comes out clean, covering the last 15 minutes of baking. Cool in pan on a wire rack. Remove from pan. Makes 1 ring.

Mrs. Joseph D. Comer, Churchville, Maryland

Apple Streusel Coffee Bread

½ cup packed brown sugar
1 teaspoon ground cinnamon
1 16-ounce loaf frozen white bread dough, thawed
2 tablespoons butter *or* margarine, softened
1½ cups finely chopped peeled apple
1 tablespoon butter *or* margarine, melted

2 tablespoons all-purpose flour
2 tablespoons sugar
1 tablespoon butter *or* margarine
⅓ cup slivered almonds (optional)

Carol recommends using a tart apple such as a Jonathan, Granny Smith, or Winesap for making this blue-ribbon bread.

In a small mixing bowl stir together the brown sugar and cinnamon. Set mixture aside.

Divide the bread dough in half. On a lightly floured surface roll each dough half into an 8-inch square. Spread *1 tablespoon* of the softened butter or margarine over *each* dough square. Arrange *half* of the apples down the center of *each* dough square. Sprinkle *half* of the brown sugar mixture over the apples. Make 2-inch cuts in dough at 1-inch intervals on both sides of the apples. Fold strips alternately over apples to give a braided appearance. Fold under ends of dough.

Place loaves on a greased 15x10x1-inch baking pan. Brush with the 1 tablespoon melted butter or margarine. For the crumb topping, in a small mixing bowl stir together flour and sugar. Cut in the 1 tablespoon butter or margarine till mixture resembles coarse crumbs. Sprinkle *half* the crumb topping over *each* loaf. Top with almonds, if desired. Cover and let rise till nearly double (45 to 60 minutes). Bake in a 350° oven about 30 minutes or till golden brown. Serve warm. Makes 2 loaves.

Carol Hedrick, Ithaca, New York

Starting from a banana-nut bread recipe given to her in the 1940s, Janet created this tasty alternative for the 1980s.

Strawberry-Walnut Bread

2 cups finely chopped walnuts
3 cups all-purpose flour
1½ teaspoons ground cinnamon
1 teaspoon baking soda
1 teaspoon ground cardamom
½ teaspoon salt
¼ teaspoon ground nutmeg

4 beaten eggs
2 cups sugar
1½ cups mashed strawberries (about 3 cups whole berries)
1 cup cooking oil
1 cup mashed banana
1 tablespoon finely shredded orange peel

Grease and flour two 9x5x3-inch loaf pans. Sprinkle ½ *cup* of the walnuts in the bottom of *each* pan. Set aside.

In a large mixing bowl stir together flour, cinnamon, baking soda, cardamom, salt, and nutmeg. In a medium mixing bowl stir together eggs, sugar, strawberries, cooking oil, banana, and orange peel. Add to flour mixture, stirring just till dry ingredients are moistened. Carefully stir in remaining nuts. Transfer batter to prepared pans. Bake in a 350° oven for 1 hour or till a wooden toothpick inserted near center comes out clean. Let cool in pans for 10 minutes. Remove loaves from pans. Cool completely on wire racks. Wrap and store overnight before serving. Makes 2 loaves.

Janet Consorti, Ventura, California

Quick Tarragon Batter Rolls

2½ cups all-purpose flour
1 package active dry yeast
1 tablespoon dried parsley flakes
1 teaspoon dried tarragon, crushed
1 teaspoon celery seed
1 cup warm water (115° to 120°)
2 tablespoons sugar
2 tablespoons cooking oil
½ teaspoon salt
1 egg

66 These no-knead rolls have a marvelously subtle herb flavor. 99

In a large mixer bowl combine *1½ cups* of the flour, yeast, parsley, tarragon, and celery seed. In a small mixing bowl stir together water, sugar, oil, and salt. Add to flour mixture, along with egg. Beat with an electric mixer on low speed for 30 seconds, scraping bowl occasionally. Beat on high speed for 3 minutes.

Use a spoon to stir in remaining flour. Cover and let rise in a warm place till double (about 30 minutes). Stir batter down. Spoon batter into 12 greased muffin cups, filling each slightly more than half full. Cover and let rise till nearly double (20 to 30 minutes). Bake rolls in a 375° oven for 15 to 18 minutes or till golden brown. Makes 12 rolls.

Dr. Arthur L. Plouff, Newburyport, Massachusetts

Shoofly Coffee Bread

2 cups packaged buttermilk pancake mix
½ teaspoon ground cinnamon
¼ teaspoon ground ginger
⅔ cup milk
⅓ cup molasses
¼ cup sugar
2 tablespoons butter *or* margarine

Like an authentic Pennsylvania Dutch Shoofly Pie, this bread contains molasses. It's popularly believed that the pie received its name because "shooing" was often used to drive away the flies frequently attracted to the molasses.

Grease a 9-inch pie plate. Set aside. In a medium mixing bowl stir together pancake mix, cinnamon, and ginger. Remove ⅓ *cup* of the dry ingredients and set aside.

In a small mixing bowl stir together milk and molasses. Add to dry ingredients, stirring just till moistened. Do not overmix. Transfer batter to prepared pie plate, spreading evenly over the bottom.

For crumb topping, in a small mixing bowl combine the reserved dry ingredients and sugar. Cut in butter or margarine till mixture resembles coarse crumbs. Sprinkle crumb topping over batter. Bake in a 350° oven about 25 minutes or till a wooden toothpick inserted near center comes out clean. Serve warm or cool. Makes 8 servings.

Beverly Myers, Cincinnati, Ohio

Pineapple-Spice Scones

3 cups all-purpose flour
⅓ cup sugar
2½ teaspoons baking powder
½ teaspoon salt
¾ cup butter *or* margarine
1 8-ounce can crushed pineapple (juice pack)

Light cream *or* milk
3 tablespoons chopped macadamia nuts *or* almonds
1 tablespoon sugar
½ teaspoon ground cinnamon

> 66 *There's nothing like the tropical touch of these scones to put us in a cheery mood.* 99

In a large mixing bowl stir together flour, the ⅓ cup sugar, baking powder, and salt. Cut in butter or margarine till mixture resembles coarse crumbs. Make a well in the center. Stir in *undrained* pineapple just till dry ingredients are moistened (dough will be sticky).

On a lightly floured surface knead dough gently 10 to 12 strokes. Roll dough ¼ inch thick. Cut dough with a floured 2½-inch biscuit cutter. Transfer scones to an ungreased baking sheet. Brush tops with light cream or milk.

For topping, stir together nuts, the 1 tablespoon sugar, and cinnamon. Sprinkle about *1 teaspoon* of the topping over *each* scone. Bake in a 425° oven about 15 minutes or till golden brown. Serve warm. Makes about 21 scones.

Susan Milotich, San Carlos, California

Poppy Seed Muffins

¾ cup sugar
¼ cup butter *or* margarine, softened
½ teaspoon finely shredded orange peel
2 eggs
2 cups all-purpose flour

2½ teaspoons baking powder
¼ teaspoon salt
¼ teaspoon ground nutmeg
1 cup milk
½ cup light raisins
½ cup chopped pecans
¼ cup poppy seed

Heidi doesn't limit these sweet muffins to the breakfast table— they're also great with lunch or dinner.

In a medium mixer bowl beat together sugar, butter or margarine, and orange peel with an electric mixer on medium speed for 30 seconds. Add the eggs, one at a time, beating well after each addition.

In a medium mixing bowl stir together flour, baking powder, salt, and nutmeg. Add flour mixture and milk alternately to beaten mixture, beating on low speed after each addition. Stir in raisins, pecans, and poppy seed. Line muffin pans with paper bake cups. Fill three-fourths full. Bake in a 400° oven for 15 to 20 minutes or till golden brown. Makes about 18 muffins.

Heidi Henderson, Olympia, Washington

Pineapple-Spice Scones

Country Scones

½ cup currants
2 cups all-purpose flour
3 tablespoons sugar
2 teaspoons baking powder
¾ teaspoon salt
½ teaspoon baking soda
⅓ cup butter *or* margarine

1 8-ounce carton dairy sour cream
1 egg yolk
1 slightly beaten egg white
1 teaspoon sugar
⅛ teaspoon ground cinnamon

The British keep their scones warm for tea time by wrapping them in a small towel, hence the phrase tea towel.

In a small mixing bowl pour enough *hot water* over currants to cover. Let stand for 5 minutes. Drain well and set aside.

Meanwhile, in a large mixing bowl stir together flour, the 3 tablespoons sugar, baking powder, salt, and soda. Cut in butter or margarine till mixture resembles coarse crumbs. Stir in currants.

In a small bowl stir together sour cream and egg yolk. Add all at once to flour mixture, stirring just till dough clings together. On a lightly floured surface knead dough gently for 10 to 12 strokes. Pat or roll dough into a 9-inch circle, about ½ inch thick. Cut dough with a floured 4-inch round cookie cutter. Transfer circles to an ungreased baking sheet. Cut each circle completely through into quarters, but do not separate the sections.

Brush tops with egg white. In a small bowl combine the 1 teaspoon sugar and cinnamon. Sprinkle sugar-cinnamon mixture over tops of circles. Bake in a 425° oven for 15 to 18 minutes or till lightly browned. Cool on a wire rack for 5 minutes. Break the circles apart. Serve warm. Makes 16 to 20 scones.

Mrs. M. McCavour, Burnaby, British Columbia, Canada

Cranberry-Apple Muffins

½ cup whole cranberry sauce
½ teaspoon finely shredded
   orange peel
1½ cups all-purpose flour
½ cup sugar
1 teaspoon ground cinnamon
½ teaspoon baking soda
¼ teaspoon baking powder
1 slightly beaten egg
1 cup shredded, peeled apple
⅓ cup milk
⅓ cup cooking oil
½ cup sifted powdered sugar
2 to 3 teaspoons orange juice

> 66 *This moist, cakelike muffin takes on a very festive appearance with the red cranberry topping and white glaze.* 99

For cranberry filling, in a small mixing bowl stir together cranberry sauce and orange peel. Set aside. In a medium mixing bowl stir together flour, sugar, cinnamon, baking soda, baking powder, and ¼ teaspoon *salt.* Make a well in the center of the dry ingredients. In a small mixing bowl stir together egg, apple, milk, and oil. Add all at once to dry ingredients, stirring just till moistened.

Fill greased muffin cups half full. Make a well in center of each with the back of a spoon. Spoon about *2 teaspoons* of the cranberry filling into *each* well. Bake in a 375° oven for 18 to 20 minutes or till done. Meanwhile, in a small bowl stir together powdered sugar and orange juice to make a glaze of drizzling consistency. Drizzle over warm muffins. Makes 12 muffins.

Priscilla Yee, Concord, California

Apple-Nut-Cheese Pan Biscuits

⅓ cup sugar
⅓ cup chopped walnuts
½ teaspoon ground cinnamon
1¾ cups packaged biscuit mix
¾ cup shredded sharp
   cheddar cheese
   (3 ounces)
1 medium apple, peeled,
   cored, and chopped
   (about ¾ cup)
⅓ cup cold water
¼ cup butter *or* margarine,
   melted

You don't need a biscuit cutter for these tasty treats. Simply mix up the dough, pinch off 18 pieces, and roll them into balls.

In a small bowl stir together sugar, nuts, and cinnamon. Set aside. In a large mixing bowl stir together biscuit mix, cheddar cheese, and chopped apple. Make a well in the center of the cheese mixture. Add water all at once, stirring just till moistened.

Form the dough into a ball. Divide into 18 pieces. Shape each piece into a ball. Roll balls in melted butter or margarine and then in the sugar mixture. Arrange balls in a greased 9x1½-inch round baking pan. Bake in a 400° oven for 25 to 30 minutes or till done. Cool in the pan for 5 minutes. Remove biscuits from pan. Cool on a wire rack. Serve warm. Makes 18 biscuits.

Mrs. Julia Coffman, Mooresville, Indiana

Three-Grain Waffles

For a treat kids will love, mold butter or margarine into interesting shapes to serve with these waffles. Press the butter into a small cookie cutter lined with plastic wrap. Freeze till firm. Then lift the butter from the mold with the wrap.

1 cup whole wheat flour
1 cup toasted wheat bran
1 cup yellow cornmeal
1 cup nonfat dry milk powder
1 package active dry yeast
¼ teaspoon salt
2½ cups water
2 eggs
3 tablespoons cooking oil
3 tablespoons honey

In a medium mixer bowl combine flour, bran, cornmeal, milk powder, yeast, and salt. Add water, eggs, oil, and honey. Beat with an electric mixer on medium speed for 1 minute. Cover bowl loosely. Refrigerate batter overnight.

Stir waffle batter. For *each* waffle, pour ½ *cup* of the batter onto a preheated waffle iron. Close the lid quickly. Do not open during baking. Cook for 5 to 6 minutes or till done. Makes 8 to 10 waffles.

Mary Love Chambers, Holly Hill, Florida

Stuffed French Toast

1 8-ounce package cream cheese, softened
1 teaspoon vanilla
½ cup chopped walnuts
1 16-ounce loaf unsliced French bread
4 eggs
1 cup whipping cream
½ teaspoon vanilla
½ teaspoon ground nutmeg
1 12-ounce jar (1½ cups) apricot preserves
½ cup orange juice

Beat together the cream cheese and the 1 teaspoon vanilla with an electric mixer on medium speed till fluffy. Stir in nuts and set aside.

Cut bread into ten to twelve 1½-inch-thick slices. For pockets, cut a slit in the center top of *each* bread slice, cutting about two-thirds of the way to, but not through, the bottom crust. Fill *each* pocket with about 1½ *tablespoons* of the cream cheese mixture.

In a small mixing bowl stir together eggs, whipping cream, the ½ teaspoon vanilla, and nutmeg. Using tongs, dip the filled bread slices into the egg mixture, coating both sides and being careful not to squeeze out the filling. Cook bread slices on a lightly greased griddle till both sides are golden brown. To keep cooked bread slices hot for serving, place them on a baking sheet in a warm oven.

Meanwhile, in a saucepan combine preserves and orange juice. Cook and stir over medium heat till preserves are melted. To serve, drizzle the apricot mixture over hot bread slices. Makes 10 to 12.

Dennis Passer, Omaha, Nebraska

Nutty-Orange Pancakes

½ cup butter *or* margarine
2 tablespoons orange juice
2 eggs
1 cup orange juice
2 tablespoons honey
1¾ cups packaged biscuit mix
½ cup ground walnuts

Necessity is the mother of invention, and the need to use up a gift of several pounds of shelled walnuts spurred Edith to create this award-winning breakfast pancake.

For orange butter, in a small mixer bowl combine butter or margarine and the 2 tablespoons orange juice. Beat with an electric mixer on medium speed till fluffy. Transfer to small serving bowl. Set aside.

For pancakes, in the same mixer bowl combine eggs, the 1 cup orange juice, and honey. Beat on low speed till combined. Add the biscuit mix and nuts. Beat on medium speed about 30 seconds or till combined. For pancakes, pour about ¼ *cup* batter onto a hot, lightly greased griddle or heavy skillet. Cook till golden brown, turning to cook other side when pancakes have a bubbly surface and slightly dry edges. Serve with orange butter. Makes 12 to 14 (4-inch) pancakes.

Edith Wilson, Gualala, California

Beer Pancakes

2 cups packaged biscuit mix
2 tablespoons sugar
½ teaspoon ground cinnamon
Dash ground nutmeg
5 beaten eggs
½ cup beer
2 tablespoons cooking oil
Butter *or* margarine
Maple-flavored syrup

Gaylord's pancakes became even more popular with his camping friends after he discovered he could substitute beer for the milk.

Stir together packaged biscuit mix, sugar, cinnamon, and nutmeg. Combine beaten eggs, beer, and cooking oil. Add egg mixture all at once to dry ingredients, stirring just till moistened. (Batter will be lumpy.) Add a little additional beer if thinner pancakes are desired.

For pancakes, pour about ¼ *cup* batter onto a hot, lightly greased griddle or heavy skillet. Cook till golden brown, turning to cook the other side when pancakes have a bubbly surface and slightly dry edges. Serve pancakes warm with butter or margarine and maple-flavored syrup. Makes 10 to 12 (4-inch) pancakes.

Gaylord Stidham, Soap Lake, Washington

KAYLEEN SLOBODEN, PUYALLUP, WASH.

Kayleen and Jim Sloboden live in beautiful upper Washington state, in a small town called Puyallup (pew-AL-up). They share a sunny, spacious home with their two daughters, Adrienne and Aimee. Kayleen works part-time in the recovery room at Riverton General Hospital in Seattle; Jim manages his own cabinet manufacturing business.

Both of the Slobodens work at staying physically fit and keeping Kayleen's cooking hobby from taking its toll on the family physique. Jim regularly squeezes in a golf game after work, and Kayleen, a former aerobics teacher, jogs a couple of miles daily in their wooded neighborhood.

Kayleen readily admits, "Cooking was a late-blooming interest for me. When I got married, I started going to bed at night reading cook books and I just taught myself to cook." She would list menus for the coming week, incorporating new recipes

66 When I got married, I started going to bed at night reading cook books and I just taught myself to cook. 99

she planned to try. "After I felt comfortable with cooking, I started changing and adding ingredients."

Kayleen became so fascinated with recipes that she started entering cooking contests—often winning finalist or grand prize status. What began eight years ago as simply a pastime has evolved into a full-time hobby that's been "a rewarding and really thrilling experience," says Kayleen. "It's a challenge to create a recipe within the guidelines of a particular set of contest rules."

Kayleen's apt to try a recipe out on her family three or four times to make sure it tastes just right for competition. "My husband and daughters are my toughest critics—they tell me exactly what they like and don't like," laughs Kayleen. Neighbors and co-workers are willing guinea pigs when the family tires of a recipe in progress.

continued

KAYLEEN SLOBODEN, PUYALLUP, WASH.

When it comes to having get-togethers with family and friends, Kayleen explains, "We enjoy smaller groups for entertaining. It's more casual and easygoing that way." The Slobodens' backyard has a spacious multilevel deck that's ideal for outdoor gatherings. There's a large window pass-through from Kayleen's kitchen, and a built-in gas grill. More

often than not, fresh salmon, caught by Jim or bought down at the Tacoma docks, is the main course—and Jim knows how to grill it to juicy perfection.

In the winter, the activities move to the Slobodens' spacious kitchen. "For a family party, we'll have a make-your-own pizza, so everyone can roll their own dough and add their favorite toppings. The kitchen counter island is perfect for it," says Kayleen.

Kids are an important part of the Slobodens' cooking scene. According to Kayleen, "Cooking is frequently a family affair. The girls love anything they can pat with their hands, like pizza dough, cookie dough, and piecrust," Kayleen relates. "We also like to go berry picking together. I use the berries for dessert sauce and homemade ice cream."

Kayleen feels the girls can learn to cook by watching their mother. "I try to have Adrienne read the recipe, and she tells me what I'm supposed to do next."

With the basic techniques down, Kayleen believes that anything's possible when she's cooking creatively.   *continued*

KAYLEEN SLOBODEN, PUYALLUP, WASH.

Kayleen developed this unusual biscuit idea especially for one of *Better Homes and Gardens*® magazine's monthly recipe contests. "I saw a recipe for a sweet bread made with zucchini," Kayleen says. "But I thought it would be nice to make it a savory bread with sweet potatoes." Adrienne and Aimee enjoy patting out the dough to make it easy to cut into finger-length sticks. The biscuits make perfect accompaniments for barbecued main dishes, chili, or salads.

Herbed Sweet-Potato Biscuits

2¼ cups all-purpose flour
1 tablespoon baking powder
½ teaspoon baking soda
½ teaspoon salt
½ teaspoon finely shredded lemon peel
¼ teaspoon dried basil, crushed
¼ teaspoon dried thyme, crushed
1 slightly beaten egg
1½ cups finely shredded peeled sweet potato (1 large potato)
½ cup finely chopped green onion
½ cup dairy sour cream
2 tablespoons butter or margarine, melted
Butter or margarine, melted

In a large mixing bowl stir together flour, baking powder, soda, salt, lemon peel, basil, and thyme. In a medium mixing bowl stir together egg, sweet potato, green onion, sour cream, and the 2 tablespoons melted butter or margarine. Add egg mixture to dry ingredients, stirring just till dry ingredients are moistened. Shape dough into a ball with hands.

On a lightly floured surface, knead dough gently for 10 to 12 strokes. Pat dough into an 8-inch square. Cut dough in half. Cut *each* half crosswise into *eight* 1-inch strips. Place strips on a greased baking sheet. Brush with additional melted butter or margarine. Bake in a 425° oven about 20 minutes or till golden. Makes 16 biscuits.

Jam and Cheese Loaf

1 package active dry yeast
½ cup warm water
   (110° to 115°)
2½ cups packaged biscuit mix
1 beaten egg
1 tablespoon sugar

1 8-ounce package cream
   cheese, softened
½ cup sugar
1 tablespoon lemon juice
¼ cup desired jam *or*
   preserves

> **66** *This bread looks like a made-from-scratch yeast braid, but it's much easier and faster to prepare.* **99**

In a mixing bowl dissolve yeast in water. Stir in biscuit mix, egg, and the 1 tablespoon sugar. Turn out onto surface dusted with additional biscuit mix. Knead gently 20 strokes. Place dough on a greased 15½x12-inch baking sheet. Pat into a 14x9-inch rectangle.

For filling, stir together cream cheese, the ½ cup sugar, and lemon juice till smooth. Spread lengthwise down center third of rectangle. Make 3-inch cuts in dough at 1-inch intervals on both sides of filling. Fold strips alternately over filling. Cover. Chill overnight. Bake in a 350° oven 20 minutes. Spoon desired jam down center of loaf. Bake 5 minutes more or till golden. Cool 10 minutes. Makes 1 loaf.

Susan J. Adams, Atlanta, Illinois

Pecan Pizza Coffee Cake

½ cup whole bran cereal,
   coarsely crushed
¼ cup sugar
1 package active dry yeast
½ cup warm water
   (110° to 115°)
1 egg
1⅔ cups all-purpose flour

1 tablespoon cooking oil
1 cup chopped pecans
⅓ cup packed brown sugar
¼ cup maple-flavored syrup
2 tablespoons butter *or*
   margarine
1 teaspoon ground cinnamon

Audrey's quick one-rise coffee cake invites easy serving and easy eating.

In a bowl combine cereal, sugar, and yeast. Stir in water. Let stand 5 minutes. Add egg, *½ cup* of the flour, oil, and ½ teaspoon *salt.* Beat with an electric mixer on low speed for 30 seconds. Beat on high speed for 3 minutes, scraping bowl often. Stir in remaining flour. Knead 1 minute on a well-floured surface. Place in greased bowl, turning once. Cover. Let rise in warm place till double (about 1 hour).

In a saucepan combine pecans, brown sugar, syrup, butter, and cinnamon. Cook and stir till sugar dissolves. *Do not boil.* Set aside. Punch dough down. Let rest for 10 minutes. With floured hands, press dough into a greased 12-inch pizza pan, forming a high edge. Spread pecan mixture to within 1 inch of edge. Place pizza pan on a baking sheet. Bake in a 400° oven 18 to 20 minutes or till golden. Serve warm. Makes 1.

Mrs. Audrey Kovalak, Springfield, Virginia

Jam and Cheese Loaf

Apple-Wheat Sourdough Rolls

Apple butter sweetens Annette's moist yeast rolls.

Sourdough Starter
3½ to 4 cups all-purpose flour
½ cup toasted wheat germ
1 package active dry yeast
¼ teaspoon baking soda
½ cup milk

¼ cup butter *or* margarine
1 tablespoon honey
¾ teaspoon salt
1 beaten egg
¾ cup apple butter
Milk

Bring ½ *cup* of the Sourdough Starter to room temperature. In a large mixing bowl combine *1½ cups* of the flour, wheat germ, yeast, and baking soda. In a small saucepan heat milk, butter or margarine, honey, and salt just till warm (115° to 120°) and butter or margarine is almost melted, stirring constantly. Add milk mixture to the flour mixture. Stir in egg, apple butter, and Sourdough Starter. Beat with an electric mixer on low speed for 30 seconds, scraping bowl often. Beat on high speed for 3 minutes, scraping bowl occasionally. Stir in as much of the remaining flour as possible.

Turn dough out onto a lightly floured surface. Knead in enough of the remaining flour to make a moderately stiff dough that is smooth and elastic (6 to 8 minutes total). Shape dough into a ball. Place in a greased bowl, turning once to grease surface. Cover. Let rest for 15 minutes. Shape dough into 2-inch balls. Place balls on greased baking sheets. Cover. Let rise till double (1 to 1½ hours). Brush tops with milk. Bake in a 375° oven 15 to 18 minutes or till golden brown. Makes 24 rolls.

Sourdough Starter: Dissolve 1 package *active dry yeast* in ½ cup warm *water* (110° to 115°). Stir in 2 cups warm *water*, 2 cups all-purpose *flour*, and 1 tablespoon *honey or sugar*. Beat till smooth. Cover with cheesecloth. *Do not cover with a tight-fitting lid.* Let stand at room temperature for 5 to 10 days or till bubbly, stirring 2 to 3 times each day. (Fermentation time depends upon room temperature. A warmer room hastens the fermentation process.)

To store, transfer Sourdough Starter to a jar, cover with cheesecloth, and refrigerate. *Do not cover jar tightly with a metal lid.* To use Starter, bring desired amount to room temperature. To replenish Starter after using, stir ¾ cup all-purpose *flour*, ¾ cup *water*, and 1 teaspoon *sugar or honey* into remaining amount. Cover. Let stand at room temperature at least 1 day or till bubbly. Refrigerate for later use. If Starter isn't used within 10 days, stir in 1 teaspoon *sugar or honey*. Repeat every 10 days until used.

Annette Tortorella Roos, Salt Lake City, Utah

Dinner Rolls Italiano

4½ to 5 cups all-purpose flour
2 packages active dry yeast
1½ teaspoons Italian seasoning
1 cup milk
½ cup water
2 tablespoons sugar
2 tablespoons butter
  or margarine
1 teaspoon garlic salt
2 eggs
¾ cup grated Parmesan
  cheese
2 tablespoons butter *or*
  margarine, melted

In a large mixer bowl combine *1½ cups* of the flour, yeast, and Italian seasoning. In a small saucepan heat milk, water, sugar, the 2 tablespoons butter or margarine, and garlic salt just till warm (115° to 120°), stirring constantly. Add the warm milk mixture to dry ingredients along with eggs. Beat with an electric mixer on low speed for 30 seconds, scraping bowl constantly. Beat on high speed for 3 minutes. Stir in *½ cup* of the Parmesan cheese. Stir in as much of the remaining flour as you can.

On a lightly floured surface, knead in enough of the remaining flour to make a moderately stiff dough (6 to 8 minutes total). Shape dough into a ball. Place dough in a lightly greased bowl, turning once to grease surface. Cover. Let rise in a warm place till double (about 45 minutes). Punch dough down. Let rest for 10 minutes.

Divide dough into 16 pieces. Shape *each* piece into a ball. Dip tops of dough balls into the 2 tablespoons melted butter or margarine, then into the remaining Parmesan cheese. Arrange dough balls in 2 greased 9x1½-inch-round baking pans. Cover. Let rise till nearly double (about 15 minutes). Bake in a 375° oven for 20 to 25 minutes or till golden. Makes 16 rolls.

Carol M. Gilley, Cookeville, Tennessee

Carrot-Whole Wheat Pretzels

Pictured at right.

3 cups whole wheat flour
2 packages active dry yeast
½ cup butter *or* margarine
½ cup honey
1 egg

1 cup grated carrot
3½ to 4 cups all-purpose flour
1 beaten egg yolk

Combine whole wheat flour and yeast. Heat and stir butter or margarine, honey, and 2 cups *water* till warm (115° to 120°). Add to flour mixture. Add the 1 egg and carrot. Beat with an electric mixer on low speed for 30 seconds, scraping bowl. Beat on high speed for 3 minutes. Stir in as much of the all-purpose flour as you can.

On a floured surface, knead in enough remaining flour to make a moderately stiff dough that is smooth and elastic (6 to 8 minutes total). Place in a greased bowl, turning once. Cover. Let rise till double (about 1 hour). Punch down. Divide dough into 4 portions. Let rest for 10 minutes. Divide *each* portion into 12 pieces. Roll pieces into 14-inch ropes. Shape into pretzels. Place on greased baking sheets. Cover. Let rise till nearly double (about 30 minutes). Combine egg yolk and 2 tablespoons *water*. Brush over pretzels. Bake in a 400° oven about 15 minutes or till golden. Cool. Makes 48 pretzels.

Ann Wolf, Sunnyvale, California

Steamed Ginger Buns

You can decorate the steamed buns by dipping small Oriental stamps or rubber stamps in red food coloring, then pressing lightly atop cooked buns. Or, try your hand at painting designs on the steamed buns. (See photo, page 71.)

1 13¾-ounce package hot roll mix
4 teaspoons sugar
1 teaspoon ground ginger

½ teaspoon finely shredded orange peel
Dash ground cinnamon
2 tablespoons butter, melted

Prepare mix according to package directions through kneading step. Cover. Let rest 5 minutes. For filling, combine sugar, ginger, orange peel, and cinnamon.

Divide dough into 8 pieces. On a lightly floured surface, roll or pat each piece into a 3½-inch circle. Brush with some of the melted butter. Sprinkle ¾ *teaspoon* of the filling in the center of *each* circle. Bring dough up around filling and pinch together well to seal. Place buns, seam side down, on a lightly greased rack of a metal or bamboo steamer so sides of buns don't touch. Pour water into a wok till the water is 1 to 1½ inches deep. Bring to boiling. Reduce heat to medium-high. Set steamer in wok. Steam buns, covered, for 15 to 20 minutes or till done. Remove from steamer. Cool slightly. Makes 8.

Alethea Sparks, Des Moines, Iowa

Easter Fruit-and-Nut Bread

3 to 3½ cups all-purpose
  flour
1 package active dry yeast
½ cup milk
¼ cup sugar
¼ cup butter *or* margarine
¼ cup water
¾ teaspoon finely shredded
  lemon peel

½ teaspoon salt
2 egg yolks
2 eggs
1 cup ground walnuts
⅓ cup sugar
2 egg whites
½ teaspoon lemon juice
⅓ cup currant jelly
¾ cup chopped pitted dates

> 66 *This recipe brings back fond memories of my childhood in Germany and the special occasions when my mother baked this delicious fruit- and nut-filled braid.* 99

In a large mixer bowl stir together *1½ cups* of the flour and yeast. In a small saucepan heat and stir milk, the ¼ cup sugar, butter or margarine, water, lemon peel, and salt just till warm (115° to 120°) and butter or margarine is almost melted. Add warm milk mixture to flour mixture. Add the 2 egg yolks and *1* of the whole eggs. Beat with an electric mixer on low speed for 30 seconds, scraping sides of bowl often. Beat on high speed for 3 minutes, scraping bowl occasionally.

Using a spoon, stir in as much of the remaining flour as you can. Turn out onto a lightly floured surface. Knead in enough of the remaining flour to make a moderately stiff dough that is smooth and elastic (6 to 8 minutes total). Shape dough into a ball. Place dough in a lightly greased bowl, turning once to grease surface. Cover. Let rise in a warm place till double (1 to 1¼ hours). Punch down. Let rest for 10 minutes. Divide dough into 6 pieces.

In a medium mixing bowl combine walnuts, the ⅓ cup sugar, egg whites, and lemon juice. Set aside. In a small mixing bowl beat remaining egg and 1 tablespoon *water.* Set aside. Roll each piece of dough into a 10x4-inch rectangle. Spread about *1 tablespoon* of the jelly lengthwise down the center third of *each* dough rectangle. Spread *2 tablespoons* of the dates atop the jelly. Spread *about 3 tablespoons* of the walnut mixture over the dates. Overlap long sides of dough over filling. Brush edges with some of the beaten egg mixture and seal. Repeat with remaining rectangles to make 6 ropes. Place *3* of the ropes, seam side down, on a baking sheet. Braid the ropes loosely, beginning in the middle and working toward the ends. Pinch and seal the ends. Repeat with remaining 3 ropes. Brush braids with some of the beaten egg mixture. Cover. Let rise in a warm place till nearly double (about 45 minutes). Brush again with remaining beaten egg mixture.

Bake braids in a 350° oven for 30 to 35 minutes or till golden, covering with foil during the last 15 minutes to prevent overbrowning. Remove braids from baking sheets. Cool. Makes 2 braids.

Dorle Ritsch, Basalt, Colorado

Garden Patch Bread

1 package active dry yeast
⅓ cup warm water
  (110° to 115°)
1 egg
¾ cup coarsely chopped
  cabbage
1 5-ounce can (⅔ cup)
  evaporated milk

1 carrot, cut up
¼ cup sliced celery
¼ cup snipped parsley
¼ cup cooking oil
2 tablespoons honey
1 teaspoon salt
3 cups whole wheat flour
1¼ cups all-purpose flour

In a large mixing bowl dissolve yeast in the warm water. In a blender container or food processor bowl combine the egg, cabbage, evaporated milk, carrot, celery, parsley, cooking oil, honey, and salt. Cover and blend or process till smooth. Stir into yeast mixture. Using a spoon, stir in all of the whole wheat flour and as much of the all-purpose flour as you can.

Turn out onto a lightly floured surface. Knead in enough of the remaining all-purpose flour to make a moderately stiff dough that is smooth and elastic (6 to 8 minutes total). Shape into a ball. Place dough in a lightly greased bowl, turning once to grease surface. Cover. Let rise in a warm place till double (about 1¼ hours). Punch dough down. Divide dough in half. Cover. Let rest for 10 minutes.

Shape dough into two 6- to 7-inch round loaves on a greased baking sheet. Cover. Let rise in a warm place till nearly double (about 30 minutes). Bake in a 350° oven about 30 minutes or till done. If necessary, cover with foil the last 10 minutes to prevent overbrowning. Cool loaves on wire racks. Serve warm. Store bread in the refrigerator. Makes 2 loaves.

Antoinette Cox, Fresno, California

Pineapple-Whole Wheat Rolls

The honey-butter glaze on these cloverleaf rolls adds a delightfully sweet touch.

1 8-ounce can crushed
  pineapple
1 cup all-purpose flour
1 package active dry yeast
⅓ cup milk
3 tablespoons brown sugar
3 tablespoons cooking oil

¼ teaspoon salt
2 to 2½ cups whole wheat
  flour
2 tablespoons honey
2 tablespoons butter *or*
  margarine, melted

Drain pineapple, reserving ⅓ cup juice. Set aside. In a large mixer bowl stir together all-purpose flour and yeast. Set aside. In a small saucepan heat reserved pineapple juice, milk, brown sugar, cooking oil, and salt just till warm (115° to 120°). (Mixture will appear curdled.) Add to flour mixture. Beat with electric mixer on low speed for 30 seconds, scraping sides of bowl constantly. Beat at high speed for 3 minutes. Stir in the pineapple and as much of the whole wheat flour as you can.

On a lightly floured surface, knead in enough remaining whole wheat flour to make a moderately stiff dough that is smooth and elastic (6 to 8 minutes total). Place dough in a lightly greased bowl. Turn once to grease surface. Cover. Let rise in a warm place till double (about 1 hour). Punch dough down. Let rest for 10 minutes.

Divide dough into thirds. Shape each third into 12 pieces. Shape each piece into a ball, pulling edges under to make a smooth top. Place 3 balls in a greased muffin cup, smooth side up. Let rise in a warm place till nearly double (about 20 minutes). Bake in a 375° oven about 15 minutes or till done. Meanwhile, in a small mixing bowl combine honey and the melted butter or margarine. Remove rolls from pan. Brush with honey mixture. Makes 12 rolls.

Mrs. Carmen Hoagland, Fremont, Michigan

Oven Barley Pilaf

3 cups water
1 cup quick-cooking barley
½ teaspoon salt (optional)
1½ cups finely chopped onion
½ cup shredded carrot

2 tablespoons cooking oil
¼ cup toasted wheat germ
¼ teaspoon garlic powder
3 tablespoons snipped
   parsley

Carole serves this versatile whole-grain side dish with chicken, beef, fish, or pork.

In a medium saucepan bring water to boiling. Add barley and salt, if desired. Return to boiling. Reduce heat and simmer, covered, for 12 to 15 minutes or till barley is tender. *Do not drain.*

Meanwhile, in another medium saucepan cook onion and carrot in cooking oil till tender but not brown. In a greased 1½-quart casserole combine *undrained* barley, cooked vegetables, wheat germ, and garlic powder. Bake, uncovered, in a 350° oven for 25 to 30 minutes or till lightly browned and water is absorbed. Fluff with a fork to serve. Sprinkle with parsley. Makes 8 servings.

Carole Kurilko, Pine Brook, New Jersey

Green Chili Rice

1 cup chopped onion
¼ cup butter *or* margarine
3 cups cooked rice
2 cups dairy sour cream
1 cup cream-style cottage
   cheese
1 bay leaf, crushed

½ teaspoon salt
⅛ teaspoon pepper
3 4-ounce cans whole green
   chili peppers
1 cup shredded cheddar
   cheese (4 ounces)
Snipped parsley

Chili peppers, cottage cheese, cheddar cheese, and sour cream are the main attractions in this show-stopping side dish.

In a small saucepan cook onion in butter or margarine till tender but not brown. In a large bowl combine cooked onion, rice, sour cream, cottage cheese, bay leaf, salt, and pepper.

Quarter green chili peppers lengthwise. Rinse and seed chili peppers. Chop *half* of the chili peppers. Stir chopped peppers into the rice mixture. Transfer mixture to a 12x7½x2-inch baking dish. Arrange remaining quartered chili peppers diagonally atop casserole. Sprinkle cheddar cheese atop. Bake, uncovered, in a 375° oven about 30 minutes or till mixture is heated through. Sprinkle with parsley. Makes 8 to 10 servings.

Doris Hoke, Stone Mountain, Georgia

If you prefer, bake Linda's elegant rice dish in an 8x1½-inch round baking dish. Just add 5 minutes to the baking time.

Brown Rice Puff

3 beaten egg yolks
½ cup milk
2 tablespoons butter *or* margarine, melted
¼ teaspoon dry mustard
Dash ground red pepper
1 cup cooked brown rice

½ cup shredded cheddar cheese (2 ounces)
½ cup shredded Monterey Jack cheese (2 ounces)
3 egg whites
Dairy sour cream (optional)
Parsley sprigs (optional)

In a medium mixing bowl combine egg yolks, milk, butter or margarine, dry mustard, and red pepper. Stir in rice, cheddar cheese, and Monterey Jack cheese.

In a small mixer bowl beat egg whites till stiff peaks form (tips stand straight). Gently fold beaten egg whites into rice mixture. Transfer mixture to 4 well-greased 8-ounce casseroles. Bake in a 300° oven about 30 minutes or till a knife inserted 1 inch from the center comes out clean. Garnish with sour cream and parsley, if desired. Makes 4 servings.

Linda Bahr, Topeka, Kansas

Rice-Stuffed Avocados

Zylpha brushes the cut avocados with Italian dressing for extra flavor and to keep them from browning.

1 5-ounce package brown and wild rice mix
¼ teaspoon ground cumin
4 medium avocados
¼ cup Italian salad dressing
1 large tomato, peeled, seeded, and chopped
½ cup cashews, coarsely chopped
8 pitted ripe olives

Prepare rice mix according to package directions, adding cumin with rice seasonings. Meanwhile, halve, seed, and peel avocados. To make halves rest firmly, cut a small slice from the rounded side of each half. Brush with salad dressing. Arrange halves on a serving platter. Stir tomato and cashews into rice mixture. Heat through. Spoon onto avocado halves. Garnish with olives. Makes 8 servings.

Zylpha Jones, San Diego, California

Orange-Almond Pilaf

Pictured on page 26.

½ cup chopped green onion
1 clove garlic, minced
¼ teaspoon dried thyme, crushed
¼ teaspoon ground cinnamon
⅛ teaspoon pepper
Several dashes ground red pepper (optional)
2 tablespoons butter *or* margarine
1 cup long grain rice
1 14½-ounce can beef broth
1 teaspoon finely shredded orange peel
1 cup sliced almonds, toasted

In a medium saucepan cook green onion, garlic, thyme, cinnamon, pepper, and red pepper, if desired, in butter or margarine till onion is tender but not brown. Stir in *uncooked* rice, beef broth, and orange peel. Simmer, covered, for 15 to 20 minutes or till rice is tender. Stir in ½ *cup* of the almonds. Garnish with remaining almonds. Serves 4.

Sharon Stilwell, Des Moines, Iowa

Spinach Pesto and Pasta Toss

Stephanie's quick side-dish uses a spinach and cottage cheese variation of the classic basil and Parmesan cheese pesto.

6 slices bacon
10 ounces spaghetti *or* other pasta
1 10-ounce package frozen chopped spinach
2 cloves garlic, minced
⅛ teaspoon pepper
½ cup cream-style cottage cheese
⅓ cup grated Parmesan cheese

In a skillet cook bacon till crisp. Drain, reserving 2 tablespoons drippings. Crumble bacon and set aside. Cook pasta in a large amount of boiling salted water for 10 to 12 minutes or till done. Drain well.

Meanwhile, in a medium saucepan cook spinach according to package directions. *Do not drain.* Place *undrained* spinach, reserved bacon drippings, garlic, and pepper in a blender container or food processor bowl. Cover and blend or process till smooth. Add *undrained* cottage cheese. Cover and blend or process till smooth.

Arrange pasta on a large serving platter. Pour spinach mixture over pasta. Toss to mix well. Sprinkle with crumbled bacon and Parmesan cheese. Serve immediately. Makes 10 to 12 servings.

Stephanie M. Williamson, Virginia Beach, Virginia

Noodles Divine

Donna designed this skillet dish to be fast, easy, and made with ingredients she had on hand.

¾ cup shredded carrot
⅓ cup chopped onion
1 tablespoon butter *or* margarine
2⅓ cups water
1 10¾-ounce can condensed cream of chicken soup
1 4-ounce can mushroom stems and pieces, drained
Dash pepper
4 cups wide egg noodles
1 cup chopped fresh broccoli
Grated Parmesan cheese

In a 10-inch skillet cook carrot and onion in butter or margarine over medium heat about 3 minutes or till vegetables are tender, stirring occasionally. Stir in water, soup, mushrooms, and pepper. Bring to boiling. Stir in noodles. Return to boiling. Reduce heat and simmer, covered, for 15 minutes. Add broccoli. Cook for 10 minutes more or till broccoli and noodles are tender, stirring occasionally. Sprinkle cheese on top. Makes 8 servings.

Donna Reed, Ramsey, Illinois

Italian-Style Pasta Salad

4 ounces spaghetti
1 6-ounce jar marinated artichoke hearts
½ of a small zucchini, halved lengthwise and sliced
1 cup shredded mozzarella cheese (4 ounces)
1 medium carrot, shredded
2 ounces sliced salami, cut into strips
2 tablespoons grated Parmesan cheese

2 tablespoons salad oil
2 tablespoons white wine vinegar
¾ teaspoon dry mustard
½ teaspoon dried oregano, crushed
½ teaspoon dried basil, crushed
1 clove garlic, minced

Serve this top-rated make-ahead salad with grilled Italian sausages, pork chops, or chicken at your next summertime outing. (Pictured at left.)

Break spaghetti in half and cook according to package directions. Drain. Set aside. Drain and coarsely chop artichoke hearts, reserving marinade. In a large bowl combine cooked spaghetti, artichokes, zucchini, mozzarella cheese, carrot, salami, and Parmesan cheese.

For dressing, in a screw-top jar combine the reserved artichoke marinade, salad oil, vinegar, mustard, oregano, basil, and garlic. Cover and shake well. Pour dressing over spaghetti mixture. Toss to coat well. Cover and chill several hours or overnight. Serves 8 to 10.

Mary Kowinsky, Petaluma, California

Fettuccine Verde

1½ cups all-purpose flour
1 cup whole wheat flour
2 eggs
1 10-ounce package frozen chopped spinach, cooked and well drained

1½ teaspoons cooking oil
2 cloves garlic, minced
½ cup butter *or* margarine
1 cup whipping cream
½ cup grated Parmesan cheese

Stir together flours and 1 teaspoon *salt*. Make a well in the center. Combine eggs, spinach, oil, and 1 tablespoon *water*. Add to dry ingredients. Mix well, adding another tablespoon *water* if necessary.

On a floured surface knead dough till smooth and elastic (8 to 10 minutes total). Divide in half. Cover. Chill 1 hour. Roll each dough half into a 21x12-inch rectangle. Cut rectangles crosswise into ¼-inch strips. Spread strips on wire racks. Dry several hours. Cook pasta in boiling water about 8 minutes or till tender. Drain. Keep warm.

Cook garlic in butter till tender. Stir in cream and cheese. Heat through. Toss with hot pasta. Makes 6 to 8 servings.

Lou Eisenbrandt, Overland Park, Kansas

BEST-EVER FRUIT AND VEGETABLE IDEAS

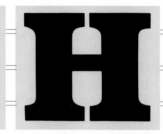

HOT OR COLD,
THERE'S A TEMPTING SIDE DISH IN THIS MÉLANGE
OF FRUIT AND VEGETABLE SPECIALTIES TO
TITILLATE YOUR TASTE BUDS. SIMPLE YET
INTRIGUING, SATISFYING YET VERSATILE—NONE
OF THESE TOP-NOTCH RECIPES WILL PLAY
SECOND FIDDLE AT YOUR MEAL.

Jicama Salad in Pepper Boats

Jicama (HEE-kuh-muh) is a juicy, mild, and slightly sweet root vegetable that's also known as the Mexican potato.

2 cups shredded jicama
2 tablespoons chopped onion
1 tablespoon lemon juice
¼ cup plain yogurt
¼ cup dairy sour cream
½ teaspoon salt
½ teaspoon chili powder
⅛ teaspoon pepper
2 large green peppers, quartered lengthwise
Snipped parsley (optional)
Cherry tomatoes (optional)

Pat shredded jicama between paper towels to remove excess liquid. In a medium mixing bowl combine jicama, onion, and lemon juice. Set aside. In a small mixing bowl combine yogurt, sour cream, salt, chili powder, and pepper. Stir into jicama mixture. Cover and chill.

Spoon jicama mixture into green pepper quarters. Garnish wtih parsley and cherry tomatoes, if desired. Makes 8 servings.

Esther M. Brown, Mesa, Arizona

Cheesy Stuffed Turnips

6 medium turnips, peeled
¾ cup crushed saltine crackers
½ cup shredded cheddar cheese (2 ounces)
¼ cup milk
3 tablespoons butter *or* margarine
Melted butter *or* margarine
Paprika
2 tablespoons butter *or* margarine
2 tablespoons all-purpose flour
¼ teaspoon salt
⅛ teaspoon pepper
1¼ cups milk

Cook turnips, covered, in boiling salted water about 25 minutes or till tender. Hollow out each turnip, leaving a ½-inch shell. Finely chop turnip centers (you should have about 1 cup chopped turnip). Set the chopped turnip aside.

In a medium mixing bowl combine crushed crackers, cheese, the ¼ cup milk, and the 3 tablespoons butter or margarine. Fill hollowed-out turnips with cheese mixture. Place in a greased 10x6x2-inch baking dish. Brush with the melted butter or margarine. Sprinkle with paprika. Bake, covered, in a 350° oven for 25 minutes. Uncover and bake for 10 minutes more.

Meanwhile, for sauce melt the 2 tablespoons butter or margarine. Stir in flour, salt, and pepper. Add the 1¼ cups milk all at once. Cook and stir till thickened and bubbly, then cook and stir 2 minutes more. Stir in chopped turnip and heat through. Spoon sauce over stuffed turnips. Makes 6 servings.

Delka F. Crawford, Wichita, Kansas

Harvest Cinnamon Beans

¼ cup chopped onion
¼ teaspoon ground cinnamon
1 tablespoon butter *or* margarine
1½ pounds fresh green beans, cut into 1-inch pieces *or* two 9-ounce packages frozen cut green beans, thawed
½ cup chicken broth
⅛ teaspoon salt
Dash pepper
2 tablespoons tomato paste
Green onion fan (optional)

With the simple addition of cinnamon and tomato paste, Deborah gave her everyday green beans an air of sophistication. (Pictured at left.)

In a medium saucepan or a 10-inch skillet cook onion and cinnamon in butter or margarine till onion is tender but not brown. Stir in green beans, chicken broth, salt, and pepper. Bring to boiling. Reduce heat and simmer, covered, about 20 minutes or till beans are tender. Gently stir in tomato paste. Garnish with a green onion fan, if desired. Serve immediately. Makes 6 servings.

Deborah Augenstein, Greeley, Colorado

Tomato and Pea Pod Vinaigrette

2 cups fresh pea pods *or* one 6-ounce package frozen pea pods, thawed
2 large tomatoes
1 green onion, thinly sliced
¼ cup salad oil
¼ cup vinegar
1 tablespoon snipped parsley
1 teaspoon dried basil, crushed
1 teaspoon sugar *or* honey
¾ teaspoon dry mustard
½ teaspoon paprika
Several dashes ground red pepper

Sharon uses the leftover delicately flavored vinaigrette dressing to complement other tossed green salads.

Bias-slice the pea pods into ½-inch pieces. Set aside. Halve tomatoes. Spoon out and reserve the pulp, removing the seeds. Invert tomato shells on paper towels. Cover and chill. Chop reserved pulp. In a small mixing bowl combine tomato pulp, pea pods, and green onion.

For dressing, in a screw-top jar combine oil, vinegar, parsley, basil, sugar or honey, mustard, paprika, red pepper, ¼ cup *water,* and ¼ teaspoon *salt.* Cover and shake well. Gently stir ¼ *cup* of the dressing into the tomato mixture. (Reserve remaining dressing for another use.) Cover and chill till serving time, stirring occasionally. To serve, use a slotted spoon to transfer tomato mixture into tomato shells. Makes 4 servings.

Sharon Stilwell, Des Moines, Iowa

Corn and Rice Salad

1 16-ounce can whole kernel corn, drained
2 cups cooked rice
¼ cup chopped red *or* green sweet pepper
¼ cup sliced green onion
¼ cup chopped pitted ripe olives
3 tablespoons olive oil *or* cooking oil
3 tablespoons white wine vinegar
2 tablespoons snipped parsley
2 tablespoons soy sauce
½ teaspoon Dijon-style mustard
¼ teaspoon garlic powder
8 cherry tomatoes, sliced
1 tablespoon grated Parmesan cheese

Planning a picnic? Toss this salad together at home, then stir in the tomatoes and top with cheese just before serving.

In a medium mixing bowl combine corn, rice, red or green pepper, onion, and olives. For dressing, in a screw-top jar combine oil, vinegar, parsley, soy sauce, mustard, and garlic powder. Cover and shake well. Pour dressing over corn mixture. Cover and chill for several hours or overnight, stirring occasionally. To serve, stir in tomatoes. Top with Parmesan cheese. Makes 8 servings.

NOTE: If using olive oil in the dressing, let the salad stand at room temperature about 20 minutes before serving.

Denise Del Monte-Thomas, El Dorado, Arkansas

J.J.'s Corn on The Cob

⅓ cup butter *or* margarine, softened
2 tablespoons prepared mustard
2 tablespoons prepared horseradish
1 teaspoon Worcestershire sauce
¼ teaspoon lemon pepper
6 fresh ears of corn, husks and silks removed

J.J. devised this recipe for a Fourth of July celebration when he was stationed in Turkey during World War II.

In a small mixing bowl combine butter or margarine, mustard, horseradish, Worcestershire sauce, and lemon pepper. Spread butter mixture over each ear of corn.

Cut six 18x12-inch pieces of *heavy* foil. Wrap each ear of corn in a piece of foil. Grill corn, on an uncovered grill, directly over *medium-hot* coals for 20 to 25 minutes or till tender, turning often. Serves 6.

J.J. McGonagle, Chatsworth, California

Golden Mushroom Fritters

How do you make a good thing even better? Try dipping these golden first-place fritters into buttermilk salad dressing.

1 cup packaged biscuit mix
1 cup chopped fresh mushrooms
2 tablespoons sliced green onion
1 tablespoon chopped pimiento
¼ teaspoon salt
¼ teaspoon celery seed
1 beaten egg yolk
¼ cup dairy sour cream
1 egg white
Cooking oil for deep-fat frying

In a large mixing bowl combine biscuit mix, mushrooms, onion, pimiento, salt, and celery seed. Combine egg yolk and sour cream. Stir into dry ingredients just till moistened.

In a small mixing bowl use a rotary beater to beat egg white till stiff peaks form (tips stand straight). Fold the beaten egg white into the mushroom mixture.

In a deep-fat fryer or heavy saucepan heat oil to 375°. Carefully drop mushroom batter by tablespoonfuls into hot oil. Fry fritters, a few at a time, about 2 minutes or till golden brown, turning once. Drain on paper towels. Serve warm. Makes 12.

Mrs. Marjorie Lindsay, Bonaparte, Iowa

Easy-Serve Salad Bundles

For her friends who like extra onion flavor, Janice stirs 2 tablespoons finely chopped onion into the salad mixture.

½ cup chopped green pepper
½ cup chopped seeded cucumber
½ cup chopped celery
½ cup chopped zucchini
6 cherry tomatoes, quartered
⅓ cup sour cream dip with toasted onion
¼ cup mayonnaise *or* salad dressing
¼ teaspoon salt
⅛ teaspoon pepper
6 hard rolls

In a large mixing bowl combine green pepper, cucumber, celery, zucchini, and tomatoes. For dressing, stir together sour cream dip, mayonnaise or salad dressing, salt, and pepper. Gently stir dressing into the vegetable mixture.

Cut a thin slice off the top of *each* roll. Remove bread in center of *each* roll, leaving a ½-inch shell. Spoon salad mixture into bread shells. Replace roll tops. Wrap sandwiches individually in foil. Chill till serving time. Makes 6 servings.

Janice S. Elder, Spartanburg, South Carolina

Tangy Brussels Sprouts

When you're buying fresh brussels sprouts, look for the ones that are small and compact, with a vivid green color.

1 pound fresh brussels sprouts *or* two 10-ounce packages frozen brussels sprouts
6 slices bacon
⅓ cup Italian salad dressing
1 3-ounce can sliced mushrooms, drained
¼ cup sliced green onion
2 tablespoons chopped pimiento
¼ cup crumbled blue cheese

If using fresh brussels sprouts, trim the stems slightly. Remove the wilted or discolored leaves and wash. Cut sprouts in half. Cook, covered, in a small amount of boiling salted water about 10 minutes or till crisp-tender. Drain. (*Or,* if using frozen brussels sprouts, cook whole sprouts according to package directions. Drain and halve.)

In a medium skillet cook bacon till crisp. Drain well. Crumble bacon and set aside. In a medium saucepan combine cooked sprouts, salad dressing, mushrooms, onion, and pimiento. Cook and stir over low heat till heated through. Remove from heat and stir in blue cheese and crumbled bacon. Makes 6 to 8 servings.

Mrs. William Strieber, Crofton, Maryland

Italian Vegetable Toss

1½ cups medium shell macaroni
2 cups broccoli flowerets
1 cup cauliflower flowerets
1 cup sliced fresh mushrooms
1 cup sliced, pitted ripe olives
1 7½-ounce can artichoke hearts, drained, rinsed, and chopped
½ cup sliced green onion
⅔ cup Italian salad dressing
1 medium avocado, seeded, peeled, and sliced
1 medium tomato, seeded and chopped

Jodie's imaginative, light-tasting salad is a potpourri of vegetables and pasta.

Cook macaroni according to package directions. Drain. Rinse with cold water. Drain well. In a large mixing bowl combine cooked macaroni, broccoli, cauliflower, mushrooms, olives, artichoke hearts, and green onion. Toss with Italian dressing. Cover and chill for several hours. Just before serving, toss vegetable mixture with avocado and tomato. Makes 12 to 16 servings.

Jodie Bacon, Boise, Idaho

Cucumber Mousse

2 envelopes unflavored gelatin
1 cup mayonnaise *or* salad dressing
1 tablespoon sliced green onion
1 tablespoon lemon juice
½ teaspoon dried dillweed
¼ teaspoon salt
Dash bottled hot pepper sauce
2 medium cucumbers, peeled and cut up
Lettuce leaves

Add a fresh touch to any summertime meal with this light and simple salad.

To soften gelatin, combine gelatin and ¼ cup *cold water.* Let stand for 5 minutes. Transfer to a blender container or food processor bowl. Add ½ cup *boiling water.* Cover and blend or process till gelatin is dissolved. Add mayonnaise or salad dressing, green onion, lemon juice, dillweed, salt, and hot pepper sauce to blender container or food processor bowl. Cover and blend or process till combined.

With blender or processor running, add cucumber, a few pieces at a time, through hole in lid. Blend or process till smooth. Pour cucumber mixture into a 4½-cup metal ring mold (8-inch diameter) or 8 individual molds. Chill about 4 hours or till firm.

To serve, unmold mousse onto a lettuce-lined serving platter or individual serving plates. Garnish with sliced cucumber and radish roses, if desired. Makes 8 servings.

Mrs. Sabina G. Lawton, Providence, Rhode Island

TERESA MITCHUM, OVERLAND PARK, KANS.

Teresa and Jim Mitchum, along with their children Stephanie and Aaron, live in suburban Overland Park, Kansas. Jim's career as a financial analyst for a pharmaceutical firm has taken the family from Indianapolis to Tennessee, back to Indiana, and on to Kansas City. With all these moves, Teresa, a full-time wife and mother who likes to be known as Terry, keeps busy refurbishing the homes her family lives in.

There's a country-style appeal in the latest Mitchum house that comes partly from the counted cross-stitch wall pieces made by Terry. One such version, outlined in red hearts, proclaims, "The best antiques are old friends."

But besides the furnishings, Terry always manages to take along her Italian cooking heritage and love for all things culinary wherever she lives. "Thank goodness I have an understanding and risk-taking family!" laughs Terry. "I do a lot of cooking by trial and error."

Terry remembers getting involved in cooking almost on impulse. "My 8th grade history teacher always kidded me about meatballs because of my (Italian) last name. So one day I brought some meatballs to class!" Her recipe for spaghetti and meatballs was a legacy brought over by her father from his family in Naples. It's fitting that making perfect pasta was Terry's first cooking lesson.

"The rule of thumb for pasta is to make one pound for each four servings," advises Terry. And how do you decide when it's done? "I eat it!" she says with enthusiasm. "Then I quickly

continued

TERESA MITCHUM, OVERLAND PARK, KANS.

pour it into a colander. I don't rinse it because that makes it soggy." Next comes an unusual serving technique. "I put the pasta in a large, shallow bowl and sprinkle a liberal dose of Parmesan cheese and pepper over it. Then I pour about a cup of sauce over the pasta and toss lightly. Finally, I sprinkle with additional cheese and pepper and pour another thin layer of sauce over the top. I serve additional sauce with it."

When they lived in Indianapolis, one of the Mitchums' favorite places to shop for their ethnic specialties was downtown at the City Market. Housed in a century-old building, it's filled with food shops, produce stands, and ethnic eateries. The little Italian market, run by Lena Palamara, offered Terry a chance to indulge in her favorites.

66 To test pasta for doneness, I eat it! Then I quickly pour it into a colander. I don't rinse it because that makes it soggy. 99

When the Mitchums' first child was born, they made a conscious effort to change some of their eating habits for the better. Terry explains, "I managed to convert many of our recipes so we could cut down on sugar, salt, additives, and preservatives." Recently, Terry discovered that she has developed some food allergies, so more than ever the family's diet centers on fresh vegetables, fruits, whole grains, and lean meat.

Now the Mitchums' standbys include lots of quiches, chicken dishes, vegetable concoctions, and rice. "We barbecue frequently in the summertime, and I've been experimenting with kabobs. I'm also intrigued by stir-frying," adds Terry. It seems obvious that wherever the Mitchums are, home is where the kitchen is.

TERESA MITCHUM, OVERLAND PARK, KANS.

This colorful vegetable dish grew out of Terry's love of pasta, vegetables, and Italian seasonings. "My maternal grandmother was from the South," Terry recalls fondly. "We never sat down at her table without having three or four vegetables." Topped with cheese, this colorful casserole makes a hearty side dish that complements chicken, fish, or many barbecued entrées.

Tomato and Broccoli Bake

4 ounces cavatelli *or* medium shell macaroni
1 cup shredded cheddar cheese (4 ounces)
1 tablespoon all-purpose flour
1 medium onion, thinly sliced
1 clove garlic, minced
2 tablespoons butter *or* margarine

5 medium tomatoes, peeled, seeded, and chopped
¼ cup snipped parsley
¼ teaspoon dried oregano, crushed
¼ teaspoon dried basil, crushed
2 cups fresh *or* frozen chopped broccoli

Cook pasta in boiling salted water for 8 to 10 minutes or till tender. Drain well. Meanwhile, combine ½ *cup* cheese and flour. Set aside.

In a large saucepan cook onion and garlic in butter or margarine till tender but not brown. Stir in the tomatoes, parsley, oregano, basil, and ¼ teaspoon *salt.* Bring to boiling. Add broccoli. Simmer, covered, for 4 minutes. Stir in cooked pasta and cheese-flour mixture.

Transfer to an 8x8x2-inch baking dish. Bake, covered, in a 375° oven for 15 minutes. Sprinkle with remaining cheese. Bake, uncovered, for 5 minutes more. Makes 6 to 8 servings.

Bulgur-Vegetable Pilaf

Barbara likes to serve this colorful vegetable pilaf as a meat accompaniment.

1 cup chopped onion
1 cup chopped celery
1 cup sliced fresh mushrooms
1 clove garlic, minced
3 tablespoons cooking oil
1 cup chicken *or* beef broth
1 cup sliced carrots

1 cup sliced zucchini
½ cup green *or* red sweet
  pepper strips
½ cup bulgur
1 teaspoon dried tarragon,
  crushed
¼ teaspoon salt

In a 3-quart saucepan cook onion, celery, mushrooms, and garlic in hot oil about 8 minutes or till vegetables are tender. Stir in chicken or beef broth, carrots, zucchini, green or red pepper strips, bulgur, tarragon, and salt. Bring to boiling. Reduce heat and simmer, covered, for 15 minutes or till vegetables are tender. Makes 8 servings.

Mrs. Barbara Milne, San Diego, California

Cauliflower-Carrot Cheese Pie

3 cups herb-seasoned
  croutons, finely crushed
3 tablespoons butter *or*
  margarine, melted
1 cup chopped onion
1 clove garlic, minced
2 tablespoons butter *or*
  margarine
4 cups cauliflower flowerets
½ cup sliced carrot
½ teaspoon dried savory,
  crushed

½ teaspoon dried oregano,
  crushed
¼ teaspoon salt
  Dash pepper
¾ cup shredded cheddar
  cheese (3 ounces)
2 slightly beaten eggs
¼ cup milk
¾ cup shredded cheddar
  cheese (3 ounces)

Stir together crushed croutons and the 3 tablespoons melted butter or margarine. Press into a lightly greased 9-inch pie plate. Bake in a 375° oven for 8 to 10 minutes or till golden. Set aside.

Meanwhile, cook onion and garlic in the 2 tablespoons butter or margarine till onion is tender but not brown. Stir in cauliflower, carrot, savory, oregano, salt, and pepper. Cook, covered, over medium-low heat about 15 minutes or till vegetables are crisp-tender.

Sprinkle ¾ cup cheddar cheese over the bottom of the baked pie shell. Spoon vegetable mixture atop. Combine eggs and milk. Carefully pour over vegetables in pie shell. Bake, uncovered, in a 375° oven for 15 minutes. Top with ¾ cup shredded cheddar cheese. Bake for 5 to 10 minutes more or till set. Makes 6 to 8 servings.

Linda Roscoe, Youngstown, Ohio

Cheesy Broccoli Casserole

When it's in season, Flora likes to make this first-place vegetable side dish with asparagus.

1½ pounds fresh broccoli
2 slightly beaten eggs
¾ cup cream-style cottage cheese
½ cup shredded cheddar cheese (2 ounces)
2 tablespoons finely chopped onion
1 teaspoon Worcestershire sauce
¼ teaspoon salt
⅛ teaspoon pepper
¼ cup fine dry bread crumbs
1 tablespoon butter *or* margarine, melted

Cut brocooli stalks into spears. Cook, covered, in a small amount of boiling water about 10 minutes or till crisp-tender. Drain well.

Meanwhile, in a medium mixing bowl combine eggs, cottage cheese, cheddar cheese, onion, Worcestershire sauce, salt, and pepper. Arrange broccoli spears in a 10x6x2-inch baking dish. Spoon cheese mixture atop. Stir together bread crumbs and melted butter or margarine. Sprinkle evenly over cheese mixture. Bake, uncovered, in a 350° oven for 15 to 20 minutes or till set. Serve immediately. Makes 4 to 6 servings.

Mrs. Flora B. Rippstein, Apple Valley, California

Romaine and Broccoli Stir-Fry

Julia's vegetable stir-fry makes a light-and-easy side dish to serve family or company.

1 medium head romaine
4 slices bacon, cut up
6 cups broccoli flowerets
¼ cup water
1 teaspoon sugar
¼ teaspoon salt

Cut romaine into ½-inch-wide strips. Set aside. In a wok or large skillet cook bacon till crisp. Remove bacon, reserving drippings in wok or skillet. Drain bacon on paper towels. Set aside.

Add broccoli to drippings in wok or skillet, stirring to coat. Stir in water, sugar, and salt. Cover and simmer for 4 minutes. Stir in romaine. Stir-fry for 3 minutes. Remove from wok or skillet. Sprinkle with bacon pieces. Makes 6 servings.

Julia A. Haciski, Baltimore, Maryland

Squash-Corn Casseroles

Barbara jazzed up the ever-popular scalloped corn with the addition of some winter squash. (Pictured at right.)

½ cup chopped onion
½ cup chopped green pepper
2 tablespoons butter *or* margarine
2 cups mashed cooked winter squash
1 17-ounce can cream-style corn
1 cup coarsely crushed saltine crackers

½ cup shredded American cheese (2 ounces)
2 tablespoons chopped pimiento
2 tablespoons coarsely crushed saltine crackers
1 teaspoon butter *or* margarine, melted

In a 1½-quart saucepan cook onion and green pepper in the 2 tablespoons butter or margarine till tender but not brown. Stir in squash, corn, the 1 cup crushed crackers, cheese, and pimiento. Spoon mixture into 6 or 8 individual casseroles. Combine the 2 tablespoons crushed crackers and the 1 teaspoon melted butter or margarine. Sprinkle over each casserole. Bake, uncovered, in a 350° oven for 30 minutes. Makes 6 to 8 servings.

Barbara York, Wichita Falls, Texas

Apple-Vegetable Stuffed Squash

Mary Jeanne mashed carrots, turnips, spices, and an apple with acorn squash for this tasty side-dish combination.

2 medium acorn squash (about 1 pound each)
2 medium carrots, chopped
2 small turnips, chopped
1 tablespoon butter *or* margarine

1 tablespoon brown sugar
½ teaspoon ground cinnamon
¼ teaspoon ground nutmeg
1 cup coarsely shredded, peeled apple

Halve and seed squash. Place squash, cut side down, in a 13x9x2-inch baking pan. Bake, covered, in a 350° oven for 30 minutes. Turn cut side up. Bake, covered, for 20 to 30 minutes more or till tender. Scoop pulp out of each squash half, keeping shells intact. Set shells aside. Place cooked pulp in a large mixer bowl.

Meanwhile, cook carrots and turnips, covered, in a small amount of boiling water about 20 minutes or till tender. Drain well. Add cooked carrots and turnips to the mixer bowl with the squash. Beat with an electric mixer on low speed till mashed. Add butter or margarine, brown sugar, cinnamon, nutmeg, and ¼ teaspoon *salt*. Beat till combined. Stir in shredded apple. Spoon mixture into squash shells. Return filled shells to baking pan. Bake in a 350° oven for 15 to 20 minutes or till heated through. Makes 8 servings.

Mary Jeanne Brooks, Chelsea, Oklahoma

Potato Royale

You can pick up the spicy hot Pickapeppa sauce in specialty food shops and large supermarkets.

4 baking potatoes
¼ cup sliced green onion
¼ cup chopped green pepper
¼ cup chopped celery
2 cloves garlic, minced
3 tablespoons butter *or* margarine
1 cup fresh *or* frozen coarsely chopped shrimp

½ cup dairy sour cream
½ cup shredded mozzarella cheese (2 ounces)
½ teaspoon lemon juice
½ teaspoon Pickapeppa sauce *or* steak sauce
Dash bottled hot pepper sauce
Grated Parmesan cheese

Scrub potatoes. Prick with a fork. Bake in a 350° oven for 70 to 80 minutes. Cool, then halve lengthwise. Scoop out insides, leaving a ¼-inch shell. Mash pulp and set aside. Place shells on a baking sheet.

In a medium saucepan cook onion, green pepper, celery, and garlic in butter or margarine till tender. Add shrimp. Cook and stir for 1 to 2 minutes more. Remove from heat and set aside.

In a medium mixing bowl combine sour cream, mozzarella cheese, lemon juice, Pickapeppa or steak sauce, and hot pepper sauce. Stir in mashed potatoes and shrimp mixture. Spoon mixture into potato shells. Sprinkle with Parmesan cheese. Bake in a 350° oven 20 to 25 minutes or till heated through. Makes 8 servings.

Mrs. Pauline M. Anisman, Houma, Louisiana

Potato-Crust Quiche

This deliciously different side-dish quiche uses vegetables from start to finish.

3 medium potatoes
¼ cup butter *or* margarine
2 cups loose-pack frozen mixed vegetables
½ cup shredded cheddar cheese (2 ounces)
2 beaten eggs

1 5-ounce can (⅔ cup) evaporated milk
1 tablespoon fine dry bread crumbs
Carrot curls
Parsley sprigs

Cook whole potatoes, covered, in boiling salted water for 20 to 25 minutes or till tender. Drain and peel. Mash with a potato masher. Measure 1⅓ cups mashed potatoes. Stir in butter or margarine. Spoon into a greased 9-inch pie plate. Spread over bottom and up sides of pie plate, building up sides with a spoon to form a crust. Arrange vegetables in bottom of potato crust. Sprinkle with cheese.

Combine eggs, milk, ¼ teaspoon *salt,* and ⅛ teaspoon *pepper.* Pour over cheese. Sprinkle with bread crumbs. Bake in a 375° oven for 40 to 50 minutes. Garnish with carrot curls and parsley. Serves 8.

Kris Heller, Hutchinson, Kansas

Fiesta Potato Salad

4 cups frozen loose-pack hash brown potatoes
½ cup finely chopped celery
½ cup chopped, pitted ripe olives
2 tablespoons chopped pimiento
2 tablespoons finely chopped onion
2 tablespoons diced canned green chili peppers
½ cup dairy sour cream
½ of a 1.25-ounce envelope (about 2 tablespoons) taco seasoning mix
1 single-serving envelope *instant* cream of chicken soup mix
¼ cup sliced radishes

In a 10-inch skillet combine frozen potatoes and ½ cup *water*. Cook, covered, over medium-low heat for 8 to 10 minutes. Drain well. In a large mixing bowl stir together celery, olives, pimiento, onion, and chili peppers. Fold in cooked and drained potatoes.

In a small mixing bowl combine sour cream and taco seasoning mix. Stir ¼ cup *hot water* into soup mix, stirring till soup is dissolved. Fold soup into sour cream mixture. Gently stir sour cream mixture into potato mixture. Transfer to a serving bowl and garnish with radishes. Serve warm. Makes 6 servings.

Mrs. Peter DuBovy, Huntington Beach, California

Fruit-and-Rice Salad

4 cups cooked brown rice
1 11-ounce can mandarin orange sections, drained
1 8-ounce can pineapple chunks (juice pack), drained
1 cup chopped carrot
1 cup seedless red grapes, halved
1 medium apple, cored and coarsely chopped
½ cup raisins
½ cup mayonnaise *or* salad dressing
½ cup whipping cream
2 tablespoons chopped chutney
1 tablespoon curry powder
1 tablespoon lemon juice
¼ teaspoon salt
¼ teaspoon pepper
½ cup chopped walnuts
½ cup pine nuts
Spinach leaves

After chilling, stir in some additional whipping cream if the salad seems a little dry. (Pictured at right.)

In a large mixing bowl combine rice, orange sections, pineapple chunks, carrot, grapes, apple, raisins, mayonnaise or salad dressing, cream, chutney, curry powder, lemon juice, salt, and pepper. Cover and chill for several hours. Just before serving, stir in walnuts and pine nuts. Serve on a spinach-lined platter. Makes 8 to 10 servings.

Mrs. Charles A. Kinell, Monterey Park, California

Sunflower Waldorf Salad

2 small apples, cored and coarsely chopped
⅓ cup sunflower nuts
¼ cup seedless green grapes, halved
¼ cup chopped celery
¼ cup vanilla yogurt
1 large banana, sliced
Lettuce leaves

For a slightly different taste twist, make this fruity salad with lemon or apple yogurt.

In a medium mixing bowl combine apples, sunflower nuts, grapes, and celery. Fold in yogurt and banana. Serve on individual lettuce-lined salad plates. Makes 4 servings.

Toni Schwer, Muncie, Indiana

Five-Fruit Salad

Jolie's first-place fruit salad features a unique pineapple-peanut butter dressing.

½ of a 6-ounce can (⅓ cup) frozen pineapple juice concentrate, thawed
2 tablespoons peanut butter
⅓ cup salad oil
½ cup seedless green grapes
½ cup fresh strawberries
4 cups torn lettuce
1 cup fresh *or* canned pineapple chunks, drained
1 cup sliced, peeled fresh peaches *or* frozen unsweetened peach slices, thawed
¼ of a medium cantaloupe, peeled and cut into wedges
Lemon juice

For dressing, in a blender container or food processor bowl combine pineapple juice concentrate and peanut butter. Cover and blend or process till smooth. With blender or processor running at high speed, gradually add oil through hole in lid. Blend or process till combined. Transfer to a storage container. Cover and store dressing in refrigerator till serving time. Stir dressing before serving.

Just before serving, halve the grapes and strawberries. Line a large platter with lettuce. Arrange grapes, berries, pineapple, peaches, and cantaloupe atop lettuce (brush peach slices with a little lemon juice to prevent darkening). Pass dressing with salad. Makes 8 servings.

Jolie Steckart, De Pere, Wisconsin

Banana-Sprout Salad

You can put together Lee's fruit salad in short order. Serve it with assorted cheeses and crackers, and it's a perfect light lunch or supper.

1 large banana, sliced
½ of a medium avocado, seeded, peeled, and chopped
1 tablespoon lemon juice
¼ cup crushed pineapple, well drained
2 tablespoons chopped walnuts
⅔ cup alfalfa sprouts
2 tablespoons mayonnaise *or* salad dressing
2 tablespoons plain yogurt
1 tablespoon toasted wheat germ
Sliced strawberries (optional)

Toss banana and avocado with lemon juice. Stir in pineapple and walnuts. Arrange alfalfa sprouts on 2 individual serving plates. Top each with some of the fruit mixture. For dressing, combine mayonnaise or salad dressing, yogurt, and wheat germ. Spoon dressing atop fruit. Garnish with strawberries, if desired. Serves 2.

Lee Pulliam, Pfafftown, North Carolina

Tangy Apple Ring

2 cups applesauce
1 6-ounce package lemon-flavored gelatin
1 12-ounce can (1½ cups) lemon-lime carbonated beverage
1 teaspoon finely shredded orange peel

¼ cup orange juice
1 medium apple, cored and chopped
2 tablespoons chopped walnuts
Mayonnaise *or* salad dressing (optional)
Watercress (optional)

In a medium saucepan heat applesauce just till it bubbles. Stir in gelatin. Cook and stir over medium-low heat till gelatin dissolves. Remove from heat and cool. Stir in carbonated beverage, orange peel, and orange juice. Chill till partially set (consistency of unbeaten egg whites). Fold in chopped apple and walnuts. Transfer to a 4- to 4½-cup ring mold. Chill till firm.

To serve, unmold onto a serving platter. Serve with mayonnaise or salad dressing and garnish with watercress, if desired. Serves 8.

Kim Hayes, Bottineau, North Dakota

Eggnog Salad

1 envelope unflavored gelatin
1 8-ounce can crushed pineapple (juice pack)
3 tablespoons lime juice
1½ cups dairy eggnog
½ cup finely chopped celery
1½ cups cranberry juice cocktail *or* apple juice

1 3-ounce package raspberry-flavored gelatin
1 14-ounce jar cranberry-orange sauce
Lettuce leaves
Frosted cranberries (optional)

Soften unflavored gelatin in the *undrained* pineapple and lime juice for 5 minutes. Cook and stir over medium heat till gelatin dissolves. Cool to room temperature. Stir in eggnog. Chill till partially set (consistency of unbeaten egg whites). Fold in celery. Transfer to a 12x7½x2-inch pan. Chill till almost firm.

Meanwhile, heat cranberry juice cocktail or apple juice to boiling. Stir in raspberry-flavored gelatin till dissolved. Chill till partially set (consistency of unbeaten egg whites). Fold in cranberry-orange sauce. Carefully spoon atop eggnog mixture in pan. Chill till firm. Cut into squares and serve on lettuce-lined plates. Garnish each serving with frosted cranberries, if desired. Makes 12 servings.

Laura Getschmann, Bremerton, Washington

MARIE BRUNO, PALM BEACH, FLA.

Just a block from the sparkling Atlantic oceanfront of Palm Beach, Florida, is the home of Marie and Al Bruno. They share their seaside residence with two daughters, Gloria and Maryann, a couple of big dogs, and one adopted cat. Originally from New Jersey, the Brunos have adapted completely to life in Florida, indulging in boating, fishing, and swimming when schedules permit. In short, they live as much outside as inside.

Marie combines her homemaking duties with a real estate brokerage business and spreads her enthusiasm for the sunshine state wherever she can. "I have a dual personality," says Marie of her two-career status. The same could also be said for Marie's unique culinary style— robust Italian dishes on the one hand and lighter, fresher meals on the other.

As a newlywed back in New Jersey, Marie recalls, "When I first got married, I couldn't cook anything. My grandmother used to live up the street, and I would run to her and say, 'Grandma, how do I do this?' Thank goodness for grandmothers!" Armed with a repertoire of hearty family dishes, Marie has mastered the art of Italian cookery. She boasts proudly, "My lasagna will knock your socks off!"

Raising a family and tending to her business in Florida has changed Marie's cooking style drastically. "Time is a big factor in my meal planning. But I've also become a more exciting, experimental cook," she says. The Brunos entertain often, too. Al says, "Marie prepares everything two or three days in advance so she can be with the guests and not have to stay in the kitchen."

The Brunos' recently remodeled kitchen is a spacious, thoughtfully designed cooking center for the entire family. It

(continued)

MARIE BRUNO, PALM BEACH, FLA.

placed so that Marie can converse with family and friends while cooking. At one end of the kitchen, there's a dining area and a huge built-in cabinet that houses a treasured antique china collection. Just outside is a terrace and a view of a large old grapefruit tree. Notes Marie, "Maintenance is a lot easier in this kitchen—and the livability is fantastic!"

Marie had a chance to explore microwave cooking while doing product demonstrations at

was a special project for Marie, who took careful notes on features she liked while viewing other homes. All of the built-in appliances and the cooktop are within easy reach, and were

her husband's appliance store. Now she wouldn't be without her microwave. "I enjoy it," says Marie. "I was ready for something different to make my cooking life easier!"

But the biggest change for the Brunos' cooking and eating habits came when Al was diagnosed as a diabetic. Marie says, "It was a shock at first, but after a week's reprogramming with the hospital dietitians, I developed a new method of cooking." The Brunos discovered

that they like eating lighter, and everyone feels great, too. "The family is on a better program, and no one suffers because of the dietary restrictions," Marie insists. As a result of the new diet, she lost 13 pounds and Al shed a whopping 70 pounds!

Marie found that many of her family favorites were adaptable to Al's special diet. "We eat a lot of fish, chicken, and salads. I use many of the sugar-free products on the market now, and if a recipe calls for sugar, I'll try to adapt it to a sugar substitute. We've basically eliminated heavy desserts—we stick to fresh fruit or sherbet."

Dining out is a favorite hobby of the Brunos, and their new eating habits haven't deterred them from sampling cuisines offered in their area. "It's very hard to put the brakes on food," Marie admits, "but we try to keep within the framework of the basic dietary guidelines. It's just a matter of making substitutions."

MARIE BRUNO, PALM BEACH, FLA.

This side-dish salad is a year-round favorite of the Brunos. "Chef's Choice Fruit Salad," says Marie, "is also very good in the winter, because the ingredients are all readily available." It's a takeoff on an old favorite, carrot-raisin salad, but with yummy additions like dates and nuts. Arranging the ingredients in a circular design makes a pretty presentation.

Chef's Choice Fruit Salad

To prevent the apple slices from darkening before serving time, toss them in a mixture of lemon juice and water. Drain well and add them to the salad as directed.

Romaine leaves
4 cups torn mixed salad greens
1 medium apple, cored and sliced
¼ cup shredded coconut
1 cup raisins, chopped pitted dates, *or* chopped dried, pitted prunes

½ cup slivered almonds
½ cup shredded carrot
½ cup mayonnaise *or* salad dressing
½ cup dairy sour cream
¼ cup orange marmalade
1 tablespoon milk

Line a large salad bowl with romaine leaves. Place torn mixed greens in center of bowl. Arrange apple slices around the edge of the bowl. Sprinkle with coconut. Arrange raisins, dates, or prunes; almonds; and carrot in a circular design atop lettuce. Cover and chill.

For dressing, combine the mayonnaise or salad dressing, sour cream, marmalade, and milk. Cover and chill.

Just before serving, spoon dressing over salad. Toss to coat. Makes 6 to 8 servings.

Easy Fruit Salad

5 fresh apricots, peeled, pitted, and cut into bite-size pieces
1 large apple, cored and coarsely chopped
1 tablespoon lemon juice
1 cup fresh *or* canned pineapple chunks, drained

1 large orange, peeled and sectioned
½ cup thinly sliced celery
¼ cup slivered almonds
½ cup dairy sour cream
2 tablespoons apricot brandy
1 cup torn lettuce

Wrong time of the year for fresh apricots? Substitute canned ones instead.

In a large salad bowl toss apricots and apple with lemon juice to prevent darkening. Add pineapple chunks, orange sections, celery, and almonds. Cover and chill. Meanwhile, for dressing stir together sour cream and apricot brandy. Cover and chill.

Just before serving, gently toss the lettuce with the fruit mixture. Spoon dressing atop and toss. Makes 6 to 8 servings.

Mrs. Esther Brightman, Central Valley, California

Rhubarb-Raspberry Jam

6 cups fresh *or* frozen unsweetened sliced rhubarb
4 cups sugar
1 tablespoon lemon juice

2 cups fresh *or* frozen red raspberries
1 3-ounce package raspberry-flavored gelatin

In a Dutch oven or large kettle combine rhubarb, sugar, and lemon juice. Let stand for 15 minutes. Bring to boiling. Boil, uncovered, for 10 minutes, stirring frequently. Stir in the raspberries. Return to boiling and boil hard, uncovered, for 5 to 6 minutes or till thick, stirring frequently. Remove from heat. Add gelatin. Stir till dissolved.

Ladle at once into hot, clean half-pint jars, leaving a ¼-inch headspace. Wipe jar rims and adjust lids. Process in boiling water bath for 15 minutes (start timing when water boils). Makes 5 to 6 half-pints.

Mrs. Roman Novak, Silver Spring, Maryland

Cherry-Berry Jam

3 cups pitted dark sweet cherries *or* frozen unsweetened pitted dark sweet cherries, thawed
2 cups fresh strawberries *or* frozen unsweetened whole strawberries, thawed

4¼ cups sugar
¾ cup water
1 1¾-ounce package powdered fruit pectin

Two favorite summer fruits star in this simple refrigerator jam.

Finely chop cherries. Measure 1½ cups. Remove stems and mash strawberries. Measure 1 cup. Combine cherries, strawberries, and sugar. Let stand for 10 minutes. Combine water and pectin. Bring to a full rolling boil (a boil that cannot be stirred down). Boil hard, uncovered, for 1 minute, stirring constantly. Stir pectin mixture into fruit mixture. Stir constantly for 3 minutes. Ladle at once into clean half-pint jars or moisture- and vaporproof freezer containers, leaving a ½-inch headspace. Seal and label. Let stand for several hours at room temperature or till jam is set. Store in refrigerator for up to 3 weeks or in freezer for up to 3 months. Makes about 5 half-pints.

Mrs. Cindy Cassidy, Swannanoa, North Carolina

Fruited Chili Relish

15 medium ripe tomatoes, peeled and chopped (11 cups)
3 medium pears, peeled, cored, and chopped (3 cups)
3 medium apples, peeled, cored, and chopped (2½ cups)
3 medium peaches, peeled, pitted, and chopped (1½ cups)

2 cups sugar
2 cups vinegar
1½ cups chopped onion
1 medium green pepper, chopped (½ cup)
1 medium red sweet pepper, chopped (½ cup)
1 tablespoon salt
¼ cup pickling spice

Toward the end of the cooking time, stir the relish mixture frequently so it doesn't stick to the bottom of the pan.

In an 8-quart Dutch oven stir together tomatoes, pears, apples, peaches, sugar, vinegar, onion, green pepper, red sweet pepper, and salt. Tie pickling spice in a cheesecloth bag. Add to Dutch oven. Bring mixture to boiling. Boil, uncovered, for 1 to 1¼ hours or till reduced by half, stirring occasionally. Remove spice bag.

Ladle hot relish into hot, clean pint jars, leaving a ½-inch headspace. Wipe jar rims and adjust lids. Process in boiling water bath for 10 minutes (start timing when water boils). Makes 5 pints.

Stacy Zarubi, Sparks, Nevada

Ruby Beet Relish

6 cups coarsely shredded red cabbage (1 medium head)
4 cups shredded, peeled cooked beets (6 medium)
1¾ cups finely chopped celery
1⅔ cups sugar
1½ cups white vinegar
1 cup chopped onion

1 cup cranberry juice cocktail
2 tablespoons prepared horseradish
½ teaspoon finely shredded orange peel
⅛ teaspoon ground red pepper

This sweet-and-sour cabbage mixture is especially good with pork burgers or any other pork entrée.

In a 4-quart Dutch oven or kettle stir together cabbage, beets, celery, sugar, vinegar, onion, cranberry juice, horseradish, orange peel, red pepper, and 1 teaspoon *salt*. Bring to boiling. Reduce heat and simmer, uncovered, for 5 minutes, stirring frequently.

Ladle hot relish into hot, clean pint jars, leaving a ½-inch headspace. Wipe rims and adjust lids. Process in boiling water bath for 15 minutes (start timing when water boils). Makes about 5 pints.

Barbara C. Gossage, Springfield, Virginia

Zippy Onion Relish

3 large onions, finely chopped (3 cups)
½ cup tomato sauce
3 tablespoons catsup
2 tablespoons water
1½ teaspoons sugar
½ teaspoon dried oregano, crushed
¼ teaspoon salt
¼ teaspoon garlic salt
¼ teaspoon crushed red pepper

At your next cookout, spoon this hot and spicy relish on your grilled franks or burgers.

In a medium saucepan combine onions, tomato sauce, catsup, water, sugar, oregano, salt, garlic salt, and red pepper. Bring to boiling. Reduce heat and simmer, covered, about 20 minutes or till the onions are just tender.

Store relish, in a tightly covered container, in the refrigerator for up to 2 weeks. Makes about 2½ cups.

Mrs. Nancy L. Mosiello, Concord, New Hampshire

Rhubarb Chutney

1 pound fresh rhubarb, chopped (3 cups)
2 cups finely chopped onion
2 cups packed brown sugar
2 cups vinegar
1 tablespoon salt
1 teaspoon ground allspice

Donna's winning relish adds pizzazz to ham, pork roast, or poultry.

In a 4-quart Dutch oven stir together rhubarb, onion, brown sugar, vinegar, salt, and allspice. Bring to boiling. Reduce heat and simmer, covered, for 30 to 40 minutes or till thick, stirring occasionally.

Ladle hot chutney into hot, clean half-pint jars, leaving a ½-inch headspace. Wipe rims and adjust lids. Process in boiling water bath for 10 minutes (start timing when water boils). Makes 3 half-pints.

Mrs. Donna Torres, Cornucopia, Wisconsin

Creamy Green Bean Dressing

½ cup cream-style cottage cheese
2 tablespoons plain yogurt
2 tablespoons milk
½ cup cooked green beans
¼ cup shredded cheddar cheese (1 ounce)
1 tablespoon finely chopped onion

1 tablespoon vinegar
Few drops bottled hot pepper sauce
1 hard-cooked egg, finely chopped
Milk
1 hard-cooked egg, finely chopped (optional)
Parsley sprig (optional)

Leave out the additional milk and you've got yourself a terrific vegetable dip! (Pictured at left.)

In a blender container or food processor bowl combine cottage cheese, yogurt, and milk. Cover and blend or process till smooth. Add *half* of the green beans, cheddar cheese, onion, vinegar, hot pepper sauce, dash *salt,* and dash *pepper.* Cover and blend or process till smooth. Add remaining green beans. Cover and blend or process just till beans are finely chopped, stopping blender as necessary to scrape down sides. Stir in hard-cooked egg. Cover and chill thoroughly.

Before serving, stir in 1 to 2 teaspoons additional milk to make dressing desired consistency. Garnish with hard-cooked egg and parsley, if desired. Makes about 1⅓ cups.

Anne Dobrinen, Fresno, California

Blender Tofu Dressing

8 ounces tofu (fresh bean curd), cubed (1½ cups)
¾ cup milk
1 0.6-ounce envelope Zesty Italian dry salad dressing mix *or* one 0.4-ounce envelope buttermilk dry salad dressing mix

1 tablespoon mayonnaise *or* salad dressing

Place tofu, *half* of the milk, salad dressing mix, and mayonnaise or salad dressing in a blender container or food processor bowl. Cover and blend or process till smooth. Add remaining milk. Cover and blend or process till combined. Cover and chill thoroughly. Serve with vegetable or main-dish salads. Makes about 1⅔ cups.

Judy Bodnick, Grand Island, New York

If watercress isn't available, use 3 tablespoons each of parsley and spinach.

Seaside Sauce

2 tablespoons finely snipped parsley
2 tablespoons finely chopped watercress
2 tablespoons finely chopped fresh spinach
1 cup mayonnaise *or* salad dressing

1 4½-ounce can shrimp, rinsed and drained
1 teaspoon capers, drained
1 teaspoon finely chopped sweet pickle
2 to 3 tablespoons milk (optional)

In a small saucepan cook parsley, watercress, and spinach, covered, in a small amount of boiling water for 2 minutes. Drain well. In a small bowl combine cooked parsley, watercress, and spinach with mayonnaise or salad dressing. Stir in shrimp, capers, and sweet pickle. Cover and chill thoroughly.

Just before serving, stir in milk for a thinner consistency, if desired. Spoon sauce atop cooked fish or steamed vegetables. Makes 1⅓ cups.

Carol E. Hedrick, Ithaca, New York

Easy Horseradish Sauce

Carol serves this versatile sauce with hot cooked vegetables such as broccoli, cabbage, and potatoes. But we found it's equally tasty on beef sandwiches or grilled burgers.

⅔ cup mayonnaise *or* salad dressing
2 tablespoons prepared horseradish
2 tablespoons milk
1 teaspoon dry mustard
¼ teaspoon freshly ground black pepper

In a small mixing bowl stir together mayonnaise or salad dresing, horseradish, milk, dry mustard, and pepper. Cover and chill thoroughly. Makes about ¾ cup.

Carol Wenger Gibbons, Philadelphia, Pennsylvania

Elegant Raspberry Sauce

The fruity flavor of this special-occasion sauce complements roast pork, ham, or poultry.

1 10-ounce package frozen red raspberries, thawed
2 tablespoons dry white wine
1 tablespoon orange liqueur
2 teaspoons cornstarch
1 tablespoon butter *or* margarine

Place raspberries in a blender container or food processor bowl. Cover and blend or process till smooth. In a 1-quart saucepan combine wine, orange liqueur, and cornstarch. Stir in raspberries and butter or margarine. Cook and stir till thickened and bubbly, then cook and stir for 2 minutes more.

Press raspberry mixture through a sieve to remove seeds. Serve warm. Makes about 1¼ cups sauce.

Carl R. Carlson, Lakewood, New York

Easy Refrigerator Pickles

Tucked into a sandwich or eaten out of the jar, these crisp, fuss-free pickles get top honors!

6 cups thinly sliced
  cucumbers
2 cups thinly sliced onions
1 clove garlic, halved
1½ cups sugar
1½ cups vinegar
½ teaspoon mustard seed
½ teaspoon celery seed
½ teaspoon ground turmeric

In a glass or crockery bowl place sliced cucumbers, onions, and garlic. In a medium saucepan combine sugar, vinegar, mustard seed, celery seed, and ground turmeric. Bring to boiling, stirring just till sugar is dissolved. Pour vinegar mixture over the cucumber mixture. Cover and chill at least 24 hours before serving. Store in the refrigerator for up to 1 month. Makes about 7 cups.

Mrs. Homer Hooks, Leesburg, Florida

Quick 'n' Easy Corn Relish

No need to wait for summer to enjoy this crunchy relish.

2 12-ounce cans whole
  kernel corn with sweet
  peppers, drained
3 tablespoons cooking oil
½ cup sugar
½ cup vinegar
2 teaspoons dried minced
  onion
¼ teaspoon salt
¼ teaspoon celery seed

In a large mixing bowl stir together drained corn and cooking oil. In a small saucepan combine sugar, vinegar, onion, salt, and celery seed. Bring to boiling. Reduce heat and simmer, covered, for 2 minutes. Stir into corn mixture. Cover and chill for several hours. Drain well before serving.

Store relish, in a tightly covered container, in the refrigerator for up to 5 days. Makes about 3 cups.

Mrs. G. V. Pedersen, Grand Island, Nebraska

Use this colorful vegetable relish to dress up a condiment tray for your next picnic.

Carrot Relish

1 pound carrots, diced (about 2¾ cups)
¼ cup chopped green pepper
1 2-ounce jar diced pimiento, drained
¼ cup vinegar
3 tablespoons honey
2 tablespoons finely chopped onion

¼ cup sugar
1 tablespoon all-purpose flour
¼ teaspoon dry mustard
¼ teaspoon celery salt
¼ teaspoon salt

In a medium saucepan cook carrots, covered, in a small amount of boiling water for 10 minutes or till crisp-tender. Drain. Return carrots to saucepan. Add green pepper, pimiento, vinegar, honey, and onion.

In a small mixing bowl combine sugar, flour, dry mustard, celery salt, and salt. Stir into vegetable mixture in saucepan. Cook and stir over medium heat till bubbly. Cook and stir for 3 minutes more. Remove from heat. Serve warm or chilled.

Store relish, in a tightly covered container, in the refrigerator for up to 5 days. Makes about 2½ cups.

Julie Austin, Madison, Wisconsin

BLUE-RIBBON DESSERTS

DESSERT IS THE GRAND FINALE TO ANY MEAL—WHETHER YOU'RE PLANNING A SIT-DOWN DINNER FOR EIGHT OR A BROWN-BAG LUNCH FOR THE KIDS. LOOKING FOR A LIGHT AND AIRY DESSERT, OR ARE YOU HUNGRY FOR SOMETHING RICH AND GOOEY? WHICHEVER THE CASE MAY BE, THIS COLLECTION OF FIRST-PLACE SWEET ENDINGS HOLDS THE SOLUTION.

Strawberry-Rice Fluff

Pictured on page 66.

1 cup light cream
½ cup milk
¼ cup long grain rice
2 tablespoons sugar
1 teaspoon finely shredded
    orange peel
½ teaspoon vanilla
1 tablespoon cold water

1 teaspoon unflavored
    gelatin
1 pint fresh strawberries
    (3 cups)
2 egg whites
¼ cup sugar
    Mint leaves (optional)

In a heavy medium saucepan combine cream and milk. Bring to boiling. Stir in *uncooked* rice. Reduce heat and simmer, covered, over low heat for 25 to 30 minutes or till rice is tender and most of the liquid is absorbed, stirring occasionally (mixture may look curdled). Stir in the 2 tablespoons sugar, orange peel, and vanilla. Set aside.

In a 1-cup measure stir together cold water and gelatin. Let stand for 5 minutes. Place measuring cup in a saucepan of water and heat over low heat, stirring constantly, till gelatin dissolves. Stir into the rice mixture. Set aside to cool.

Meanwhile, chop strawberries, reserving a few whole berries for garnish. Stir chopped strawberries into cooled rice mixture. Chill till mixture starts to mound when spooned, stirring occasionally. Remove from refrigerator (gelatin will continue to set). Immediately begin beating egg whites with an electric mixer on medium speed till soft peaks form (tips curl). Gradually add the ¼ cup sugar and continue beating till stiff peaks form (tips stand straight). Gently fold egg white mixture into gelatin mixture. Spoon into dessert dishes. Chill for 3 to 24 hours. Slice reserved berries. Garnish each serving with reserved strawberries and mint leaves, if desired. Makes 4 servings.

Sharyl Heiken, Des Moines, Iowa

Sugar-Almond Wafers

Create Alethea's delicate cookie confection without turning on the oven! (Pictured on page 71.)

½ cup sliced almonds, toasted
¼ cup sifted powdered sugar
2 teaspoons water

¼ teaspoon finely shredded
    orange peel
¼ teaspoon vanilla

Place almonds in a blender container or food processor bowl. Cover and blend or process till finely ground. In a small mixing bowl stir together ground almonds, powdered sugar, water, orange peel, and vanilla. Stir till well combined and mixture is a stiff paste. Cover and chill about 1 hour or till dough is easy to handle. Shape dough into eight 1¼-inch-diameter wafers. Chill till serving time. Makes 8 wafers.

Alethea Sparks, Des Moines, Iowa

Grape and Pear Pie

2 cups sliced, peeled fresh
  pears (4 medium)
2 tablespoons lemon juice
¾ cup sugar
¼ cup all-purpose flour *or*
  2 tablespoons quick-
  cooking tapioca
1 teaspoon finely shredded
  lemon peel
¼ teaspoon ground ginger
2 cups seedless red *or* green
  grapes, halved
Pastry for Double-Crust Pie
1 tablespoon butter *or*
  margarine
Frosted red grapes
  (optional)
Lime peel (optional)

The frosted red grapes that adorn Lois' fresh-fruit pie may look elaborate, but they're easy to do. Combine one slightly beaten egg white with 2 tablespoons water. Brush small grape clusters with the egg white mixture. Sprinkle with sugar and place on a wire rack to dry for several hours. (Pictured at right.)

Sprinkle pears with lemon juice. Set aside. In a medium mixing bowl stir together sugar, flour or tapioca, shredded lemon peel, and ginger. Stir in sliced pears and grapes. (If using tapioca, let stand for 5 minutes to soften tapioca.)

For the bottom crust, on a lightly floured surface flatten *half* of the pastry with your hands. Roll dough from center to edge, forming a circle about 12 inches in diameter. Gently wrap pastry around rolling pin. Carefully unroll pastry onto a 9-inch pie plate. Ease the pastry into the pie plate, being careful not to stretch pastry. Trim to ½ inch beyond the edge of the pie plate. Transfer the fruit mixture into the bottom crust. Dot with butter or margarine. Set aside.

Roll out remaining pastry as for bottom crust. Cut into ½-inch-wide strips. Weave strips atop fruit filling to make a lattice crust. Press ends of strips into rim of crust. Fold bottom pastry over the lattice strips to build up edge. Seal and flute edges. Cover edges with foil to prevent overbrowning. Bake in a 375° oven for 25 minutes. Remove foil. Bake about 25 minutes more or till golden. Cool on wire rack. Garnish with frosted grapes and lime peel, if desired. Serves 8.

Pastry for Double-Crust Pie: In a medium mixing bowl stir together 2 cups *all-purpose flour* and ½ teaspoon *salt*. Cut in ⅔ cup *shortening or lard* till pieces are the size of small peas. Sprinkle 1 tablespoon cold *water* over part of the mixture. Gently toss with a fork. Push to one side of the bowl. Repeat with 5 to 6 additional tablespoons cold *water* till all is moistened. Form dough into a ball. Divide dough in half.

Lois Kilokowski, Newark, Ohio

Lemon Pie Hawaiian

When Sylvia created this variation of a lemon meringue pie, she packed it with a pineapple punch.

1 8¼-ounce can crushed pineapple, drained
¼ cup packed brown sugar
¼ cup coconut
2 tablespoons butter *or* margarine, softened
1 unbaked 9-inch pastry shell
1 4-serving-size package *regular* lemon pudding mix

½ cup sugar
1¾ cups water
2 slightly beaten egg yolks
2 tablespoons lemon juice
1 tablespoon butter *or* margarine
2 egg whites
¼ cup sugar
Toasted coconut (optional)

In a small mixing bowl stir together pineapple, brown sugar, the ¼ cup coconut, and the 2 tablespoons butter or margarine. Mix well. Spread pineapple mixture evenly over the bottom of the pastry shell. Cover edge of pastry with foil. Bake in a 425° oven for 5 minutes. Remove foil. Continue baking about 10 minutes more or till golden. Cool completely on a wire rack.

Meanwhile, for filling in a medium saucepan stir together pudding mix and the ½ cup sugar. Stir in water and egg yolks. Cook and stir till mixture is thickened and bubbly. Remove from heat. Stir in lemon juice and the 1 tablespoon butter or margarine. Cover with clear plastic wrap. Set aside to cool for 1 hour, stirring occasionally.

Beat egg whites with an electric mixer on medium speed till soft peaks form (tips curl). Gradually beat in the the ¼ cup sugar till stiff peaks form (tips stand straight). Carefully fold beaten egg whites mixture into cooled filling. Spoon mixture into prepared pastry shell. Chill for at least 4 hours or till filling is set. Garnish with toasted coconut, if desired. Makes 8 servings.

Mrs. Sylvia Watson, Dagsboro, Delaware

Three-Layer Mocha Pie

1 stick piecrust mix, crumbled
¾ cup finely chopped walnuts
¼ cup packed brown sugar
1 square (1 ounce) unsweetened chocolate, finely shredded
2 tablespoons warm water
1 teaspoon vanilla
1 pint coffee ice cream, softened
1 pint chocolate ice cream, softened
1 cup whipping cream
2 tablespoons powdered sugar
2 teaspoons instant coffee crystals

In a bowl stir together piecrust mix, nuts, brown sugar, and chocolate. Stir together water and vanilla. Add to piecrust mixture, a little at a time, tossing with a fork till all is moistened. On a floured surface roll pastry to a 12-inch circle. Ease into a 9-inch pie plate. Trim to ½ inch beyond rim. Flute edge. Bake in a 375° oven about 20 minutes or till lightly browned. Cool on wire rack. Chill. Spread coffee ice cream evenly in prepared crust. Freeze. Spread chocolate ice cream atop. Freeze. Beat whipping cream with powdered sugar and coffee crystals till soft peaks form. Spread atop ice cream. Freeze firm. Serves 8.

Mrs. Carol Bloch, Owings Mills, Maryland

Key Lime-Chocolate Pie

16 chocolate sandwich cookies, crushed (½ cup)
½ cup coconut
2 tablespoons butter, melted
3 egg yolks
1 14-ounce can (1¼ cups) *sweetened condensed milk*
2 envelopes (2 ounces) premelted unsweetened chocolate product
⅓ cup lime juice
3 egg whites
1 7-ounce jar marshmallow creme

Traditionally, Key Lime Pie is made by combining sweetened condensed milk with the juice of Key limes—small, lemon-yellow, strongly flavored limes native to Florida. June added a touch of chocolate to make an even tastier version of this time-honored pie.

Combine crushed cookies, coconut, and butter. Spread evenly in a 9-inch pie plate. Press onto bottom and up sides to form a firm, even crust. Bake in a 375° oven about 8 minutes or till done. Cool.

Meanwhile, beat egg yolks about 4 minutes or till thick and lemon colored. Add sweetened condensed milk, chocolate, and lime juice. Beat till combined. Pour into prepared crust.

Wash beaters. Beat egg whites till soft peaks form. Gradually add marshmallow creme, beating till stiff peaks form. Spread over filling, sealing to edges of crust. Bake in a 350° oven for 12 to 15 minutes or till meringue is golden. Cool slightly. Chill. Makes 8 servings.

Mrs. June Harton, Los Angeles, California

Fresh Raspberry Tart

¾ cup sugar
1 tablespoon quick-cooking tapioca
1½ cups fresh raspberries, crushed
1 baked 9-inch pastry shell
1 cup whipping cream
2 tablespoons sugar
2 cups fresh raspberries
3 egg whites
½ cup sifted powdered sugar

Because of the whipped cream filling, this rich and fluffy dessert needs to be served immediately. So plan to serve it when you've got eight hungry people gathered who'll devour every bit of it! (Pictured at left.)

Combine the ¾ cup sugar and tapioca. Stir in the 1½ cups crushed raspberries. Let stand for 15 minutes. Cook and stir till mixture boils. Remove from heat. Let stand for 20 minutes. Cover and chill.

Transfer chilled raspberry mixture to pastry shell. Beat whipping cream with the 2 tablespoons sugar till soft peaks form. Spread over raspberry mixture. Arrange the 2 cups fresh raspberries atop. Cover and chill about 1 hour before serving.

For meringue, beat egg whites till soft peaks form (tips curl). Gradually add powdered sugar, beating till stiff peaks form (tips stand straight). Spread meringue atop, sealing to edge of pastry. Broil 3 to 4 inches from heat for 1 to 2 minutes or till lightly browned. Serve at once. Makes 8 servings.

Mrs. Percy Lasselle, Forest Grove, Oregon

Frozen Toffee Cream Pie

1½ cups finely crushed chocolate wafers (about 25 wafers)
⅓ cup butter *or* margarine, melted
1 cup whipping cream
⅔ cup *sweetened condensed milk*
¼ cup water
1 teaspoon instant coffee crystals
½ teaspoon vanilla
2 1⅛-ounce bars chocolate-covered English toffee, crushed (about ½ cup)

Save time by tucking this delectable coffee-toffee filling into a purchased chocolate-flavored crumb pie shell.

In a small bowl combine crushed wafers and melted butter or margarine. Spread mixture evenly in a 9-inch pie plate. Press onto the bottom and 1 inch up the sides to form a firm, even crust. Chill.

Meanwhile, beat cream, sweetened condensed milk, water, coffee crystals, and vanilla with an electric mixer on low speed till combined. Beat on medium speed about 5 minutes or just till thickened and soft peaks form (tips curl). Reserve *2 tablespoons* of the crushed toffee bars. Stir remaining crushed toffee bars into whipped cream mixture. Transfer mixture to prepared crust. Sprinkle with the reserved crushed toffee bars. Freeze for several hours or overnight. Serves 8.

Mrs. H. B. Parmenter, Vincennes, Indiana

Lemon Custard-Strawberry Supreme

Although a flan pan with a removable bottom makes serving easier, a 9-inch pie plate also works well.

Pastry for Single-Crust Pie
½ cup sugar
4 teaspoons cornstarch
2 tablespoons butter *or* margarine
1 beaten egg yolk
3 tablespoons lemon juice
3 cups sliced fresh strawberries

2 3-ounce packages cream cheese, softened
¼ cup sifted powdered sugar
⅓ cup coconut
¾ cup whipping cream
¼ cup coconut, toasted

On a lightly floured surface flatten dough with your hands. Roll dough from center to edge, forming a circle about 12 inches in diameter. Gently wrap pastry around rolling pin. Carefully unroll onto a 10x1½-inch flan pan with removable bottom. Ease pastry into pan, being careful not to stretch pastry. Press against the bottom and up sides of pan. Trim excess pastry even with rim of pan. Prick bottom and sides of shell with a fork. Bake in a 450° oven for 10 to 12 minutes or till golden. Cool on a wire rack.

Meanwhile, in a saucepan stir together sugar and cornstarch. Add butter or margarine, egg yolk, and ½ cup *water.* Cook and stir till thickened and bubbly, then cook and stir for 2 minutes more. Remove from heat. Stir in lemon juice. Transfer to prepared pastry shell. Cool. Top with strawberries.

In a mixer bowl beat cream cheese and powdered sugar with an electric mixer till well combined. Fold in the ⅓ cup coconut. In another mixer bowl beat whipping cream to soft peaks (tips curl). Fold into cream cheese mixture till well combined. Spread atop berries. Sprinkle with the ¼ cup toasted coconut. Chill for 4 hours or overnight. Makes 8 to 10 servings.

Pastry for Single-Crust Pie: In a medium mixing bowl stir together 1¼ cups *all-purpose flour* and ¼ teaspoon *salt.* Cut in ⅓ cup *shortening or lard* till pieces are the size of small peas. Sprinkle 1 tablespoon cold *water* over part of the mixture. Gently toss with a fork. Push to one side of bowl. Repeat with 2 to 3 additional tablespoons of cold *water* till all is moistened. Form into a ball.

Margaret L. Smith, Inverness, Illinois

Dark sweet cherries, nestled in pastry shells and topped with whipped cream and toasted almonds, take center stage in Nellie's enticing dessert.

Cherry and Almond Tarts

Pastry for Double-Crust Pie
(see recipe, page 186)
1 16-ounce package frozen
   unsweetened pitted dark
   sweet cherries, thawed
1 6-ounce can frozen apple
   juice concentrate

2 tablespoons water
1 tablespoon cornstarch
   Few drops almond extract
   Whipped cream
   Chopped almonds, toasted

On a lightly floured surface roll *half* of the pastry to ⅛-inch thickness. Cut pastry into six 4½- or 5-inch circles. Carefully ease pastry circles into 2¾-inch muffin cups, being careful not to stretch pastry. Crimp edges. Repeat with remaining pastry. Prick pastry shells with the tines of a fork. Bake in a 450° oven for 10 to 12 minutes or till golden. Cool in pans on a wire rack. Carefully remove shells from pans.

Meanwhile, drain cherries. In a medium saucepan stir together apple juice concentrate, water, and cornstarch. Cook and stir till mixture is thickened and bubbly, then cook and stir for 2 minutes more. Stir in cherries and almond extract. Cool slightly. Spoon cherry mixture into prepared pastry shells. Chill till set. Just before serving, top tarts with whipped cream and sprinkle with toasted chopped almonds. Makes 12 tarts.

Nellie Cusworth, Thousand Oaks, California

Opposites do attract! Jackie has tucked creamy vanilla filling into chocolate pastry shells for a striking meal finale.

Chocolate and Vanilla Tarts

1½ cups all-purpose flour
3 tablespoons sugar
3 tablespoons unsweetened cocoa powder
½ cup butter *or* margarine
2 tablespoons shortening
3 to 4 tablespoons cold water
2 3-ounce packages cream cheese

¼ cup sifted powdered sugar
1 8-ounce carton vanilla yogurt
1 teaspoon vanilla
½ of a 4-ounce container frozen whipped dessert topping, thawed
Fresh strawberries

For pastry, combine flour, sugar, and cocoa. Cut in butter and shortening till pieces are the size of small peas. Sprinkle *1 tablespoon* water over part of the mixture. Gently toss with a fork. Push to side of bowl. Repeat till all is moistened. Form into a ball.

On a floured surface roll dough to ⅛-inch thickness. Cut pastry into twelve 5-inch circles. Carefully ease pastry circles into 2¾-inch muffin cups, being careful not to stretch pastry. Crimp edges. Bake in a 400° oven for 12 to 15 minutes or till done. Carefully remove from pans. Cool on a wire rack.

For filling, beat cream cheese and powdered sugar till well combined. Beat in yogurt and vanilla. Fold in dessert topping. Spoon filling into shells. Chill. Top with fresh strawberries. Makes 12 tarts.

Jacqueline McComas, Frazer, Pennsylvania

Toasted Almond Soufflé

2 tablespoons butter *or* margarine
3 tablespoons all-purpose flour
Dash salt
½ cup light cream
¾ teaspoon finely shredded orange peel

¼ cup orange juice
3 egg yolks
¼ cup finely chopped almonds, toasted
3 egg whites
3 tablespoons sugar
Strawberry-Orange Sauce

Our Test Kitchen has a secret for successful soufflés: Don't open the oven door before you're ready to test the soufflé for doneness. A sudden rush of cooler air before the soufflé is set may cause it to fall.

In a small saucepan melt butter or margarine. Stir in flour and salt. Add cream all at once. Cook and stir over medium heat till mixture is thickened and bubbly, then cook and stir for 1 minute more. (Mixture will be very thick.) Remove from heat. Stir in orange peel and orange juice. Mix well. Set aside to cool slightly.

In a mixer bowl beat egg yolks with an electric mixer on high speed about 5 minutes or till thick and lemon colored. Gradually beat orange mixture into beaten yolks. Gently stir in the toasted almonds. Wash beaters thoroughly.

In a large mixer bowl beat egg whites with an electric mixer on medium speed till soft peaks form (tips curl). Gradually add sugar, beating till stiff peaks form (tips stand straight). Gently fold the orange-almond mixture into beaten egg white mixture. Carefully transfer egg white mixture to an ungreased 1½-quart soufflé dish. Bake in a 325° oven about 40 minutes or till golden and a knife inserted near center comes out clean. Serve soufflé immediately with Strawberry-Orange Sauce. Makes 4 servings.

Strawberry-Orange Sauce: In a medium saucepan stir together 3 tablespoons *sugar,* 1 teaspoon *cornstarch,* and dash *salt.* Stir in ½ cup *orange juice.* Cook and stir till mixture is thickened and bubbly, then cook and stir for 2 minutes more. Remove from heat. Stir in 2 teaspoons *butter or margarine* till melted. Stir in 1 cup fresh *strawberries,* halved. Cover surface with clear plastic wrap or waxed paper. Let stand at room temperature till serving time. Makes about 1¼ cups sauce.

Pat Teberg, Des Moines, Iowa

Easy Pumpkin Cheesecake

1 10½- *or* 11-ounce
  package cheesecake mix
1 teaspoon ground cinnamon
½ teaspoon ground nutmeg
¼ teaspoon ground cloves
¾ cup canned *or* mashed
  cooked pumpkin
¾ cup milk
½ teaspoon vanilla
  Whipped cream (optional)
  Ground cinnamon
  (optional)

66 *I love cheesecake and pumpkin pie. One day I put them together and, like magic, I had a wonderful dessert in a jiffy!* 99

Prepare the graham cracker crust in the cheesecake mix according to package directions. Spread evenly in a 9-inch pie plate. Press onto the bottom and up the sides of the pie plate to form a firm, even crust. Chill in freezer while preparing filling.

For filling, in small mixer bowl combine cheesecake filling mix, the 1 teaspoon cinnamon, nutmeg, and cloves. Add pumpkin, milk, and vanilla. Beat with an electric mixer on low speed till combined, scraping bowl constantly. Beat for 3 minutes on medium speed, scraping bowl occasionally. Pour mixture into prepared crust. Chill for at least 1 hour or till set. Let stand for 5 minutes before serving. Garnish with whipped cream and sprinkle with additional cinnamon, if desired. Makes 8 servings.

Jean Cox, Denver, Colorado

Honey-Cinnamon Cheesecake Pie

1½ cups all-purpose flour
3 tablespoons sugar
1½ teaspoons baking powder
⅓ cup butter *or* margarine
5 to 6 tablespoons cold water
2 8-ounce packages cream
  cheese, softened
¼ cup sugar
1½ teaspoons ground
  cinnamon
⅔ cup honey
4 eggs

Sugar and spice and everything nice describes Sara's pleasing cheesecake dessert.

Stir together flour, the 3 tablespoons sugar, baking powder, and ½ teaspoon *salt.* Cut in butter or margarine till mixture resembles coarse crumbs. Add water, a little at a time, till all is moistened. Form dough into a ball. On a lightly floured surface roll dough into a 12-inch circle. Ease pastry into a 10-inch flan pan, being careful not to stretch pastry. Trim pastry even with pan edge. Set aside.

In a large mixer bowl beat cream cheese, the ¼ cup sugar, and cinnamon with an electric mixer on medium speed till combined. Gradually add honey, beating till smooth. Add eggs and beat just till combined. Pour into prepared pastry. Bake in a 350° oven about 50 minutes or till set. Cool. Remove sides from flan pan. Chill. Serves 12.

Sara Iles Johnston, Ithaca, New York

Caramel-Pecan Cheesecake

Beverly's creamy quick 'n' easy topper of caramel ice-cream topping and sour cream would be just as scrumptious on a purchased cheesecake from your favorite bakery.

1 cup finely crushed graham crackers (about 14 crackers)
¾ cup ground pecans
¼ cup sugar
¼ cup butter *or* margarine, melted

12 ounces cream cheese, softened
¾ cup caramel ice cream topping
3 eggs
2 tablespoons milk
½ cup dairy sour cream

Combine crushed crackers, pecans, sugar, and butter. Spread in an 8-inch springform pan. Press onto bottom and 1½ inches up sides to form a firm, even crust. Beat cream cheese till fluffy. Gradually beat in ½ *cup* of the caramel topping. Add eggs and milk. Beat just till combined. Transfer mixture to crust-lined pan. Bake in a 350° oven for 40 to 45 minutes or till center is set. Cool in pan for 15 minutes.

Stir together sour cream and the remaining caramel topping. Spoon atop cheesecake. Loosen sides of cheesecake from pan. Cool 30 minutes more. Remove sides of pan. Cool completely. Chill. Makes 10 to 12 servings.

Beverly Hill, Santee, California

Peanut Butter and Chocolate Cheesecakes

These miniature cheesecakes are great for buffet-style entertaining.

¾ cup finely crushed chocolate-covered graham crackers (about 11 crackers)
1 8-ounce package cream cheese, softened
1 3-ounce package cream cheese, softened
½ cup sugar

1 teaspoon vanilla
½ cup milk
2 eggs
⅓ cup peanut butter
½ cup semisweet chocolate pieces, melted and slightly cooled

Line muffin cups with paper bake cups. Spread about *1 tablespoon* crushed crackers in *each* cup. Set aside. Beat cream cheese till smooth. Add sugar and vanilla. Beat till fluffy. Beat in milk. Add eggs, beating just till combined. Divide mixture in half.

Gradually stir peanut butter into *half* of the cheese mixture. Stir chocolate into the remaining cheese mixture. Spread *2 tablespoons* of the peanut butter mixture evenly over cracker crumbs in *each* muffin cup. Top *each* with *2 tablespoons* of the chocolate mixture. Bake in a 325° oven for 20 to 25 minutes or till set. Cool on a wire rack. Chill. To serve, peel off paper cups and invert. Makes 12.

Mrs. Becky Hofner, Rockford, Ohio

Chocolate Fried Pies

½ cup sugar
¼ cup all-purpose flour
1 tablespoon unsweetened cocoa powder
½ cup milk
2 tablespoons butter *or* margarine
½ teaspoon vanilla
2 cups packaged biscuit mix
⅓ cup milk
Cooking oil
Sifted powdered sugar

Bite into one of Bobbie's pillowlike pastries and discover the velvety chocolate cream filling. (Pictured at left.)

For filling, in a saucepan stir together sugar, flour, and cocoa powder. Stir in the ½ cup milk and butter. Cook and stir till thickened and bubbly, then cook and stir for 1 minute more. Stir in vanilla. Cool.

Meanwhile, stir together biscuit mix and the ⅓ cup milk (knead in with hands if necessary). Form into a ball. On a lightly floured surface roll dough to ⅛-inch thickness. Cut ten 4-inch circles, rolling dough again if necessary. Place about *1 tablespoon* of the filling in center of *each* circle. Moisten edges of circles with *water*. Fold dough over filling to form half-circles. Seal edges with the tines of a fork. In a heavy skillet heat 1 inch of cooking oil over medium-high heat. Fry pastries, several at a time, for 1 to 2 minutes on each side or till golden. Cool. Sprinkle with powdered sugar. Makes 10.

Mrs. Bobbie J. Napper, Tomball, Texas

Pineapple-Orange Squares

¾ cup all-purpose flour
½ cup coconut
⅓ cup butter *or* margarine, melted
2 tablespoons brown sugar
1 quart vanilla ice cream
1 8-ounce package cream cheese, softened
½ of a 6-ounce can (⅓ cup) frozen orange juice concentrate, thawed
1 8¼-ounce can crushed pineapple, drained
Pineapple slices (optional)

Stir together flour, coconut, butter, and brown sugar. Spread evenly in an 8x8x2-inch baking pan. Press onto bottom of pan to form a firm, even crust. Bake in a 325° oven about 20 minutes or till golden. Cool.

Meanwhile, stir ice cream to soften. Beat cream cheese and orange juice concentrate till fluffy. Add ice cream by spoonfuls, beating till smooth after each addition. Stir in crushed pineapple. Spoon into prepared crust. Freeze 8 hours or overnight. Let stand 10 minutes before serving. Garnish with pineapple slices, if desired. Serves 8 or 9.

Linda Brooks, St. Paul, Minnesota

Peanut-Mocha Dessert

½ cup butter *or* margarine
1 cup all-purpose flour
1 cup finely chopped peanuts
1 8-ounce package cream cheese, softened
1 cup sifted powdered sugar
1 4-ounce container frozen whipped dessert topping, thawed
3 cups milk
3 to 4 teaspoons instant coffee crystals
1 4-serving-size package *instant* chocolate pudding mix
1 4-serving-size package *instant* vanilla pudding mix
Grated chocolate

For crust, in a medium mixing bowl cut butter or margarine into flour till mixture resembles coarse crumbs. Stir in *¾ cup* of the peanuts. Spread mixture evenly in a 13x9x2-inch baking dish. Press onto the bottom of the pan to form a firm, even crust. Bake in a 350° oven about 20 minutes or till golden. Cool.

Meanwhile, in a mixer bowl beat cream cheese on low speed of an electric mixer till fluffy. Add powdered sugar and *half* of the thawed whipped topping. Beat till combined. Spread over crust. Chill.

Meanwhile, in a mixer bowl combine milk and coffee crystals, stirring to dissolve crystals. Add chocolate and vanilla pudding mixes. Beat with an electric mixer on low speed for 1 to 2 minutes or till smooth. Spoon atop cream cheese layer. Chill about 3 hours or till firm. (*Or,* freeze overnight or till firm. Let stand 20 to 25 minutes before serving.) Top with the remaining whipped topping, grated chocolate, and remaining chopped peanuts. Serves 16.

Donna B. Morrison, Syracuse, New York

Strawberry-Banana Freeze

It's no trouble to double Diane's light and refreshing drink. At only 97 calories per serving, share it with a crowd of calorie-counters!

1 cup frozen unsweetened whole strawberries
2 ripe small bananas
Lemon juice (optional)
½ cup evaporated skim milk
½ teaspoon vanilla

If desired, reserve *1* berry, sliced, and *4* thin banana slices, brushed with lemon juice, for garnish. Set aside. Cut remaining bananas into chunks. Wrap in plastic wrap. Freeze till firm. In a blender container or food processor bowl combine frozen bananas, evaporated milk, and vanilla. Cover and blend or process till smooth. With blender or food processor running, gradually add remaining berries, blending till smooth. Garnish with reserved fruit. Serve at once. Serves 4.

Diane Meyer-Hesler, West Chicago, Illinois

Peanut Butter-Ice Cream Squares

Cut down on salt but not flavor when you make the tasty filling with unsalted dry roasted peanuts.

1¼ cups finely crushed graham crackers (about 18 cracker squares)
¼ cup sugar
⅓ cup butter *or* margarine, melted
1 cup dry roasted peanuts, chopped
½ cup light corn syrup
⅓ cup chunky peanut butter
1 quart vanilla ice cream

For crust, in a small mixing bowl stir together crushed crackers and sugar. Stir in melted butter or margarine. Mix well. Spread crumb mixture evenly in a 9x9x2-inch baking pan. Press onto the bottom of the pan to form a firm, even crust. Place crust in the freezer for 30 minutes to chill.

Meanwhile, in a small mixing bowl stir together ⅔ *cup* of the chopped peanuts, corn syrup, and peanut butter. Stir ice cream to soften. Spoon *half* of the softened ice cream evenly over chilled crust. Spread the peanut butter mixture atop. Carefully spread remaining ice cream over all. Sprinkle with the remaining chopped peanuts. Cover and freeze till firm. Let stand at room temperature for 10 to 15 minutes before serving. Makes 9 servings.

Mrs. A. M. Matteson, La Plata, Missouri

Frozen Pumpkin Mousse

There are two easy steps to unmolding Lynne's refreshing make-ahead dessert. First, wrap the mold in a warm, damp towel to soften the edges of the frozen mousse. Then just invert the mousse onto a serving plate.

2 cups whipping cream
1½ cups canned *or* mashed cooked pumpkin
1 cup packed brown sugar
1 cup milk
¼ cup brandy *or* apple juice
3 tablespoons crystallized ginger, finely chopped
1 teaspoon ground cinnamon
1 teaspoon vanilla
¼ teaspoon salt
⅛ teaspoon ground cloves

Place a large mixer bowl and a 6½-cup mold in freezer to chill. Meanwhile, in a large mixing bowl stir together whipping cream, pumpkin, brown sugar, milk, brandy or apple juice, ginger, cinnamon, vanilla, salt, and cloves. Transfer mixture to a 13x9x2-inch baking pan. Freeze till firm.

Break frozen pumpkin mixture into chunks. Transfer chunks to chilled mixer bowl. Beat with an electric mixer on medium speed till smooth. Spoon mixture into chilled 6½-cup mold. Cover and freeze till firm. Unmold and serve. Makes 8 to 10 servings.

Lynne Lederman, Rye, New York

PRISCILLA YEE, CONCORD, CALIF.

Priscilla Yee resides comfortably in a roomy 4-bedroom home in Concord, California, with a fluffy gray cat named Hubie. Why does this petite single woman need such a large domain? "I wanted a big kitchen, and big kitchens don't usually come in small houses," says Priscilla. "So you can see where my priorities are. There's no more rewarding or satisfying hobby for me than cooking."

Priscilla grew up in California with a father who worked in the restaurant business and a mother who encouraged her children to cook. Of her father's talent, Priscilla recalls, "I was always amazed when he would disappear into the kitchen, throw things into a bowl, and surprise us with wonderful pies!" To appease her inherited sweet tooth, Priscilla began making pies and cookies. "She is the pastry chef of the family," says sister Judy. "We have a lot of get-togethers and there are always more people around if they know Priscilla is going to be there with dessert!"

When Priscilla entered her first cooking contest at age 18 and found herself a national finalist, her cooking hobby literally began to pay off. Now she enters cooking competitions about once a month and enjoys creating exciting new recipes

that conform to contest guidelines. Priscilla has been well rewarded for her efforts, regularly winning prizes and usually achieving at least finalist status. But winning prizes isn't the only impetus for Priscilla's cooking pastime. "It's also a way of sharing my efforts with other people, and they seem to enjoy my hobby, too," says Priscilla.

Working in San Francisco as a computer project director, Priscilla has developed a reputation among her co-workers for bringing in sweet surprises for them to taste. They—and her family—are Priscilla's critics.

The city of cable cars has proven time and time again to be the source of new ideas for recipes. Priscilla has taken a few

continued

PRISCILLA YEE, CONCORD, CALIF.

> *Some of my best recipe ideas come from browsing at food demonstrations in large department stores or from checking out food displays on my lunch hour.*

cooking classes on such varied subjects as Chinese Dim Sum and Italian pasta dishes, and also takes advantage of the frequent cooking demonstrations in San Francisco's department stores. Priscilla finds that new recipe ideas often gel during her 45-minute commute to and from work. "Then I just have to get home and try them right away," she laughs.

Cooking for one is a challenge that Priscilla has learned to overcome with characteristic common sense and generous dashes of creativity. "It's a bit of an extra challenge," she admits, "but I don't believe it means compromising on quality or variety in food." She has found that the key lies in learning to cut down any recipe. "For example," notes Priscilla, "to divide a recipe, one just needs to

keep in mind that there are sixteen tablespoons in a cup and three teaspoons in a tablespoon." She's been known to split an egg in half, measuring it out in tablespoons. "For many recipes, such precision is not even necessary. Just a little thought and a set of small pots and pans is all that's needed." Priscilla thinks it's an advantage to cook just for oneself. "The way I see it," she says, "I have more time for cooking than someone who has children to care for." You can bet that it's definitely time well spent!

PRISCILLA YEE, CONCORD, CALIF.

To celebrate a friend's June birthday, Priscilla set to work improving a recipe published in the newspaper. This show-stopping strawberry- and whipped-cream-filled cake is delicious proof of Priscilla's prizewinning culinary reputation.

Strawberry Silhouette Cake

3 egg yolks
1 cup sugar
1 teaspoon finely shredded lemon peel
2 tablespoons lemon juice
½ cup sifted cake flour *or* sifted all-purpose flour
3 egg whites

6 cups whole strawberries
1 envelope unflavored gelatin
2½ cups whipping cream
3 tablespoons powdered sugar
1 teaspoon vanilla
Strawberry leaves

Beat yolks for 1 minute. Gradually add *½ cup* sugar. Beat 5 minutes or till thick. Add peel and juice. Beat till combined. Gradually add flour, beating till combined. Beat whites till stiff peaks form. Fold *one-fourth* of the beaten whites into yolk mixture. Gently fold yolk mixture into remaining whites just till combined. Spread evenly in an ungreased 9-inch springform pan. Bake in a 350° oven for 20 to 25 minutes or till top springs back when lightly touched. Invert to cool.

Reserve *4* berries for garnish. Crush *1¼ cups* of the remaining berries. Stir in remaining sugar. Set aside. Combine gelatin and ¼ cup cold *water*. Let stand 5 minutes. Cook and stir till gelatin is dissolved. Stir in crushed berries. Remove from heat. Cool.

Meanwhile, cut around sides of pan to loosen cake. Remove pan sides. Cut between bottom of cake and pan. Remove pan bottom. Cut cake in half horizontally. Wash and reassemble pan. Beat *1 cup* whipping cream till stiff peaks form. Fold into cooled gelatin mixture. Chill till mixture mounds when spooned.

Place bottom cake layer in pan, cut side up. Arrange remaining berries, pointed ends up, evenly atop. Spread gelatin mixture evenly over berries. Top with second cake layer, cut side down. Cover. Chill several hours or till gelatin mixture is firm. Cut around sides of cake to loosen. Remove pan sides and bottom. Place on a serving plate. Beat remaining whipping cream, powdered sugar, and vanilla till stiff peaks form. Frost top and sides. Garnish with reserved berries and strawberry leaves. Makes 8 to 10 servings.

Velvety Coconut-Spice Cake

2½ cups all-purpose flour
1½ teaspoons baking powder
1½ teaspoons ground cinnamon
¾ teaspoon baking soda
¼ teaspoon ground cloves
¼ teaspoon ground nutmeg
¼ teaspoon ground allspice
⅛ teaspoon ground ginger
½ cup butter *or* margarine
½ cup sugar
½ cup packed brown sugar
1 teaspoon vanilla

4 eggs
1¼ cups light cream
¼ cup molasses
1¼ cups coconut, toasted
⅔ cup orange marmalade
½ of an 8-ounce package cream cheese, softened
½ cup butter *or* margarine, softened
Few drops orange extract
2⅔ cups sifted powdered sugar
Toasted coconut

Cinnamon, cloves, nutmeg, allspice, and ginger spice up Rhonda's triple-decker delight.

Grease and lightly flour three 8x1½-inch round baking pans. Set aside. In a medium mixing bowl stir together flour, baking powder, cinnamon, baking soda, cloves, nutmeg, allspice, and ginger. Mix well. Set aside.

In a large mixer bowl beat ½ cup butter or margarine with an electric mixer on medium speed for 30 seconds. Add sugar, brown sugar, and vanilla. Beat till fluffy. Add eggs, one at a time, beating well after each addition.

In a small mixing bowl stir together light cream and molasses. Add dry ingredients and molasses mixture alternately to beaten mixture, beating on low speed after each addition just till combined. Stir in the 1¼ cups toasted coconut. Transfer batter to prepared pans. Bake in a 350° oven for 20 to 25 minutes or till a wooden toothpick inserted near the center comes out clean. Cool in pans for 10 minutes on wire racks. Remove from pans. Cool completely.

To assemble cake, spread *half* of the orange marmalade over *1* of the cake layers. Place a second cake layer on top. Spread remaining orange marmalade over the top of the second layer. Top with remaining cake layer.

For frosting, in a medium mixer bowl beat cream cheese, ½ cup butter or margarine, and orange extract with an electric mixer on medium speed till light and fluffy. Gradually add the powdered sugar, beating till smooth and creamy. Frost top and sides of cake. Sprinkle top and sides of cake with toasted coconut. Chill. Makes 12 servings.

Rhonda D. Thomas, Oak Harbor, Washington

Yogurt-Rhubarb Cake

Did you realize rhubarb is really considered a vegetable? Over the years, it has more often been used as a fruit in pies and tarts. Here rhubarb makes this cake moist and memorable.

½ cup packed brown sugar
½ cup chopped pecans
¼ cup all-purpose flour
2 tablespoons butter *or* margarine, melted
1 teaspoon ground cinnamon
1 cup all-purpose flour
1 cup whole wheat flour
1½ teaspoons baking powder
1 teaspoon ground cinnamon
½ teaspoon baking soda

½ teaspoon salt
1 8-ounce carton cherry-vanilla yogurt
3 tablespoons milk
½ cup butter *or* margarine
1 cup packed brown sugar
2 eggs
1 teaspoon vanilla
2½ cups chopped fresh *or* frozen rhubarb, thawed

Grease and lightly flour a 13x9x2-inch baking pan. Set aside. For crumb topping, in a small mixing bowl stir together the ½ cup brown sugar, chopped pecans, the ¼ cup all-purpose flour, the 2 tablespoons melted butter or margarine, and 1 teaspoon cinnamon. Mix well. Set mixture aside.

For cake, in a medium mixing bowl stir together the 1 cup all-purpose flour, whole wheat flour, baking powder, 1 teaspoon cinnamon, baking soda, and salt. Set aside. In a small mixing bowl stir together yogurt and milk. Set aside.

In a large mixer bowl beat the ½ cup butter or margarine with an electric mixer on medium speed for 30 seconds. Add the 1 cup brown sugar and beat till fluffy. Add eggs and vanilla and beat well. Add the dry ingredients and the yogurt mixture alternately to the beaten mixture, beating on low speed after each addition till combined. Fold in the chopped rhubarb.

Pour batter into the prepared pan. Sprinkle the crumb topping evenly over the batter. Bake in a 350° oven for 40 to 45 minutes or till a wooden toothpick inserted near center comes out clean. Serve warm or cool. Makes 15 servings.

Mrs. A. J. Ponzi, Denver, Colorado

Elegant Nectarine Torte

Celebrate the fresh-fruit season with Bobbie's sensational four-layer torte. Pinch hit with peeled and pitted peaches if you haven't any nectarines. (Pictured at left.)

1 package 2-layer-size spice *or* white cake mix
1 3-ounce package orange-pineapple-flavored *or* lemon-flavored gelatin
1 cup boiling water
¾ cup cold water
5 small nectarines, pitted

Grease and flour two 9x1½-inch round cake pans. Prepare cake mix according to package directions. Transfer batter to prepared pans. Bake in a 350° oven for 25 to 30 minutes or till a wooden toothpick inserted near the center comes out clean. Cool 10 minutes in pans on wire racks. Remove from pans. Cool completely.

In a medium mixing bowl combine gelatin and boiling water. Stir to dissolve gelatin. Stir in the cold water. Chill mixture till partially set (consistency of unbeaten egg whites). Reserve ⅓ cup of the gelatin mixture and set aside. Finely chop enough of the nectarines to measure 1½ cups. Stir chopped fruit into partially set gelatin. Chill till almost firm.

To assemble torte, cut cake layers in half horizontally. Spread ⅓ of the gelatin-nectarine mixture over *1* cake layer. Repeat layers 2 more times. Top with final cake layer. Thinly slice the remaining nectarines and arrange in a swirl pattern on top of cake. Drizzle the ⅓ cup reserved gelatin mixture over sliced nectarines. Cover and chill till set. Makes 10 to 12 servings.

Bobbie Mae Cooley, Bowen, Illinois

Fruit and Angel Dessert

Make short work of Dorothy's ready-when-you-are dessert by purchasing an angel cake from your favorite grocery store.

1 large angel cake (about 10 ounces)
1 15¼-ounce can crushed pineapple
1 6-ounce jar maraschino cherries, drained and chopped
1 12-ounce container frozen whipped dessert topping, thawed
1 3½-ounce can (1⅓ cups) flaked coconut, toasted

Tear cake into bite-size pieces (you should have about 8 cups). Arrange *half* of the cake pieces in the bottom of a 13x9x2-inch baking pan. Top with *half* of the *undrained* pineapple and *half* of the chopped cherries. Spread *half* of the dessert topping over all and sprinkle *half* of the coconut atop. Repeat layers. Cover and refrigerate overnight. Makes 12 servings.

Mrs. Dorothy Burnette, Tuscaloosa, Alabama

Applesauce-Raisin Cake

Anna relied on molasses and applesauce to give her homemade cake a sweet, down-home country flavor.

2½ cups all-purpose flour
1 teaspoon baking soda
1 teaspoon ground cinnamon
½ cup butter *or* margarine
1 beaten egg
1 cup molasses

1 8½-ounce can
    (1 scant cup) applesauce
½ cup raisins
¾ cup sifted powdered sugar
4 teaspoons lemon juice

Grease and flour a 9x9x2-inch baking pan. Set aside. In a large mixing bowl stir together flour, baking soda, and cinnamon. Cut in butter or margarine till mixture resembles coarse crumbs. In a medium mixing bowl stir together egg, molasses, and applesauce. Stir in dry ingredients just till moistened. Stir in raisins.

Transfer batter to prepared pan. Bake in a 350° oven for 40 to 45 minutes or till a wooden toothpick inserted near the center comes out clean. Cool cake in pan for 15 minutes. Meanwhile, in a small mixing bowl stir together powdered sugar and lemon juice. Spread over warm cake. Serve warm or cool. Makes 9 servings.

Mrs. Anna McSwain, Pensacola, Florida

Caramel-Pear Pudding Cake

When fresh pears aren't in season, Cathy substitutes a 16-ounce can of pears, drained and cut up.

1 cup all-purpose flour
⅔ cup sugar
1½ teaspoons baking powder
½ teaspoon ground cinnamon
¼ teaspoon salt
    Dash ground cloves
½ cup milk
4 medium pears, peeled,
    halved, cored, and cut
    into ½-inch pieces
    (about 2 cups)

½ cup chopped pecans
¾ cup packed brown sugar
¾ cup boiling water
¼ cup butter *or* margarine
    Ice cream *or* whipped
        cream (optional)

In a large mixing bowl stir together flour, sugar, baking powder, cinnamon, salt, and cloves. Stir in milk till smooth. Stir in pears and pecans. Transfer batter to an ungreased 2-quart casserole. Set aside.

In another mixing bowl stir together brown sugar, boiling water, and butter or margarine. Mix well. Pour evenly over batter in casserole.

Bake in a 375° oven about 45 minutes or till top springs back when lightly touched. Serve immediately with ice cream or whipped cream, if desired. Makes 8 servings.

Cathy Goodlock, Hudson, Michigan

Royal Chocolate Cake

2 cups all-purpose flour
1 teaspoon baking powder
1 teaspoon baking soda
½ teaspoon salt
½ cup butter *or* margarine
1½ cups sugar
1 teaspoon vanilla
2 eggs

2 squares (2 ounces)
   unsweetened chocolate,
   melted and slightly
   cooled
1 cup water
   Fruit Filling
   Chocolate Frosting

Grease and flour two 9x1½-inch round baking pans. Set aside. In a medium mixing bowl stir together flour, baking powder, baking soda, and salt. Set aside.

In a large mixer bowl beat butter or margarine with an electric mixer on medium speed for 30 seconds. Add sugar and vanilla. Beat till combined. Add eggs, one at a time, beating well after each addition. Add melted chocolate and beat till combined. Add dry ingredients and water alternately to beaten mixture, beating on low speed after each addition just till combined.

Transfer batter to the prepared pans. Bake in a 350° oven for 30 to 35 minutes or till a wooden toothpick inserted near the center comes out clean. Cool in pans for 10 minutes on wire racks. Remove from pans. Cool completely on wire racks. Spread Fruit Filling between layers. Frost with Chocolate Frosting. Makes 12 servings.

Fruit Filling: In a medium saucepan stir together ¾ cup *water* and 1 tablespoon *cornstarch.* Stir in ½ cup *light raisins,* ½ cup chopped pitted *dates,* ¼ cup *sugar,* 2 tablespoons chopped *maraschino cherries,* and 1 tablespoon chopped *crystallized ginger.* Cook and stir till mixture is thickened and bubbly, then cook and stir for 2 minutes more. Stir in 1 teaspoon *lemon juice.* Remove from heat. Cool.

Chocolate Frosting: In a medium mixer bowl beat ⅓ cup *butter or margarine* with an electric mixer on medium speed for 30 seconds. Add ¾ cup sifted *powdered sugar,* 1 *egg,* and 1 teaspoon *vanilla.* Beat till fluffy. Add ¾ cup sifted *powdered sugar.* Beat till smooth. Add 2 squares (2 ounces) *unsweetened chocolate,* melted and slightly cooled. Beat till combined.

Mrs. Dorothy M. Stranix, Victoria, British Columbia

Cherry-Pecan Dessert

(Pictured at left.)

1 16-ounce can pitted tart
   red cherries (water pack)
1 cup all-purpose flour
1 teaspoon ground cinnamon
½ teaspoon baking soda
1 egg

1 cup sugar
1 tablespoon butter *or*
   margarine, melted
½ teaspoon almond extract
½ cup pecans, chopped
   Cherry Sauce

Drain cherries, reserving liquid. Add enough *water* to cherry liquid to equal 1 cup. Set aside to use in Cherry Sauce.

Combine flour, cinnamon, soda, and ¼ teaspoon *salt.* Combine cherries and *2 tablespoons* of the dry ingredients. Beat egg till thick and lemon colored. Gradually add sugar. Beat for 5 minutes. Stir in remaining dry ingredients till combined. Stir in the melted butter and almond extract. Stir in cherry mixture. Transfer batter to a greased 9x9x2-inch baking pan. Top with pecans. Bake in a 325° oven for 45 to 50 minutes or till golden. Serve with Cherry Sauce. Serves 9.

Cherry Sauce: Stir together ¼ cup *sugar,* 1 tablespoon *cornstarch,* and ¼ teaspoon *salt.* Stir in reserved cherry liquid. Cook and stir till mixture is thickened and bubbly, then cook and stir for 2 minutes more. Remove from heat. Stir in 1 tablespoon *butter or margarine* and 2 drops *almond extract.*

Elizabeth S. Bridgwater, Louisville, Kentucky

Date Fluff

Although LaVerna's date-and-peanut-butter pudding tastes marvelously rich, it has a mere 142 calories per creamy serving.

½ of an envelope unflavored
   gelatin (1¼ teaspoons)
1½ cups skim milk
 2 slightly beaten egg yolks
 2 tablespoons sugar
 1 tablespoon creamy peanut
   butter

⅓ cup pitted whole dates,
   snipped
½ teaspoon vanilla
 2 stiffly beaten egg whites

In a saucepan sprinkle gelatin over milk. Let stand for 5 minutes. Cook and stir over medium heat till gelatin is dissolved. Slowly stir *half* of the hot gelatin mixture into the beaten egg yolks. Return all to saucepan. Cook and stir over medium heat for 1 to 2 minutes or till slightly thickened. Remove from heat. Stir in sugar and peanut butter. Stir in dates and vanilla. Chill till partially set.

Carefully fold beaten egg whites into gelatin mixture. Spoon mixture into 6 individual dessert dishes. Chill till firm. Serves 6.

Mrs. LaVerna Mjones, Moorhead, Minnesota

Perfect Pecan Pudding

½ cup all-purpose flour
⅛ teaspooon cream of tartar
3 eggs
1 cup dark corn syrup
½ cup sugar
2 tablespoons butter *or* margarine, melted

1 teaspoon vanilla
1 cup chopped pecans
Powdered sugar
Light cream (optional)

In a small mixing bowl stir together flour and cream of tartar. Set aside. In a small mixer bowl beat eggs with an electric mixer on high speed about 5 minutes or till thick and lemon colored. Add corn syrup, sugar, butter or margarine, and vanilla. Beat well. Fold flour mixture into egg mixture. Fold in *half* the pecans. Transfer to a greased 10x6x2-inch baking dish. Sprinkle remaining pecans atop. Bake in a 375° oven for 30 to 35 minutes or till done.

To serve, spoon into dessert dishes. Sift powdered sugar over each serving. Serve with light cream, if desired. Makes 6 to 8 servings.

Melicia Montemayor, Santa Maria, California

Peanut Butter-Brown Rice Pudding

Joan dolled up old-fashioned rice pudding with brown rice, peanut butter, and honey, and nabbed first-place for her efforts.

3 slightly beaten eggs
2 cups cooked brown rice
½ cup peanut butter
⅓ cup honey
1 teaspoon ground cinnamon

2 cups milk
½ cup raisins *or* chopped pitted dates
Whipped cream (optional)
Peanuts (optional)

In a large mixing bowl combine eggs, cooked rice, peanut butter, honey, and cinnamon. Stir in milk and raisins or dates. Transfer to a 10x6x2-inch baking dish. Place dish in a 13x9x2-inch baking pan. Place baking pan on oven rack. Pour hot water into larger pan to a depth of 1 inch. Bake in a 350° oven for 25 minutes. Stir rice mixture. Continue baking for 20 to 25 minutes more or till a knife inserted near center comes out clean. Serve warm or chilled with whipped cream and peanuts, if desired. Makes 8 servings.

Joan Leviness, Winsted, Connecticut

Nutty Pumpkin Bread Pudding

Suzanne serves hot spiced cider along with this rich, date-studded dessert.

2 slightly beaten egg yolks
1 cup canned pumpkin
½ cup packed brown sugar
2 tablespoons brandy (optional)
1 teapoon ground cinnamon
½ teaspoon ground nutmeg
2 cups milk

4 cups whole wheat bread cubes
½ cup chopped pecans
½ cup chopped pitted dates
2 stiffly beaten egg whites
Light cream *or* whipped cream

In a large mixing bowl combine egg yolks; pumpkin; brown sugar; brandy, if desired; cinnamon; and nutmeg. Stir in milk. Gently stir in bread cubes, pecans, and dates. Fold in stiffly beaten egg whites. Transfer mixture to a 10x6x2-inch baking dish. Bake in a 325° oven for 45 to 50 minutes or till a knife inserted near center comes out clean. Serve warm with light cream or whipped cream. Serves 8.

Suzanne Adams, Laguna Hills, California

Cocoa-Rum Pudding

Dessert at a New England roadside inn inspired Marcia's mouth-watering pudding.

2 cups French bread cubes
2 cups milk
1 cup sugar
½ cup unsweetened cocoa powder
½ teaspoon ground cinnamon

2 slightly beaten eggs
½ cup raisins
1 tablespoon butter *or* margarine, melted
2 teaspoons vanilla
Sweet Rum Hard Sauce

Place bread cubes in a large mixing bowl. Add milk and let stand for 10 minutes. Meanwhile, in a small mixing bowl stir together sugar, cocoa powder, and cinnamon. In a medium mixing bowl stir together eggs, raisins, butter or margarine, and vanilla. Add sugar mixture and mix well. Stir egg mixture into bread cube mixture. Pour into an ungreased 10x6x2-inch baking dish.

Bake in a 375° oven for 40 to 45 minutes or till a knife inserted near center comes out clean. Serve warm with Sweet Rum Hard Sauce. Makes 6 to 8 servings.

Sweet Rum Hard Sauce: In a small mixer bowl beat together 1 cup sifted *powdered sugar* and ½ cup *butter or margarine*. Add 1 tablespoon *rum or* ½ teaspoon *rum extract* and beat till fluffy. Cover and chill. Makes about ¾ cup.

Marcia Webster, Palatine, Illinois

Baked Cottage Cheese Custard

For a smoother texture, use small-curd cottage cheese in this baked custard.

3 eggs
1½ cups milk
1 cup cream-style cottage
   cheese
½ cup sugar
1 teaspoon vanilla
Ground nutmeg
Cherry preserves *or* jam

In a medium mixing bowl lightly beat eggs. Stir in milk, cottage cheese, sugar, and vanilla. Beat with a rotary beater till combined. Place six 6-ounce custard cups in a 13x9x2-inch baking pan on an oven rack. Divide custard mixture among the custard cups. Sprinkle with nutmeg.

Pour boiling water into pan around custard cups to a depth of 1 inch. Bake in a 350° oven for 30 to 35 minutes or till a knife inserted near center comes out clean. Serve warm or chilled. Top with preserves or jam. Makes 6 servings.

Mrs. Barbara C. Gossage, Springfield, Virginia

Individual Baked Strawberry Custards

Barbara's rendition of home-style egg custard offers a subtle almond flavor. (Pictured at left.)

4 eggs
2⅓ cups milk
½ cup sugar
½ teaspoon almond extract
2 cups fresh sliced
   strawberries *or* frozen
   sliced strawberries,
   thawed
Ground cinnamon
   (optional)
Whipped cream

In a medium mixing bowl lightly beat eggs. Stir in milk, sugar, and almond extract. Stir in *1½ cups* strawberries. Place six 6-ounce custard cups in a 13x9x2-inch baking pan on an oven rack. Divide custard mixture among the custard cups (cups will be nearly full). Sprinkle with cinnamon, if desired.

Pour boiling water into pan around custard cups to a depth of 1 inch. Bake in a 325° oven for 50 to 60 minutes or till a knife inserted near center comes out clean. Chill well. Just before serving, dollop with whipped cream. Garnish with remaining strawberries. Serves 6.

Barbara Woods, Hewitt, New Jersey

Apple-Almond Dessert

You'll need about 4 slices of bread to get 3 cups of soft bread crumbs.

3 cups soft bread crumbs
¼ cup butter *or* margarine, melted
3 tablespoons sugar
½ cup whipping cream
1 tablespoon sugar
¼ teaspoon vanilla
1 15-ounce jar chunk-style applesauce
⅓ cup chopped almonds (toasted, if desired)
2 tablespoons raspberry jam

In a medium mixing bowl toss together bread crumbs, butter or margarine, and the 3 tablespoons sugar. Spread in a 13x9x2-inch baking pan. Bake in a 375° oven for 15 to 20 minutes or till lightly toasted, stirring once or twice. Meanwhile, in a small mixer bowl beat whipping cream with the 1 tablespoon sugar and vanilla just till soft peaks form (tips curl).

In a 1-quart serving bowl, layer *one-third* of the crumb mixture, *half* of the applesauce, *half* of the almonds, and *half* of the whipped cream. Repeat layers, ending with crumbs. Cover and chill thoroughly. To serve, melt jam and drizzle atop. Makes 8 servings.

Mrs. Paul L'Ecuyer, Essex Junction, Vermont

Applescotch Dessert

Serve this cobblerlike dessert with a scoop of vanilla ice cream or a dollop of whipped cream.

1¼ cups packed brown sugar
1 tablespoon cornstarch
¼ cup butter *or* margarine
1½ teaspoons vanilla
2 cups all-purpose flour
¼ cup sugar
1 tablespoon baking powder
⅓ cup shortening
3 cups chopped, peeled apple
¾ cup milk
1 tablespoon sugar
½ teaspoon ground cinnamon

For syrup, in a medium saucepan combine brown sugar and cornstarch. Stir in 2 cups *cold water*. Cook and stir till thickened and bubbly, then cook and stir 2 minutes more. Stir in *2 tablespoons* butter or margarine and *1 teaspoon* vanilla. Pour into a 13x9x2-inch baking dish.

For biscuit topper, in a medium mixing bowl combine flour, the ¼ cup sugar, baking powder, and ¼ teaspoon *salt*. Cut in shortening till pieces are the size of small peas. Stir in chopped apple. Stir in milk and remaining vanilla till moistened. Drop by tablespoons over syrup in baking dish. Combine the 1 tablespoon sugar and cinnamon. Sprinkle over topper. Dot with remaining butter or margarine. Bake in a 350° oven for 50 to 55 minutes. Makes 10 to 12 servings.

Margaret R. Nebel, Davenport, Iowa

Apple Strudel Crepe Stack

Crepes
¾ cup fine dry bread crumbs
⅓ cup butter *or* margarine, melted
3 cups finely chopped, peeled cooking apple
¼ cup packed brown sugar
1 teaspoon finely shredded lemon peel
½ teaspoon ground cinnamon
¼ teaspoon ground nutmeg
3 tablespoons chopped walnuts
1 tablespoon sugar
Whipped cream (optional)

No rule says you must make crepes the same day you serve them. In fact, you can make them a day, a week, or up to 4 months ahead and store them in your freezer. Just make a stack, alternating each crepe with 2 layers of waxed paper. Then wrap the stack in a moisture- and vaporproof bag and freeze. Let the crepes thaw at room temperature about 1 hour.

Prepare crepes. Set aside. For apple filling, combine bread crumbs with melted butter or margarine. Reserve *3 tablespoons* bread crumb mixture. Combine remaining crumb mixture with apple, brown sugar, lemon peel, cinnamon, and nutmeg.

To assemble, place 1 crepe, browned side up, in a greased 9-inch pie plate. Top with about *½ cup* apple filling. Alternately layer crepes and apple filling, ending with a crepe. Combine reserved crumbs, walnuts, and sugar. Sprinkle over top. Bake in a 375° oven for 30 minutes. Serve warm with whipped cream, if desired. Makes 6 servings.

Crepes: In a mixing bowl combine 2 *eggs*, 1 cup all-purpose *flour*, ½ cup *milk*, ½ cup *apple juice*, 2 tablespoons melted *butter or margarine*, and ¼ teaspoon *salt*. Beat with a rotary beater till combined. Heat a lightly greased 8-inch skillet. Remove from heat. Spoon in a scant ¼ cup batter. Lift and tilt the skillet to spread the batter. Return to heat. Brown on one side (do not turn). Invert the skillet over paper towels. Remove the crepe. Repeat with remaining batter, greasing skillet as needed. Makes about 9 crepes.

Sandy Cohen, Brooklyn, New York

LUANA IMPELLIZZERI, JAMESVILLE, N.Y.

L uana and Tony Impellizzeri and their two teenage boys inhabit the small town of Jamesville, in upstate New York. Unlike the quiet town of Jamesville, the Impellizzeri household is anything but quiet.

From the time the boys were little, the Impellizzeris have been concerned about nutrition. Says Tony, "We started to cultivate homegrown fruits and vegetables, and discovered that the quality of our own produce was really good—much better than store-bought."

Today the garden, an 80x50-foot plot, is an annual family affair. Besides fruit trees and concord grapes, there are squashes of all kinds, tomatoes, greens, and an ever-changing variety of vegetables and fragrant fresh herbs. During the annual fall "explosion" of ripe-and-ready produce, Tony and Luana busily can and freeze everything from tomato sauce to pesto to grape jelly.

With so much freshness available in her own backyard, Luana loves to read cookbooks, try new recipes, and invent new versions of old favorites. "I never stick to a recipe," she says. "I always wind up changing them a little bit—ad-libbing with what's

available." Breads and desserts, especially pies and cakes, are her forte. She once supplied her family with all the bread and ice cream that they ate. You might say Luana's motto is: "There's nothing like homemade!" Now that Luana's schedule is

more hectic, she's had to compromise. Still, when she entertains, there are always two homemade desserts to choose from. "I like to indulge in fabulous creations with chocolate and whipped cream!

(continued)

LUANA IMPELLIZZERI, JAMESVILLE, N.Y.

And people usually request my homemade bread," she says proudly. As for the rest of the menu, Luana says, "My favorite way to cook for guests is to have a six-course gourmet meal."

Fall marks another busy activity for Luana and Tony—that of entering their own specialties in the New York State Fair Culinary Arts Competition. Luana became "addicted" 17 years ago when she entered her pies and cakes and won first prize. Then Tony caught the bug and started entering his canned goods. Now both of the Impellizzeris have acquired a winning reputation. Hundreds of ribbons and other prizes attest to their cooking talents.

❝ I never stick to a recipe. I always wind up changing them a little bit—ad-libbing with what's available. ❞

Luana picked up her baking expertise both from her blind grandmother ("she cooked everything by touch and by feel") and an adult education class. She soon become an instructor and has shared her baking skills and her love of gourmet cooking for eight years running.

That teaching experience and her associate degree in food service administration led her to her current job as Dining Center Supervisor in one of the dining halls at Syracuse University. Luana explains, "My responsibilities include supervision of breakfast and lunch production. Our hall serves about 1,200 to 1,400 meals a day."

LUANA IMPELLIZZERI, JAMESVILLE, N.Y.

With all of her experience and education, how does Luana choose a recipe that's worth trying? "It's gut feeling," she says simply. "And a lot of trial and error to learn what tastes good and what your own preferences are." This Honey-Applesauce Cake is a deliciously hearty example of Luana's emphasis on quality. It's definitely a blue-ribbon special!

Honey-Applesauce Cake

2¼ cups whole wheat flour
¼ cup nonfat dry milk powder
1½ teaspoons baking soda
¼ teaspoon baking powder
½ teaspoon salt
½ teaspoon ground cinnamon
¼ teaspoon ground cloves
1 cup honey
½ cup shortening

2 eggs
1 cup applesauce
1 cup raisins
1 cup chopped walnuts
¾ cup sifted powdered sugar
¼ teaspoon vanilla
Milk
Walnuts (optional)

Grease and flour a 10-inch fluted tube pan. Set aside. In a large mixing bowl stir together flour, nonfat dry milk powder, soda, baking powder, salt, cinnamon, and cloves. Set aside.

In a large mixer bowl beat honey and shortening with an electric mixer on medium speed till light and fluffy. Beat in eggs, one at a time, beating well after each addition. On low speed add flour mixture and applesauce alternately to beaten mixture, beating just till combined after each addition. Fold in raisins and nuts.

Pour batter into prepared pan. Bake in a 325° oven for 40 to 45 minutes or till cake tests done. Immediately invert onto a wire rack. Remove pan. Cool thoroughly.

In a small mixing bowl stir together powdered sugar, vanilla, and enough milk to make of drizzling consistency (about 2 teaspoons). Drizzle over top of cooled cake. If desired, garnish with walnuts. Makes 12 servings.

Apple Chiffon Squares

Serve this fluffy, top-notch dessert the same day you prepare it so the apples don't turn brown.

1 cup finely crushed graham crackers (14 crackers)
3 tablespoons sugar
¼ cup butter *or* margarine, melted
1 envelope unflavored gelatin
2 tablespoons sugar
¼ teaspoon salt
¼ teaspoon ground nutmeg
¾ cup apple juice *or* cider
3 slightly beaten egg yolks
1 teaspoon finely shredded lemon peel
1 tablespoon lemon juice
2 medium apples, peeled, cored, and shredded (2 cups)
3 egg whites
¼ cup sugar

In a small mixing bowl stir together crushed crackers and the 3 tablespoons sugar. Stir melted butter or margarine into crumb mixture. Toss till thoroughly combined. Reserve ¼ cup crumb mixture for topping. Pat remaining crumb mixture firmly into the bottom of a 10x6x2-inch baking dish. Chill about 1 hour or till firm.

Meanwhile, in a saucepan combine gelatin, the 2 tablespoons sugar, salt, and nutmeg. Stir in apple juice or cider, egg yolks, lemon peel, and lemon juice. Cook and stir over medium-low heat till gelatin dissolves and mixture comes just to boiling. Remove from heat. Cool gelatin mixture slightly. Stir shredded apple into gelatin mixture. Chill till partially set (the consistency of unbeaten egg whites), stirring occasionally. Transfer gelatin mixture to a large mixing bowl.

In a small mixer bowl beat egg whites till soft peaks form (tips curl). Gradually add the ¼ cup sugar, beating till stiff peaks form (tips stand straight). Fold stiffly beaten egg whites into gelatin mixture. If necessary, chill till mixture mounds when spooned. Transfer to prepared crust. Sprinkle with reserved crumb mixture. Cover and chill for several hours. Makes 6 servings.

Irya E. McLearn, Altamonte Springs, Florida

Tutti-Frutti Strudel

3 tablespoons rum
1 cup mixed dried fruit bits
½ cup sugar
⅓ cup all-purpose flour
2 teaspoons ground cinnamon
¼ teaspoon ground nutmeg
¼ cup butter *or* margarine

7 sheets frozen phyllo dough (18x13-inch rectangles), thawed
⅓ cup butter *or* margarine, melted
½ cup sliced almonds, toasted
1 beaten egg white
1 teaspoon water
Sugar

In a saucepan heat rum just till warm. Stir in dried fruit bits. Cover and let stand for 10 minutes. In a small mixing bowl combine the ½ cup sugar, flour, cinnamon, and nutmeg. Cut in the ¼ cup butter or margarine till mixture resembles fine crumbs. Set aside.

Place one rectangle of the phyllo dough on a pastry cloth. Brush with some of the ⅓ cup melted butter or margarine. Top with a second rectangle of phyllo and brush again with butter or margarine. Repeat with remaining phyllo and butter or margarine. Sprinkle toasted almonds over phyllo. Top with the crumb mixture and *undrained* fruit bits.

Roll up, jelly-roll style, starting from one of the long sides. Tuck ends under to seal. Place roll, seam side down, on a baking sheet. Score top layers of phyllo at 1-inch intervals.

Combine egg white and water and brush over roll. Sprinkle with sugar. Bake in a 375° oven for 15 to 20 minutes or till golden brown. Serve warm or cool. Makes 16 servings.

Judee Disco, Preston, Connecticut

Yogurt-Topped Fruit

You can have this light-and-easy fruit dessert ready in no time!

½ of an 8-ounce carton plain yogurt
1 teaspoon honey
¼ teaspoon finely shredded orange peel

2 cups fresh strawberries, sliced
2 medium oranges, peeled, sectioned, and cut in half

In a small mixing bowl combine yogurt, honey, and orange peel. Cover and chill. Arrange sliced strawberries and orange sections on a small plate. Drizzle yogurt mixture atop fruit. Makes 4 servings.

Alethea Sparks, Des Moines, Iowa

Strawberries Brûlée

What a winning dessert—fabulous tasting and extra-easy to make! (Pictured at left.)

2 3-ounce packages cream cheese, softened
1 cup dairy sour cream
2 tablespoons brown sugar
4 cups fresh strawberries
¼ cup packed brown sugar

In a small mixer bowl beat cream cheese with an electric mixer till fluffy. Add sour cream and the 2 tablespoons brown sugar. Beat till smooth. Reserve 1 strawberry for garnish. Halve remaining berries and arrange evenly in the bottom of a shallow 8-inch round broiler-proof dish.

Spoon cream cheese mixture over berries. Sieve the ¼ cup brown sugar evenly over cream cheese mixture. Broil 4 to 5 inches from heat for 1 to 2 minutes or till sugar turns golden brown. Slice reserved berry; arrange atop dessert. Serve immediately. Serves 8.

Alicia Kuhl, Seattle, Washington

Spicy Poached Pears

Barbara also likes to serve this fresh pear dessert with chocolate ice cream.

¾ cup dry white wine
⅓ cup orange juice
¼ cup packed brown sugar
2½ inches stick cinnamon
    or 1 teaspoon ground cinnamon
6 large pears, peeled, cored, and halved
Vanilla ice cream

In a 3-quart saucepan combine wine, orange juice, brown sugar, and stick cinnamon or ground cinnamon. Cook and stir over medium-low heat till sugar is dissolved. Add pear halves. Cover and cook for 8 to 10 minutes or till pears are barely tender. Uncover and cook about 20 minutes more or till pears are translucent. Remove stick cinnamon. Serve pears warm with vanilla ice cream. Makes 6 to 8 servings.

Mrs. Barbara Keenan, Fort Morgan, Colorado

Pear Clafouti

3 eggs
1¼ cups milk
⅔ cup all-purpose flour
⅓ cup sugar
2 teaspoons vanilla
¼ teaspoon rum extract
⅛ teaspoon salt
⅛ teaspoon ground nutmeg
2 medium pears, peeled, halved, cored, and chopped
Whipped cream

This classic, French, oven-baked pancake puffs while it's baking, then falls slightly when it comes out of the oven.

For batter in a small mixer bowl beat eggs with an electric mixer till foamy. Add milk, flour, sugar, vanilla, rum extract, salt, and nutmeg. Beat till smooth.

Grease bottom and sides of a 9- or 10-inch quiche dish or pie plate. Arrange chopped pears in prepared dish. Pour batter over pears. Bake in a 350° oven for 50 to 60 minutes or till evenly puffed and lightly browned. Let stand 15 minutes. Garnish with whipped cream. Makes 8 servings.

Margaret T. Anderson, Jamestown, New York

Macaroon-Almond Baked Pears

1 29-ounce can pear halves, drained
⅓ cup apricot preserves
¼ cup orange liqueur
1 cup crumbled soft macaroons
¼ cup sliced almonds
Whipped cream

Here's proof that a scrumptious dessert doesn't have to take hours to prepare. Half an hour is all this one takes.

Arrange pear halves, cut side up, in a 10x6x2-inch or 12x7½x2-inch baking dish. In a small mixing bowl combine apricot preserves and orange liqueur. Pour over pear halves in dish. Sprinkle macaroon crumbs and almonds atop.

Bake in a 350° oven for 20 to 25 minutes or till heated through. Serve warm with whipped cream. Makes 6 to 8 servings.

Maile Locke, San Rafael, California

Fresh-Fruit Cups

¾ teaspoon cornstarch
⅛ teaspoon salt
3 tablespoons honey
4 teaspoons lemon juice
1 slightly beaten egg yolk
1 8-ounce carton plain
   yogurt

½ cup whipping cream
4 cups desired fresh
   fruit*
1 cup granola

*A great summertime dessert—
your favorite fresh fruit layered
between crunchy granola and a
smooth, rich, honey-yogurt sauce.*

In a small saucepan combine cornstarch and salt. Stir in honey and lemon juice. Cook and stir till thickened and bubbly, then cook and stir 2 minutes more. Gradually stir about *half* of the hot mixture into the beaten egg yolk. Return egg mixture to saucepan. Cook and stir over low heat for 2 minutes more. Remove from heat and stir in yogurt. Cool completely.

In a small mixer bowl beat whipping cream till soft peaks form (tips curl). Fold whipped cream into yogurt mixture. Chill thoroughly.

Just before serving, layer yogurt mixture, desired fruit, and granola into 8 individual dessert dishes. Makes 8 servings.
* Choose any combination of the following: peeled and sliced peaches, bananas, or pineapple; or berries (halve large strawberries).

Karen Thauer, Kentwood, Michigan

Toasted Almond Cream

2 tablespoons honey
1 tablespoon Amaretto
1 teaspoon vanilla
2 apples, cored and chopped
¼ cup chopped almonds,
   toasted

½ cup whipping cream
Slivered almonds, toasted
   (optional)
Apple slices (optional)

*Impress dinner guests with this
speedy and special dessert.*

In a small mixing bowl stir together honey, Amaretto, and vanilla. Toss apples and chopped almonds with the honey mixture. Beat whipping cream till soft peaks form (tips curl). Fold whipped cream into apple mixture.

Spoon mixture into 4 individual dessert dishes. Garnish with slivered almonds and apple slices, if desired. Serve immediately. Makes 4 servings.

Linda D. Willis, Elkton, Maryland

Berry-Honey Ice Cream

Experiment with different berries—any will make this sinfully rich ice cream hard to turn down. (Pictured at left.)

1½ cups fresh *or* frozen unsweetened boysenberries, thawed
3 egg yolks
½ teaspoon finely shredded lemon peel
2 tablespoons lemon juice
⅛ teaspoon salt
¼ cup honey
1 cup whipping cream

Place the berries in a blender container or food processor bowl. Cover and blend or process till pureed. (*Or,* mash the berries in a small mixing bowl with the back of a spoon.)

In a small mixer bowl beat egg yolks about 5 minutes or till thick and lemon colored. Beat in lemon peel, lemon juice, and salt. Beat in pureed berries and honey.

Beat whipping cream till soft peaks form (tips curl). Fold whipped cream into berry mixture. Transfer mixture into an 8x8x2-inch baking pan. Cover and freeze for several hours or till almost firm. Break frozen mixture into chunks. Transfer to a chilled mixer bowl. Beat with an electric mixer till smooth, but not melted. Return mixture to cold pan. Cover and freeze till firm. Makes about 3 cups.

Mrs. Jo Hostetler, Fresno, California

Fruited Raspberry Sherbet

Marshmallows, fruit bits, and nuts dress up purchased sherbet to make Ann's simple, yet special, winning dessert.

½ gallon raspberry *or* pineapple sherbet
1 10-ounce package frozen red raspberries, thawed
1¼ cups tiny marshmallows
1 8-ounce can pineapple tidbits (juice pack), drained
½ cup maraschino cherries, chopped
½ cup chopped pecans
2 bananas, finely chopped

In a chilled bowl stir sherbet to soften. Stir in *undrained* raspberries, marshmallows, pineapple, cherries, and pecans. Mix well. Gently stir bananas into sherbet mixture. Transfer mixture to a 13x9x2-inch baking pan. Freeze till firm. Let stand about 20 minutes at room temperature before serving. Makes about 3 quarts (24 servings).

Ann K. Andersen, Mount Edgecumbe, Alaska

Cherry-Chocolate Ice Cream

Kathy's top-rated summertime treat is packed full of fruit and milk chocolate chunks.

3 slightly beaten eggs
4 cups milk
2 cups whipping cream
1 cup sugar
1 cup chocolate-flavored syrup
1 10-ounce jar maraschino cherries, drained and chopped
3 1- to 1½-ounce bars milk chocolate, chopped
1 tablespoon vanilla

In a large mixing bowl combine eggs, milk, whipping cream, sugar, chocolate-flavored syrup, cherries, chopped chocolate bars, and vanilla. Freeze in a 4- or 5-quart ice cream freezer according to manufacturer's directions. Makes about 3 quarts (24 servings).

Kathy Wierman, Fordland, Missouri

Strawberry Ice

Prompted by a restaurant dessert, Michelle and her mother created this enticing and refreshing mealtime finale.

1 cup water
¾ cup sugar
4 cups fresh *or* frozen strawberries *or* raspberries, thawed
2 cups pink lemonade
2 cups raspberry-cranberry juice drink

For sugar syrup, in a small saucepan combine water and sugar. Cook over medium heat till boiling. Boil gently for 10 minutes. Cool.

Meanwhile, place berries in a blender container or food processor bowl. Cover and blend or process till smooth. Strain through a sieve to remove seeds. Stir together cooled sugar syrup, sieved berries, lemonade, and raspberry-cranberry drink. Pour into a 13x9x2-inch baking pan. Cover and freeze several hours or till almost firm.

Break frozen mixture into chunks. Transfer to a chilled mixer bowl. Beat with an electic mixer till nearly smooth, but not melted. Return mixture to cold pan. Cover and freeze till firm. Makes 8 to 10 cups.

Michelle Mitchell, Plain City, Ohio

Chocolate Pecan-Pie Bars

A trip to New Orleans inspired these Southern-style bourbon-flavored bar cookies.

1¼ cups all-purpose flour
¼ cup sugar
½ teaspoon baking powder
½ teaspoon ground cinnamon
½ cup butter *or* margarine
1 cup finely chopped pecans
¼ cup butter *or* margarine

1 square (1 ounce) semisweet chocolate
3 beaten eggs
1¼ cups packed brown sugar
2 tablespoons bourbon *or* water
1 teaspoon vanilla

For crust, combine flour, sugar, baking powder, and cinnamon. Cut in the ½ cup butter or margarine till mixture resembles coarse crumbs. Stir in pecans. Press crust mixture into the bottom of an ungreased 13x9x2-inch baking pan. Bake in a 350° oven for 10 minutes.

Meanwhile, in a small heavy saucepan combine the ¼ cup butter or margarine and chocolate. Heat and stir over low heat till chocolate melts. Combine eggs, brown sugar, bourbon, vanilla, and melted chocolate mixture. Stir till combined. Pour over crust. Return to oven. Bake 20 minutes more or till set. Cool. Cut into bars. Makes 36.

Debbie Vanni, Libertyville, Illinois

Tropical Fruit Bars

Joan likes to serve her teenagers these moist and tangy bars as an after-school snack.

1 cup boiling water
½ cup finely snipped dried apricots
1 cup all-purpose flour
½ teaspoon baking powder
¼ teaspoon baking soda
¼ cup butter *or* margarine
½ cup packed brown sugar

1 egg
½ teaspoon finely shredded lime peel
1 tablespoon lime juice
½ cup milk
½ cup finely chopped walnuts
Lime Frosting

Pour boiling water over dried apricots. Let stand 5 minutes. Drain and set aside. Combine flour, baking powder, and soda. In a small mixer bowl beat butter or margarine for 30 seconds. Add brown sugar and beat till fluffy. Add egg, lime peel, and lime juice; beat well. Add dry ingredients and milk alternately to beaten mixture, beating after each addition. Stir in nuts and apricots. Spread evenly in a greased 12x7½x2-inch baking pan. Bake in a 350° oven for 20 to 25 minutes or till done. Cool. Frost with Lime Frosting. Cut into bars. Makes 28.

Lime Frosting: Beat together 1½ cups sifted *powdered sugar*; 1 tablespoon softened *butter or margarine*; ¼ teaspoon finely shredded *lime peel*, optional; and 1 tablespoon *lime juice*. Add enough *milk* (about 1 tablespoon) to make spreadable.

Joan Romney, Bountiful, Utah

It's easy to cut bar cookies into squares, but it's just as easy to cut them into diamond shapes. First make straight parallel cuts 1 to 1½ inches apart down the length of your pan. Then make diagonal cuts across the pan (at a 45-degree angle), keeping the lines as parallel as you can.

Maple-Coconut Bars

¾ cup all-purpose flour
½ teaspoon baking powder
¼ teaspoon salt
¼ cup butter *or* margarine
¾ cup sugar
 1 egg
½ teaspoon maple flavoring

1 cup shredded coconut, finely chopped
¼ cup chopped walnuts
½ cup shredded coconut
1 tablespoon butter *or* margarine, melted

In a mixing bowl stir together flour, baking powder, and salt. Set aside. In a medium mixer bowl beat the ¼ cup butter or margarine with an electric mixer on medium speed for 30 seconds. Add sugar and beat till combined. Add egg and maple flavoring. Beat on low speed just till combined. Add dry ingredients to beaten mixture, beating just till combined. Stir in the 1 cup coconut and nuts.

Spread batter into a greased 8x8x2-inch baking pan. Stir together the ½ cup coconut and the 1 tablespoon melted butter or margarine. Sprinkle over batter in pan. Bake in a 350° oven about 30 minutes or till done. Cut into bars. Makes 24.

Mrs. Ann P. Flood, Rochester, New York

Apple-Orange Brownies

1¼ cups all-purpose flour
1 teaspoon baking powder
½ teaspoon salt
¼ teaspoon baking soda
1 cup packed brown sugar
⅓ cup butter *or* margarine
1 beaten egg
½ cup applesauce
1 teaspoon finely shredded orange peel
1 teaspoon vanilla
½ cup chopped pecans
Orange Glaze

Combine flour, baking powder, salt, and baking soda. Set aside. In a saucepan combine brown sugar and butter or margarine. Heat and stir till butter is melted. Stir in egg, applesauce, orange peel, and vanilla. Stir applesauce mixture and nuts into dry ingredients.

Spread batter into a greased 12x7½x2-inch baking dish. Bake in a 350° oven about 25 minutes or till done. While warm, top with Orange Glaze. Cut into bars. Makes 36.

Orange Glaze: Stir together 1½ cups sifted *powdered sugar,* 2 tablespoons *orange juice,* and ½ teaspoon *vanilla* till smooth.

Mrs. Anna Mae Pritchyk, Clarks Summit, Pennsylvania

Whole Wheat, Chip, and Coffee Bars

Enjoy these moist, cakelike treats with a cup of hot coffee or a glass of cold milk—whichever strikes your fancy.

2 cups all-purpose flour
1 cup whole wheat flour
1 teaspoon baking soda
½ teaspoon salt
2 eggs
2 cups packed brown sugar
1 cup cooking oil
2 teaspoons vanilla
2 teaspoons instant coffee crystals
1 cup cold water
1 6-ounce package (1 cup) semisweet chocolate pieces
1 cup chopped walnuts
Coffee Glaze

In a mixing bowl stir together flours, soda, and salt. In a large mixer bowl beat eggs till light and fluffy. Gradually add brown sugar, oil, and vanilla. Beat well. Dissolve coffee crystals in cold water. Gradually stir into egg mixture. Add dry ingredients, beating till combined.

Pour batter into a greased 15x10x1-inch baking pan. Sprinkle chocolate pieces and nuts evenly atop. Bake in a 350° oven for 25 to 30 minutes or till done. Cool slightly. Drizzle with Coffee Glaze. Cut into squares. Makes 36.

Coffee Glaze: Dissolve ½ teaspoon *instant coffee crystals* in 4 teaspoons *water.* Combine 1 cup sifted *powdered sugar,* 1 tablespoon softened *butter or margarine,* and the coffee mixture till smooth. (If necessary, add more *water* for drizzling consistency.)

Ena N. Allen, Fairfield, Connecticut

Shortcut Napoleans

Instead of making Napoleans with traditional puff pastry, Jeannie cuts the work short with piecrust mix. And for variety, she likes to alter the flavor of the jam and the pudding filling.

1 4-serving-size package *regular* vanilla pudding mix
1½ cups milk
½ of a 4-ounce container frozen whipped dessert topping, thawed
2 sticks piecrust mix

¼ cup seedless red raspberry jam
1½ cups sifted powdered sugar
2 to 3 tablespoons milk
2 squares (2 ounces) semisweet chocolate
2 to 3 teaspoons shortening

In a medium mixing bowl combine pudding mix and the 1½ cups milk. Cook according to package directions. Cover surface and cool. Fold in dessert topping. Cover and chill.

Meanwhile, prepare piecrust mix according to package directions. Roll *half* of the pastry into a 14x9-inch rectangle. Cut lengthwise into six 1½-inch-wide strips. Cut each strip crosswise into quarters. Place strips on baking sheets. Prick with a fork. Repeat with remaining pastry. Bake in a 425° oven for 8 to 10 minutes. Cool on a wire rack.

To assemble, spread about ½ *teaspoon* jam over *each* of 24 strips. Top *each* with about *1 tablespoon* pudding mixture.

For frosting, in a small mixing bowl stir together powdered sugar and the 2 to 3 tablespoons milk. Spread about *1 teaspoon* frosting over *each* of the 24 remaining strips. Place frosted strips on top of pudding-topped strips.

In a small heavy saucepan melt chocolate and shortening over low heat, stirring often. Drizzle chocolate over frosted strips. If desired, swirl chocolate through the frosting with a knife. Chill well. Makes 24.

Jeannie Hobel, San Diego, California

Who says pie has to be fattening? This top-notch refrigerator pie is about 128 calories per slice.

Heaven-Light Lemon Pie

Nonstick spray coating
2 egg whites
½ teaspoon vinegar
½ teaspoon vanilla
3 tablespoons sugar
2 beaten eggs
¼ cup sugar
1 tablespoon finely shredded lemon peel
¼ cup lemon juice
1 tablespoon butter *or* margarine
1 1.4-ounce envelope whipped dessert topping mix
½ cup skim milk
½ teaspoon vanilla

Spray a 9-inch pie plate with nonstick spray coating. For meringue crust, in a small mixer bowl combine the 2 egg whites, vinegar, ½ teaspoon vanilla, and dash *salt*. Beat till soft peaks form. Gradually add the 3 tablespoons sugar, beating till stiff peaks form. Spread the meringue over the bottom and up the sides of the pie plate, forming a crust. Bake in a 325° oven about 25 minutes or till golden. Cool.

For filling, in a small saucepan combine the 2 eggs, the ¼ cup sugar, lemon peel, lemon juice, and butter or margarine. Cook and stir over low heat till slightly thickened. Spread *one-fourth* of the filling over crust. Prepare the dessert topping mix according to package directions using skim milk and ½ teaspoon vanilla. Spread *half* of the whipped topping over the filling. Fold together the remaining whipped topping and the remaining filling. Spoon into pie plate. Cover and chill 6 hours or overnight. Garnish with a lemon twist, if desired. Serves 8.

Mrs. Kenneth R. Wykle, Colorado Springs, Colorado

MICROWAVE SPECIALTIES

IN THE WINK OF AN
EYE, THESE APPETIZERS, MAIN DISHES,
AND SIDE DISHES GO FROM OVEN TO TABLE—
MICROWAVE OVEN THAT IS. BUSY COOKS LIKE
YOU RELY MORE AND MORE ON MICROWAVE
OVENS WHEN IT COMES TO SAVING TIME AND
ENERGY—WITHOUT SACRIFICING GOOD TASTE.
SO GO AHEAD, SIMPLIFY YOUR LIFE WITH
THESE AWARD-WINNING RECIPES THAT'LL BE
READY IN MINUTES.

Recipes with microwave directions were tested in countertop microwave ovens that operate on 600 to 700 watts. Times are approximate since microwave ovens vary by manufacturer.

Wheat Chip Nachos

1 cup whole wheat flour
1 tablespoon sesame seed
⅓ cup butter *or* margarine
3 tablespoons cold water
¾ pound bulk Italian sausage, cooked and drained
1 cup sliced, pitted ripe olives
⅓ cup sliced jalapeño peppers
2 cups shredded cheddar *or* Monterey Jack cheese
Chili powder

Combine flour and sesame seed. Cut in butter till pieces are the size of small peas. Add water, 1 tablespoon at a time, gently tossing with a fork till all is moistened. Form dough into a ball. Divide into thirds.

On a lightly floured surface flatten one portion of dough with your hands. Roll from center to edge to form an 8-inch circle. Place pastry on a large microwave-safe plate. With a fork, prick dough deeply to make 6 or 8 pie-shape wedges. Micro-cook pricked pastry, uncovered, on 100% power (high) for 3 to 4 minutes or till set, rotating plate a half-turn every minute. Remove dough from plate and place on a wire rack to cool. Repeat with remaining dough.

For nachos, carefully break the baked pastry rounds into wedges. Arrange wedges on microwave-safe plate. Top with sausage, olives, and peppers. Sprinkle with cheese and chili powder. Cook, uncovered, on high for 2 to 3 minutes or till cheese melts, rotating plate a half-turn every 30 seconds. Serve immediately. Makes 18 to 24 wedges.

Artis Robinson, Brookhaven, Mississippi

Appetizer Roll-Ups

Norma's family prefers to make these Oriental-like appetizers with pork, but they're very tasty with beef, too.

½ pound pork tenderloin (4½ to 5 inches long)
3 tablespoons soy sauce
2 tablespoons dry sherry
1 teaspoon grated gingerroot
½ teaspoon brown sugar
½ teaspoon Kitchen Bouquet
⅛ teaspoon seasoned salt
1 clove garlic, minced
20 walnut halves

Partially freeze pork. Slice meat lengthwise into very thin strips. Halve the larger strips lengthwise so all meat strips measure 4½ to 5 inches long and ¾ inch wide.

For marinade, combine soy sauce, dry sherry, gingerroot, brown sugar, Kitchen Bouquet, seasoned salt, and garlic. Add pork strips. Cover and marinate in refrigerator for 1 to 3 hours. Drain well.

Roll *1* meat strip around *each* walnut half. Place on a 12-inch microwave-safe platter. Micro-cook, uncovered, on 100% power (high) for 4 to 5 minutes, rearranging roll-ups after every minute. Makes 20.

Norma J. Keleher, Pacific Grove, California

Double Cheese and Cauliflower Soup

Instant mashed potatoes thicken Joan's rich and creamy vegetable and cheese potage. (Pictured at left.)

4 cups cauliflower flowerets
1 8-ounce package cream cheese, cut up
1 5-ounce jar sharp American cheese spread
½ of a 2½-ounce jar sliced dried beef, rinsed and chopped
½ cup instant mashed potato flakes *or* buds

In a large microwave-safe mixing bowl combine cauliflower and ½ cup *water*. Cover with vented microwave-safe plastic wrap. Micro-cook on 100% power (high) for 8 minutes, stirring after 4 minutes. Set aside.

In a 2-quart microwave-safe casserole combine cream cheese, cheese spread, dried beef, potato flakes or buds, and 1½ cups *water*. Cook, uncovered, on high for 10 to 12 minutes or till mixture is smooth and cheeses are melted, stirring after 5 minutes. Stir till combined. Stir in the *undrained* cauliflower. Cook on high for 2 to 3 minutes more or till heated through. Makes 4 main-dish servings.

Joan Gillespie, Tempe, Arizona

Spicy Fish-and-Okra Stew

1 pound frozen red snapper fillets
1 tablespoon butter *or* margarine
1 small onion, chopped
1 clove garlic, minced
1 10-ounce package frozen mixed vegetables
½ of a 10-ounce package frozen cut okra
1 cup dry white wine
1 cup peeled and chopped tomato
1 6-ounce can tomato paste
1 tablespoon sugar
1 tablespoon curry powder
½ teaspoon ground ginger
½ teaspoon ground coriander
¼ teaspoon ground allspice
½ cup broken cashews
Hot cooked rice

Place fish in a 10x6x2-inch microwave-safe baking dish. Cover with vented microwave-safe plastic wrap. Micro-cook on 100% power (high) for 3 minutes. Cut fish into cubes. Set aside.

In a 3-quart microwave-safe casserole cook butter or margarine on high for 30 seconds. Add onion and garlic. Cook, covered, for 1½ minutes. Stir in mixed vegetables, okra, wine, chopped tomato, tomato paste, sugar, curry powder, ginger, coriander, allspice, ½ cup *water*, ½ teaspoon *salt*, and fish cubes. Cook, covered, on high for 12 to 15 minutes, stirring after every 5 minutes. Stir in cashews. Serve with rice. Makes 4 to 6 main-dish servings.

Mrs. J. F. Finnegan, Minneota, Minnesota

Quick Minestrone Soup

3 slices bacon, cut up
½ cup chopped onion
1 clove garlic, minced
¼ cup sliced carrot
¼ cup chopped celery
½ of a 15½-ounce jar spaghetti sauce
1 8-ounce can red kidney beans, drained
¼ cup tiny shell macaroni
1½ teaspoons instant beef bouillon granules
¼ cup chopped zucchini

The microwave oven puts Elaine's top-notch homemade soup on the table in just about 25 minutes.

Place bacon in a 2-quart microwave-safe casserole. Micro-cook, covered, on 100% power (high) about 2½ minutes or till almost crisp, stirring once. Add onion and garlic. Cook, covered, on high for 2 minutes or till onion is tender. Drain and set aside.

In the same casserole combine carrot, celery, and 1 tablespoon *water.* Cook, covered, on high for 2 to 3 minutes or till vegetables are tender. Stir in bacon mixture, spaghetti sauce, beans, macaroni, bouillon granules, 3 cups *water,* and ¼ teaspoon *pepper.* Cook, covered, on high for 10 minutes, stirring once. Stir in zucchini. Cook, covered, on high for 5 to 8 minutes more or till macaroni is tender. Sprinkle each serving with snipped parsley and Parmesan cheese, if desired. Makes 3 to 4 main-dish servings.

Elaine Trzpuc, Center, North Dakota

Taco Salad Pie

2 cups cheddar croutons
1 beaten egg
½ cup hot taco sauce
½ pound lean ground beef
½ cup sliced green onion
3 beaten eggs
1 15½-ounce can chili with beans
1 cup shredded cheddar cheese (4 ounces)

❝ Just micro-cook the ground beef "crust" with a bean filling. Then top it off with lettuce, tomatoes, olives, and sour cream. ❞

Crush croutons. Set aside. Combine the 1 beaten egg and taco sauce. Stir in croutons. Let stand for 5 minutes or till liquid is absorbed. Add beef and ¼ *cup* onion. Mix well. Press into bottom and up sides of a 9-inch microwave-safe pie plate to form a shell. Set aside.

For filling, in a microwave-safe bowl combine the 3 beaten eggs, *undrained* chili with beans, cheese, and remaining onion. Micro-cook, uncovered, on 100% power (high) for 3 minutes, stirring after every minute. Pour filling into meat shell. Cook, uncovered, on high for 12 to 13 minutes or till filling is almost set, giving dish a quarter-turn after every 4 minutes. Let stand 5 minutes. Top each serving with shredded lettuce, chopped tomatoes, ripe olives, and sour cream, if desired. Makes 6 main-dish servings.

Mrs. Jean W. Sanderson, Leawood, Kansas

Shape meatballs into a uniform size by patting the meat mixture into a square on waxed paper. Then cut the meat-mixture square into even-size cubes and roll each cube into a ball.

Oriental-Style Meatballs

1 beaten egg	1 10-ounce package frozen
½ cup finely chopped fresh	peas and carrots
spinach	4 teaspoons cornstarch
⅓ cup fine dry bread crumbs	1 cup beef broth
¼ cup soy sauce	1 8-ounce can bamboo
1 tablespoon milk	shoots, drained
½ pound ground beef	Hot cooked rice
½ pound ground pork	

In a medium mixing bowl combine egg, spinach, bread crumbs, *2 tablespoons* soy sauce, milk, and dash *pepper.* Add ground beef and ground pork and mix well. Shape meat mixture into 36 meatballs.

Arrange meatballs in a 12x7½x2-inch microwave-safe baking dish. Cover with vented clear plastic wrap. Micro-cook on 100% power (high) for 7 to 9 minutes or till no pink remains, rearranging and turning meatballs over once. Drain and set aside.

In a 2-quart microwave-safe casserole, combine frozen vegetables and 2 tablespoons *water.* Cook, covered, on high for 4 minutes. Combine cornstarch and remaining soy sauce. Stir into vegetables along with beef broth. Cook, uncovered, on high for 5 to 6 minutes, stirring after every minute. Stir in meatballs and bamboo shoots. Cook, uncovered, on high for 2 to 3 minutes or till heated through. Serve over rice. Makes 4 to 5 main-dish servings.

Diane Shabino, Kalamazoo, Michigan

Instant Reuben Casserole

4 slices rye bread
1 tablespoon prepared
   mustard
1 12-ounce can corned beef
1 16-ounce can sauerkraut,
   drained and snipped

1 10¾-ounce can condensed
   tomato soup
3 tablespoons sweet pickle
   relish
5 slices process Swiss
   cheese, halved diagonally

66 There's next to no measuring involved—the ultimate in pantry put-togethers. 99

Spread bread with mustard. Cut bread into cubes (you should have about 2½ cups). Place cubes in the bottom of a buttered 8x8x2-inch microwave-safe baking dish. Crumble corned beef evenly over bread.

Stir together sauerkraut, tomato soup, pickle relish, and ¼ cup *water.* Spoon atop corned beef. Micro-cook, covered, on 100% power (high) for 10 to 12 minutes, giving dish a quarter-turn after 5 minutes. Arrange cheese slices over the top. Cook on high about 1 minute more or till cheese melts. Makes 6 main-dish servings.

Patricia Lanier, Durham, North Carolina

Can Opener Enchiladas

1 10¾-ounce can condensed
   cream of chicken soup
1 8¾-ounce can cream-style
   corn
½ cup sliced green onion
1 tablespoon chili powder
2 5-ounce cans chunk-
   style chicken, drained
   and flaked

½ cup dairy sour cream
¼ cup milk
12 6-inch flour tortillas
1½ cups shredded cheddar
   cheese (6 ounces)
   Green pepper rings
   (optional)
   Ripe olives (optional)

66 Thirty minutes after I began opening cans, I served this casserole to my hungry family. They gobbled it up, and the dish is now a favorite. 99

In a microwave-safe bowl combine soup, corn, green onion, and chili powder. Micro-cook, uncovered, on 100% power (high) for 4 minutes or till hot, stirring after 2 minutes. Stir in chicken, sour cream, and milk. Spread about *1¼ cups* of the chicken mixture in the bottom of a 12x7½x2-inch microwave-safe baking dish. Set aside.

Slit the tortilla package. Cook on high for 1 minute or till tortillas are softened. Spread a scant *¼ cup* chicken mixture on *each* tortilla. Top *each* with about *1 tablespoon* cheese. Roll tortillas up. Place, seam side down, in baking dish.

Cook, uncovered, on high for 6 to 8 minutes or till heated through. Top with remaining cheese. Cook on high about 1 minute more or till cheese melts. Garnish with green pepper rings and ripe olives, if desired. Makes 6 main-dish servings.

Sally J. Hertel, Spokane, Washington

Easy Stuffed Pork Chops

Apples, bread crumbs, raisins, and seasonings combine for a moist yet crunchy stuffing.

1 tablespoon butter *or* margarine
¼ cup fine dry bread crumbs
½ of a small apple, peeled, cored, and chopped (about ¼ cup)
1 tablespoon raisins
1 tablespoon finely chopped onion
¼ teaspoon salt

⅛ teaspoon pepper
⅛ teaspoon poultry seasoning
1 tablespoon apple cider *or* apple juice
4 pork loin chops, cut ½ inch thick
¼ of a 0.87-ounce envelope (2½ teaspoons) brown gravy mix

For stuffing, in a 2-cup microwave-safe measure micro-cook butter or margarine, uncovered, on 100% power (high) for 30 to 45 seconds or till melted. Stir in bread crumbs, chopped apple, raisins, onion, salt, pepper, and poultry seasoning. Add *1½ teaspoons* apple cider or apple juice to moisten.

Arrange *2* chops in an 8x8x2-inch microwave-safe baking dish. Spoon *half* of the stuffing mixture over *each* chop. Place the remaining chops atop stuffing.

In a small mixing bowl combine gravy mix with remaining 1½ teaspoons cider or apple juice. Brush *half* of the gravy mixture over chops. Cover with vented microwave-safe plastic wrap. Cook on 30% power (medium-low) for 10 minutes. Give dish a half-turn and turn chops over. Brush chops with remaining gravy mixture. Cook, covered, on medium-low for 10 to 12 minutes more or till chops are tender and no pink remains. Makes 2 main-dish servings.

Mrs. Amelia Shearouse, Orlando, Florida

Curried Fish Fillets

Curried Fish Fillets

1½ pounds fresh *or* frozen cod *or* haddock fillets, cut ¾ inch thick
2 tablespoons honey
2 tablespoons Dijon-style mustard
1 tablespoon lemon juice
½ to ¾ teaspoon curry powder
⅛ teaspoon salt
Snipped chives
Snipped parsley

66 *We serve fish often, so I was looking for a simple, yet different, way of fixing it.* **99**

Thaw fish, if frozen. Place fish in a microwave-safe 12x7½x2-inch baking dish. Set aside. In a small mixing bowl combine honey, mustard, lemon juice, curry powder, and salt. Spread honey mixture over fish. Cover with vented microwave-safe plastic wrap.

Micro-cook on 100% power (high) for 7 to 9 minutes, or till fish flakes easily with a fork, turning fish over after 4 minutes. Sprinkle with chives and parsley. Makes 6 main-dish servings.

Lynn Sametz, Dorchester, Maine

Lemony Waldorf Fillets

1 16-ounce package frozen cod *or* other fish fillets
1 cup chopped apple
½ cup thinly sliced celery
1 tablespoon butter *or* margarine
1 cup herb-seasoned stuffing mix
¼ cup chopped walnuts
¼ cup mayonnaise *or* salad dressing
1 tablespoon lemon juice

Mrs. Finnegan credits her daughter with the idea for this tasty microwave entrée.

Thaw block of frozen fish. Set aside. For stuffing, in a 1-quart microwave-safe bowl combine apple, celery, and butter or margarine. Micro-cook, covered, on 100% power (high) for 2 to 3 minutes or till celery is crisp-tender. Stir in stuffing mix, walnuts, mayonnaise or salad dressing, and lemon juice. Set stuffing aside.

Place fish in a 12x7½x2-inch microwave-safe baking dish. Cook, covered with vented clear plastic wrap, on high for 5 minutes, giving the dish a half-turn after 3 minutes. Drain off juices.

Place stuffing in 4 mounds around fish. Cook, uncovered, on high for 2 to 3 minutes more or till fish flakes easily with a fork and stuffing is heated through. Makes 4 main-dish servings.

Mrs. J. F. Finnegan, Minneota, Minnesota

Amarillo Squash

2 pounds yellow summer squash *or* zucchini, cut into ¼-inch slices (8 cups)
1 medium onion, chopped
2 tablespoons water
2 cups shredded Monterey Jack cheese (8 ounces)
1 8-ounce carton dairy sour cream
1 4-ounce can diced green chili peppers, drained
1 2-ounce jar sliced pimiento, drained and chopped (¼ cup)
1½ cups cheese-flavored tortilla chips, crushed (about 6 ounces)
Paprika

Green chili peppers add zip to Cheryl's yummy side dish.

In a 3-quart microwave-safe casserole combine squash, onion, and water. Micro-cook, covered, on 100% power (high) for 9 to 10 minutes, stirring after 5 minutes. Drain and set aside.

In a medium mixing bowl stir together cheese, sour cream, chili peppers, and pimiento. In a 12x7½x2-inch microwave-safe baking dish layer *half* of the squash mixture, *half* of the cheese mixture, then *half* of the chips. Repeat layers. Sprinkle with paprika.

Cook, uncovered, on 70% power (medium-high) about 10 minutes or till heated through, giving dish a half-turn once. Dollop with sour cream and squash slices, if desired. Makes 8 side-dish servings.

Cheryl L. Dixon, Arlington, Texas

Mushroom Sauté

2 tablespoons butter *or* margarine
2 tablespoons dry sherry
1 tablespoon dried minced onion
1 tablespoon lime juice
1 teaspoon fines herbes, crushed
¼ teaspoon garlic salt
1 pound fresh mushrooms, halved (5½ cups)

Debra created this savory side dish for her microwave cooking class. She likes serving it with steak or poultry.

In a 2-quart microwave-safe casserole combine butter or margarine, sherry, onion, lime juice, fines herbes, and garlic salt. Micro-cook, uncovered, on 100% power (high) for 1 minute, stirring once.

Stir in mushrooms. Cook, covered, on high for 6 to 8 minutes or till the mushrooms are tender, stirring after every 2 minutes. Makes 4 to 5 side-dish servings.

Debra Tito, Diamond Bar, California

Lima Bean and Apple Casserole

2 10-ounce packages frozen baby lima beans
1 medium apple, cored and chopped
2 tablespoons water
½ cup mayonnaise *or* salad dressing
½ cup dairy sour cream

1 teaspoon finely shredded lemon peel
¼ teaspoon salt
¼ teaspoon ground nutmeg
⅛ teaspoon pepper
¼ cup coarsely chopped walnuts

Mayonnaise and sour cream provide a rich base for this saucy fruit and vegetable mixture.

In a 2-quart microwave-safe casserole combine frozen lima beans, apple, and water. Micro-cook, covered, on 100% power (high) for 10 to 12 minutes or till beans are tender, stirring after every 3 minutes.

In a small mixing bowl combine mayonnaise or salad dressing, sour cream, lemon peel, salt, nutmeg, and pepper. Stir into lima bean mixture. Cook, uncovered, on high for 1 to 2 minutes or till mixture is heated through, stirring once. *Do not boil.* Sprinkle with walnuts. Makes 8 to 10 side-dish servings.

F. Hill, Long Beach, California

Creamy Carrot Casserole

4 cups sliced carrot
¾ cup mayonnaise *or* salad dressing
¼ cup chopped onion
1 tablespoon prepared horseradish
¼ teaspoon salt
¼ teaspoon pepper

14 saltine crackers, crushed (½ cup)
2 tablespoons snipped parsley
1 tablespoon butter *or* margarine, melted
½ cup shredded American cheese (2 ounces)

An abundant carrot crop inspired Shirlee to create this colorful side dish. She finds it great for buffets and potluck dinners.

In a 1½-quart microwave-safe casserole combine carrots and 2 tablespoons *water*. Micro-cook, covered, on 100% power (high) for 10 to 12 minutes or till tender, stirring after 5 minutes. Drain.

Meanwhile, in a small mixing bowl stir together mayonnaise or salad dressing, onion, horseradish, salt, and pepper. Stir the horseradish mixture into the drained carrots.

In a small mixing bowl toss together crushed crackers, parsley, and butter or margarine. Sprinkle over carrots.

Cook, uncovered, on high for 3 minutes. Sprinkle with cheese. Cook, uncovered, on high about 1 minute more or till cheese melts and mixture is heated through. Makes 6 to 8 side-dish servings.

Shirlee Nelson, Marcus, Iowa

TREASURED HOLIDAY RECIPES

WHEN VISIONS OF SUGAR PLUMS DANCE IN YOUR HEAD, YOU KNOW THE DELIGHTFULLY LONG HOLIDAY SEASON HAS ARRIVED! BUT WHAT DO YOU SERVE THIS YEAR THAT YOU HAVEN'T SERVED BEFORE TO THE SAME GUESTS? WHETHER YOU'RE HUNTING FOR AN APPETIZER OR DESSERT—OR SOMETHING IN BETWEEN—THIS YEAR TRY A NEW TASTE TREAT FROM THIS REGAL ASSORTMENT OF YULETIDE RECIPES THAT ARE SURE TO BECOME HOLIDAY FAMILY FAVORITES.

Tarragon-Wine Mustard Sauce

As a gift for special friends, Linda fills small attractive jars with this tangy, all-purpose sauce.

½ cup Dijon-style mustard
⅓ cup olive oil *or* cooking oil
¼ cup white vinegar
¼ cup dry white wine
2 tablespoons dry mustard
1 teaspoon dried basil, crushed
1 teaspoon dried tarragon, crushed

In a small mixing bowl combine Dijon-style mustard, olive oil or cooking oil, vinegar, wine, dry mustard, basil, and tarragon. Cover and chill. Serve with meats or vegetables. Makes about 1⅓ cups.

Linda Slater, Arvada, Colorado

Gingered Holiday Chutney

Short on time? Skip the canning procedure and store Margery's colorful chutney in the refrigerator or freezer for a couple of months.

2 cups packed brown sugar
¾ cup vinegar
½ teaspoon salt
¼ teaspoon ground cinnamon
¼ teaspoon ground red pepper
1 lime
1 lemon
1 pound fresh Anjou pears, peeled, cored, and coarsely chopped (about 3 cups)
1 cup chopped green pepper
1 cup chopped red sweet pepper
1 cup chopped onion
1 tablespoon chopped crystallized ginger
1 cup light raisins

For syrup, in a large saucepan combine brown sugar, vinegar, salt, cinnamon, and ground red pepper. Bring to boiling. Reduce heat and simmer, uncovered, for 10 minutes.

Meanwhile, finely shred peel from lime and lemon. Squeeze juice from each. In a large bowl combine lime and lemon peels and juices, pears, green pepper, red sweet pepper, onion, and ginger. Add raisins, mixing gently. Add mixture to hot syrup. Heat to boiling. Reduce heat and simmer, uncovered, about 1 hour or till thick.

Ladle chutney at once into hot, clean pint jars, leaving a ¼-inch headspace. Wipe jar rims and adjust lids. Process in boiling water bath for 15 minutes (start timing when water boils). Makes 2 pints.

Margery Mulkey, Boise, Idaho

Stuffed Pork Chops Flambé

Pictured at left.

¾ cup prepared mincemeat
½ cup soft bread crumbs
1 small apple, finely chopped
2 tablespoons chopped
walnuts
½ cup orange juice

6 pork loin chops, cut
1¼ inches thick
(about 4 pounds)
1 tablespoon cooking oil
¼ cup orange liqueur

For stuffing, in a medium mixing bowl combine mincemeat, bread crumbs, apple, and nuts. Stir in *2 tablespoons* orange juice.

Cut a pocket in each chop by cutting from fat side almost to bone. Spoon about ¼ *cup* stuffing into *each* pocket. Fasten pocket openings with wooden toothpicks, if necessary.

In a large skillet brown the chops, 3 at a time, in hot oil. Arrange chops in a 13x9x2-inch baking dish. Season with salt and pepper. Pour remaining orange juice over chops. Bake, covered, in a 350° oven about 1 hour or till tender.

Transfer chops to a heatproof platter. Heat orange liqueur just till hot. Remove from heat. Using a long match, ignite liqueur and pour over chops. Makes 6 servings.

Carley Lindsay, Iowa City, Iowa

Orange-Glazed Turkey Roast

A yule-worthy entrée that's bound to become a holiday tradition at your house.

1 4- to 6-pound frozen
boneless turkey roast
¾ cup butter *or* margarine,
melted
6 small oranges

¼ cup water
2 tablespoons all-purpose
flour
¼ teaspoon ground nutmeg
2 tablespoons orange liqueur

Thaw turkey roast. Place on a rack in a shallow roasting pan. Brush with some of the butter. Roast according to package directions.

Meanwhile, finely shred peel from *1* orange to get *1 tablespoon* peel. Set peel aside. Squeeze juice from all of the oranges (should have about 2 cups juice). Combine orange juice and remaining butter. Baste turkey with some of the orange juice mixture frequently during the last 30 minutes. Transfer turkey to a platter. Cover; keep warm.

For sauce, combine pan juices and remaining orange juice mixture. Add *water,* if necessary, to make 2 cups. Set aside. In a saucepan combine the ¼ cup water and flour. Stir in orange juice mixture, nutmeg, and orange peel. Cook and stir till thickened and bubbly, then cook and stir 2 minutes more. Stir in orange liqueur. Spoon some sauce over turkey. Pass remaining. Makes 12 to 16 servings.

Mary Lynn Brown, Upland, California

Chicken Breasts À l'Orange

2 tablespoons apple juice
2 tablespoons apricot brandy
Dash ground allspice
Dash ground cinnamon
Dash ground cloves
½ cup chopped mixed dried fruit
⅓ cup chopped onion
1 tablespoon butter *or* margarine
¼ teaspoon salt
¼ teaspoon poultry seasoning
Dash pepper
½ cup cooked brown rice
4 whole medium chicken breasts (about 3 pounds total), skinned, halved lengthwise, and boned
Orange Sauce
¼ cup snipped parsley
3 tablespoons sliced almonds, toasted

Clayre trimmed the holiday bird down to size. Now the stars of her meal are these rice-stuffed chicken breasts.

In a small mixing bowl combine apple juice, brandy, allspice, cinnamon, and cloves. Stir in dried fruit. Let stand for 2 hours.

For stuffing, in a small saucepan cook onion in butter or margarine till tender. Add salt, poultry seasoning, and pepper. Remove from heat. Stir in the cooked rice. Drain fruit, reserving liquid for Orange Sauce. Stir fruit into stuffing mixture.

Rinse chicken; pat dry. Place each chicken breast between 2 pieces of clear plastic wrap. Working from the center to the edges, pound lightly with a meat mallet to ¼ inch thick. Remove plastic wrap.

Place about 2 *tablespoons* stuffing in the center of *each* chicken piece. Fold in sides and roll chicken around stuffing, forming a bundle. Place chicken bundles, seam side down, in a 12x7½x2-inch baking dish.

Prepare Orange Sauce. Pour over chicken bundles. Bake, covered, in a 350° oven for 30 to 40 minutes or till chicken is tender. Sprinkle with parsley and almonds. Makes 8 servings.

Orange Sauce: In a small saucepan melt 2 tablespoons *butter or margarine.* Stir in 2 tablespoons *all-purpose flour,* 1 teaspoon ground *cinnamon,* ¾ teaspoon finely shredded *orange peel,* and several dashes bottled *hot pepper sauce.* Stir in 1¼ cups *orange juice* and the reserved liquid from the dried fruit. Cook and stir till thickened and bubbly, then cook and stir for 1 minute more.

Clayre M. Heaslip, Redlands, California

Adorned with poached apple slices, this leg of lamb makes an impressive holiday feast.

Holiday Festive Lamb

¾ teaspoon dried rosemary, crushed
½ teaspoon garlic powder
1 4- to 5-pound leg of lamb
⅓ cup sugar
⅓ cup vinegar
3 tablespoons light corn syrup
3 tablespoons water
2 inches stick cinnamon

½ teaspoon whole cloves
¼ teaspoon ground ginger
3 medium apples, cored and sliced
½ cup packed brown sugar
⅓ cup frozen orange juice concentrate, thawed
2 teaspoons prepared mustard
¾ teaspoon ground cinnamon

Combine rosemary and garlic powder. Rub over lamb. Place lamb on a rack in a shallow roasting pan. Insert a meat thermometer in the thickest portion of the meat. Roast, uncovered, in a 325° oven for 2¼ to 2½ hours or till meat thermometer registers 160°.

Meanwhile, in a medium skillet combine sugar, vinegar, corn syrup, water, stick cinnamon, cloves, and ginger. Bring to boiling. Reduce heat and simmer, covered, for 4 minutes. Add apple slices and simmer for 4 minutes. Remove apples slices. Reserve 2 tablespoons poaching liquid. Halve 4 or 5 of the apple slices. Set aside.

For glaze, combine brown sugar, orange juice concentrate, mustard, ground cinnamon, and reserved poaching liquid.

Remove roast from oven. Cut 3-inch slits in top of roast. Insert halved apple slices in slits. Spoon some of the glaze over roast. Return meat to oven and roast for 20 minutes more, spooning glaze over top once or twice.

To serve, arrange remaining apple slices on a serving platter with roast. Drizzle any remaining glaze over meat. Garnish with parsley sprigs, if desired. Makes 10 servings.

Mrs. Glen Malenke, Austin, Minnesota

Edam Cheese Spread

> **❝** *Tasteful, but simple—that's the kind of cooking I like, especially when it comes to holiday entertaining.* **❞**

1¾ pounds Edam cheese
¾ cup beer
¾ cup milk
¼ cup butter *or* margarine, softened
2 teaspoons caraway seed
2 teaspoons dry mustard
½ teaspoon celery salt
Assorted fresh fruit
Assorted crackers

Using a sharp knife, cut paraffin coating away from cheese. Finely shred cheese (you should have about 7 cups). Let shredded cheese stand at room temperature, covered, for 3 to 4 hours to soften.

In a large mixer bowl stir together cheese, beer, milk, butter or margarine, caraway seed, mustard, and celery salt. Beat with an electric mixer for 3 to 5 minutes or till combined. Transfer cheese mixture to a serving container. Cover tightly and chill.

Let cheese mixture stand at room temperature for 3 to 4 hours before serving. Serve with fruit and crackers. Makes about 4½ cups.

Linda Joan Smith, Des Moines, Iowa

Cheeseball with Everything

Having two holiday parties? This recipe makes enough for both. Just shape the cheese mixture into two small balls instead of one large one. They'll keep in the refrigerator for up to two weeks.

2 cups shredded Swiss cheese (8 ounces)
2 cups shredded cheddar cheese (8 ounces)
1 8-ounce package cream cheese, softened
½ cup dairy sour cream
10 slices bacon, crisp-cooked, drained, and crumbled
½ cup finely chopped onion
½ cup finely chopped pecans
1 2-ounce jar diced pimiento
2 tablespoons sweet pickle relish
Dash salt
Dash pepper
¼ cup snipped parsley
1 tablespoon poppy seed
Assorted crackers

Bring Swiss cheese and cheddar cheese to room temperature. In a large mixer bowl beat together cream cheese and sour cream till fluffy. Beat in Swiss cheese, cheddar cheese, *half* of the bacon, onion, *half* of the pecans, *undrained* pimiento, pickle relish, salt, and pepper till combined. Cover and chill for several hours or till firm.

In a small mixing bowl combine remaining bacon, remaining pecans, parsley, and poppy seed. Shape cheese mixture into a ball, then roll in bacon mixture. Wrap tightly and chill.

Let cheese ball stand at room temperature about 30 minutes before serving. Serve with crackers. Makes 1 large ball.

Bonnie Jean Edwards, Fargo, North Dakota

Grandma's Salami Pie

Party guests will devour this hot appetizer in no time!

3½ cups all-purpose flour
½ teaspoon salt
1 cup shortening
2 tablespoons cooking oil
⅓ to ½ cup cold water
12 ounces salami, diced (2½ cups)

3 cups shredded Swiss cheese (12 ounces)
5 hard-cooked eggs, sliced
1 cup grated Romano cheese
4 beaten eggs
½ teaspoon pepper

Combine flour and salt. Cut in shortening till pieces are the size of small peas. Stir in oil. Sprinkle *1 or 2 tablespoons* water over part of the flour mixture. Gently toss with a fork. Push to side of bowl. Repeat till all is moistened. Form dough into a ball.

On a lightly floured surface, roll out *two-thirds* of the dough to form a 16x12-inch rectangle. Press dough into bottom and up sides of a 13x9x2-inch baking pan. Sprinkle salami over dough. Top with Swiss cheese, hard-cooked eggs, and Romano cheese. Combine eggs and pepper. Pour egg mixture over ingredients in pan.

On a lightly floured surface, roll remaining dough into a 14x10-inch rectangle. Place dough over filling in pan for top crust. Seal top and bottom edges together by rolling edges toward center. Flute edges. Prick top crust. Bake in a 375° oven about 65 minutes or till golden. Let stand 45 minutes. Cut into small rectangles. Makes 32 pieces.

Rose Strohmaier, Port Murray, New Jersey

Stuffed Bacon Rolls

Arrange these easy-to-make hors d'oeuvres on a serving platter along with colorful vegetable crudités.

2 cups soft bread crumbs (about 3 slices bread)
1 medium cooking apple, cored and finely chopped (1 cup)
1 tablespoon finely chopped onion

1 tablespoon snipped parsley
⅛ teaspoon salt
1 beaten egg
¼ cup milk
10 *or* 11 slices bacon

Combine bread crumbs, apple, onion, parsley, salt, and ⅛ teaspoon *pepper*. Add egg and milk. Mix well. Shape crumb mixture into balls, using about *1 rounded tablespoon* for *each* ball.

Cut each slice of bacon in half crosswise. Wrap *half* of a bacon slice around *each* ball. Secure with a metal pick or wooden toothpick.

Place on a wire rack set in a 15x10x1-inch baking pan. Bake in a 375° oven for 30 to 35 minutes or till bacon is brown. Serve immediately. Makes 20 to 22 appetizers.

Mrs. E. Graddick Stokes, Florence, South Carolina

Festive Citrus Salad

3 medium oranges, peeled
3 small grapefruit, peeled
2 avocados, halved, seeded, peeled, and sliced
1 medium cucumber, thinly sliced
1 small onion, thinly sliced and separated into rings

Orange juice
⅔ cup wine vinegar
⅓ cup sugar
¼ teaspoon salt
¼ teaspoon pepper
Lettuce leaves
Orange peel twist (optional)

Hang on to any leftover citrus marinade. It's great atop any fresh, tossed green salad. (Pictured at left.)

Section oranges and grapefruit over a small bowl to catch juices. Reserve juices. In a large mixing bowl combine orange and grapefruit sections, avocado slices, cucumber slices, and onion rings. For marinade, measure reserved fruit juices. Add orange juice to make 1 cup. Combine juice mixture, vinegar, sugar, salt, and pepper. Pour over fruit-vegetable mixture. Cover and marinate in refrigerator for 2 to 3 hours, stirring occasionally.

Just before serving, use a slotted spoon to remove fruit-vegetable mixture from marinade. Arrange on individual lettuce-lined plates. Drizzle a little marinade over each salad. Garnish with an orange peel twist, if desired. Makes 8 to 10 servings.

Lucille Randall, Columbus, Ohio

Lemon-Parsley Stuffing

10 cups dry bread cubes (about 14 slices bread)
1 cup finely chopped onion
1 cup snipped parsley
4 teaspoons finely shredded lemon peel
2 teaspoons dried marjoram, crushed

1 teaspoon dried thyme, crushed
2 cloves garlic, minced
1 cup butter *or* margarine, melted
2 slightly beaten eggs
⅓ cup water
¼ cup lemon juice

Try Elise's sophisticated yet simple stuffing with your holiday meal. It's fresh and lemony—a blue-ribbon winner.

In a large mixing bowl combine bread cubes, onion, parsley, lemon peel, marjoram, thyme, garlic, ½ teaspoon *salt,* and ½ teaspoon *pepper*. Mix well. In a small mixing bowl combine butter or margarine, eggs, water, and lemon juice. Toss with bread mixture.

Use to stuff one 10- to 12-pound turkey, or two 3-pound broiler-fryer chickens. (*Or,* spoon stuffing into a 2-quart casserole. Bake, uncovered, in a 325° oven for 30 to 40 minutes or till heated through.) Makes about 10 servings.

Elise Roberts, Henderson, Texas

DEBBIE VANNI, LIBERTYVILLE, ILL.

Libertyville, Illinois, lies just 35 miles north of Chicago. But this charming village has a quintessential small-town atmosphere. It's a hub of activity, especially in the winter, with snowmobiling, cross-country skiing, and ice skating at the nearby parks. And there's

also an annual Christmas show sponsored by the local dance theater. It's here, in Libertyville, that Bill and Debbie Vanni, plus daughters Kristina and Kara, share a large and cheerful home.

Both Bill and Debbie are active in community and church affairs. Bill, a structural engineer by day, is also an elected official on the Village Board. Debbie, a busy wife and mother, volunteers her time to their church and the local Arts and Cultural Center. She finds that being active in the community gives her lots of opportunities to do what she likes best—cook!

Weekends are busy for Debbie, particularly during the holidays, since she caters a few parties and dinners on her own. "I like to follow the theme of the season," says Debbie, "by designing a special menu with my own recipes." One fall dinner menu included a shrimp bisque, grilled duck with wild mushrooms, wild rice, glazed cranberries, and autumn vegetables. But the dessert was the real showstopper: poached cheese-stuffed pears floating in both dark and white chocolate sauces.

For her own holiday get-togethers, she's apt to try "something different—I never make the same thing twice," Debbie says. "I prefer a small dinner party so that I can spend more time decorating the food. Food has to look good as well as taste delicious," Debbie says. "I like to spend time on the presentation. I want my food to dazzle!"

> 66 *I like to spend time on the presentation. I want my food to dazzle!* 99

"When Libertyville celebrated its centennial in 1982, I organized a local baking contest," says Debbie. Her enthusiasm for the project helped make it a tremendous success. "We received several hundred entries. After the contest, I wrote a cookbook of the winning recipes." The idea was so popular that the books sold out within two hours.

(continued)

DEBBIE VANNI, LIBERTYVILLE, ILL.

To Debbie, cooking is a creative outlet and an art. The volunteer catering she does for church weddings and art show receptions gives her a chance to put her creativity to work and prepare elegant food tailored to the occasion. "For example," she relates, "I might get a request to make hors d'oeuvres. Rather than making cheese and crackers as they suggest, I'll do something special—like putting aspic over the cheese."

Where do Debbie's food ideas come from? For starters, there's her collection of 600 cookbooks. "And since grade school, I've been clipping and collecting recipes from magazines," adds Debbie. She sometimes cooks from recipes, but more often *creates* from them.

It's no wonder that Debbie has garnered a local reputation for being a cook extraordinaire. The Lake County Fair, along with local and national cooking contests, have offered her more opportunities to cook up a storm. As a result, Debbie has collected almost more ribbons than she can count. "And we have a couple of shelves full of appliance prizes in the basement," she laughs. But Debbie has a special motive for entering contests. "I'd like to have my own food-related business someday, and a big prize would help me do that."

DEBBIE VANNI, LIBERTYVILLE, ILL.

Debbie's recipe for Harvest Sugar Cookies was adapted from her grandmother's sugar cookie recipe. "Someone requested cookies shaped like vegetables for a party, so I drew some designs freehand and used an egg yolk wash to paint them," says Debbie. The cookie has become a standard at the Vanni house at Christmastime, when

Debbie and Kristina use the same recipe to make a giant Santa Claus cookie.

"Kristina has been taking art lessons since she was three," says Debbie. "So we started painting designs on cookies. The Santa Claus cookie was her inspiraton." Sounds like a scrumptious idea for artists of all ages!

Harvest Sugar Cookies

3 cups all-purpose flour
½ teaspoon baking powder
½ teaspoon baking soda
¼ teaspoon salt
1 cup butter
1 cup sugar
2 eggs

1 teaspoon lemon extract *or* vanilla
3 cups sifted powdered sugar
2 egg whites
2 tablespoons water
Paste food coloring

In a large mixing bowl stir together flour, baking powder, soda, and salt. Set aside. In a large mixer bowl beat butter with an electric mixer on medium speed for 30 seconds. Add sugar and beat till fluffy. Add eggs and lemon extract or vanilla and beat well. Add dry ingredients and beat till combined. (You may have to stir in the last part of the dry indredients by hand.) Cover and chill about 1 hour or till easy to handle.

On a lightly floured surface, roll *one-fourth* of the dough ⅛ inch thick. Cut into vegetable shapes. Place on a greased cookie sheet. Bake in a 375° oven for 5 to 6 minutes or till bottoms are lightly browned. Remove and cool completely on wire racks.

Meanwhile, for frosting, in a medium mixing bowl combine powdered sugar, egg whites, and water. Beat till smooth. Divide frosting into the number of colors desired and tint with paste food coloring. Frost cookies to resemble vegetables. Makes about 60.

Chocolate Nog

Purchased eggnog and canned chocolate-flavored syrup make Shirley's thirst-quencher a rich, delicious, and quick-to-fix holiday beverage.

1 quart dairy eggnog
1 5½-ounce can chocolate-flavored syrup

¼ cup crème de cacao
1 cup whipping cream
Chocolate curls (optional)

In a large pitcher stir together eggnog, chocolate-flavored syrup, and crème de cacao. Cover and chill.

Just before serving, beat whipping cream till soft peaks form (tips curl). Reserve ½ cup of the whipped cream for garnish. Fold the remaining whipped cream into the eggnog mixture. Pour into serving glasses. Dollop with reserved whipped cream. Garnish with chocolate curls, if desired. Makes about 12 (4-ounce) servings.

Mrs. Shirley Strieber, Tucson Arizona

Cherry Slush

Change the character and color of this cool refresher by spiking it with any flavored vodka and varying the frozen concentrate.

3½ cups boiling water
½ cup sugar
1 tea bag

1 cup cherry-flavored vodka
1 6-ounce can frozen orange juice concentrate
Carbonated water

In a large saucepan combine boiling water and sugar, stirring constantly till sugar dissolves. Add tea bag and steep for 3 to 5 minutes. Remove and discard tea bag. Cool.

Stir vodka and orange juice concentrate into sugar mixture. Pour into a 9x5x3-inch baking pan. Freeze overnight.

Before serving, use a large spoon to scrape across the surface of the frozen mixture. Spoon into chilled glasses. Pour carbonated water over mixture in glasses and stir gently to make a slush. Makes about 10 (4-ounce) servings.

Nita Preheim, Marion, South Dakota

Chill the fruit, juice, and water thoroughly before blending this light-tasting drink.

Sparkling Peaches And Cream

1 16-ounce can peach slices, chilled
½ cup unsweetened pineapple juice, chilled
1 egg
4 ice cubes

1 tablespoon lemon juice
1 teaspoon vanilla
⅓ cup light cream
⅔ cup carbonated water, chilled
Sliced almonds (optional)

In a blender container combine *undrained* peach slices, pineapple juice, egg, ice cubes, lemon juice, and vanilla. Cover and blend till smooth. Stir in light cream. Slowly pour in carbonated water, stirring with an up-and-down motion. Pour into chilled glasses. Garnish with sliced almonds, if desired. Makes about 8 (4-ounce) servings.

Clara Beth Negoro, Hawthorne, California

Vienna Brioche Loaf

1 package active dry yeast
½ cup warm water (110°
   to 115°)
1 cup butter *or* margarine
¼ cup sugar
1 teaspoon finely shredded
   lemon peel
1 teaspoon salt
4½ cups all-purpose flour
6 eggs

⅔ cup packed brown sugar
2 beaten egg yolks
½ cup butter *or* margarine,
   melted
2 tablespoons milk
¼ teaspoon vanilla
2 cups chopped walnuts
   Sifted powdered sugar
   (optional)

> 66 *I am not sure of its original beginning, but this bread is now a part of our family breakfast every Christmas morning.* 99

Soften yeast in warm water. In a large mixer bowl beat together the 1 cup butter or margarine, sugar, lemon peel, and salt. Add *1 cup* flour, the 6 eggs, and softened yeast. Beat well. Stir in the remaining flour till smooth, forming a soft dough. Place in a lightly greased bowl. Turn once to grease surface. Cover and let rise in a warm place till double (about 2 hours). Cover. Chill overnight. Stir dough down.

For filling, in a medium mixing bowl stir together brown sugar, egg yolks, and *3 tablespoons* melted butter or margarine. Stir in milk and vanilla. Add nuts. Punch dough down. Return half of the dough to the refrigerator. Transfer other half to a floured surface. Roll into a 14x9-inch rectangle. Brush with *1 tablespoon* of the remaining melted butter or margarine. Spread with *half* of the filling. Starting from the short sides, roll each side up, jelly-roll style, to center. Place loaf, rolled side up, in a greased 9x5x3-inch loaf pan. Brush with some of the remaining melted butter or margarine. Repeat with remaining dough, butter or margarine, and filling. Cover and let rise in a warm place till nearly double (about 1½ hours).

Bake in a 350° oven about 35 minutes or till golden brown. Remove from pans. Cool on wire racks. Sift powdered sugar over loaves, if desired. Makes 2 loaves.

Mrs. Betsy Anderson, Mount Vernon, Ohio

Cranberry-Pumpkin Ring

1¾ to 2¼ cups all-purpose
   flour
1 package active dry yeast
½ cup milk
⅓ cup sugar
¼ cup butter *or* margarine
1 teaspoon ground cinnamon
½ teaspoon ground nutmeg
¼ teaspoon ground cloves
¾ teaspoon salt
1 egg
½ cup canned pumpkin

1¼ cups whole wheat flour
1¼ cups cranberries
⅓ cup sugar
1 teaspoon finely shredded
   orange peel
½ teaspoon ground cinnamon
1 tablespoon water
2 tablespons butter *or*
   margarine, softened
1 cup sifted powdered sugar
4 teaspoons milk
¼ teaspoon orange extract

Distinctive holiday flavors—cranberry and pumpkin—team up in this spiral coffee bread.

In a large mixer bowl combine ½ *cup* all-purpose flour and yeast. In a saucepan heat the ½ cup milk, ⅓ cup sugar, the ¼ cup butter or margarine, the 1 teaspoon cinnamon, nutmeg, cloves, and salt just till warm (115°to 120°) and butter is almost melted, stirring constantly. Add to flour mixture.

Beat with an electric mixer on low speed for 30 seconds, scraping sides of bowl. Add egg and pumpkin. Beat on high speed for 3 minutes. Using a spoon, stir in whole wheat flour and as much of the remaining all-purpose flour as you can.

Turn out onto a lightly floured surface. Knead in enough remaining all-purpose flour to make a moderately stiff dough that is smooth and elastic (6 to 8 minutes total). Shape into a ball. Place in a greased bowl; turn once to grease surface. Cover and let rise in a warm place till double (about 1 hour).

For filling, in a saucepan combine cranberries, ⅓ cup sugar, orange peel, the ½ teaspoon cinnamon, and water. Cook and stir over medium heat till cranberries pop. Transfer to a bowl. Cover and chill.

Punch dough down. Let rest 10 minutes. On a lightly floured surface, roll dough into a 15x10-inch rectangle. Spread with the 2 tablespoons softened butter or margarine. Spread with cranberry filling. Roll up, jelly-roll style, starting from one of the long sides. Pinch edges to seal well. Bring ends together to form a ring. Place dough, seam side down, on a greased baking sheet. With kitchen shears, make cuts in dough at about 1-inch intervals around edge. Cover and let rise till nearly double (about 30 minutes).

Bake in a 375° oven for 25 to 30 minutes, covering with foil the last 10 minutes to prevent overbrowning. Remove from baking sheet and cool on a wire rack.

For icing, combine powdered sugar, the 4 teaspoons milk, and orange extract. Drizzle icing over ring. Makes 1 ring.

Elizabeth Domkowski, Knoxville, Tennessee

Nutcracker Tarts

A sinfully rich holiday dessert bedecked with an extraordinary raspberry sauce.

3⅓ cups all-purpose flour
¼ cup sugar
1 cup butter *or* margarine
2 slightly beaten egg yolks
⅓ cup water
1 cup sugar
½ cup water
⅓ cup honey
3½ cups chopped pistachio nuts (about 1 pound)
1 cup milk
¼ cup butter *or* margarine
⅓ cup seedless red raspberry jam
2 tablespoons crème de cassis
¼ cup finely chopped pistachio nuts (about 1 ounce)

In a large mixing bowl stir together flour and the ¼ cup sugar. Cut in the 1 cup butter or margarine till pieces are the size of small peas. Add egg yolks and the ⅓ cup water, tossing with a fork till moistened. Form dough into a ball. Wrap and chill.

Meanwhile, for filling, in a saucepan combine the 1 cup sugar, the ½ cup water, and honey. Bring to boiling, stirring till sugar is dissolved. Reduce heat to low. Boil gently about 25 minutes or till caramel color. Stir in the 3½ cups nuts, milk, and the ¼ cup butter or margarine. Return to boiling. Reduce heat to low. Boil gently for 15 minutes more.

For bottom crust, on a lightly floured surface, roll *one-fourth* of the chilled dough into an 11-inch circle. Ease dough into a 9-inch flan pan, quiche dish, or cake pan. Roll out another *one-fourth* of the dough to an 11-inch circle. Cut slits for escape of steam. Pour *half* of the filling mixture into crust. Top with pastry for top crust. Trim top crust ½ inch beyond edge of pan. Fold extra pastry over top crust. Flute edges, sealing well. Repeat for second tart.

Bake in a 425° oven for 30 to 35 minutes. Cool. Invert onto a serving platter. In a small saucepan combine jam and crème de cassis. Heat and stir till jam is melted. Spoon jam mixture over tarts in a swirl design. Garnish *each* with the ¼ cup nuts. Chill. Makes 2 tarts.

Linda Ann Rohr, Stamford, Connecticut

Mocha-Nut Divinity

Instant Swiss-style coffee powder adds a delightful difference to this creamy divinity.

2½ cups sugar
½ cup light corn syrup
½ cup water
¼ cup instant Swiss-style
     coffee powder

2 egg whites
1 cup chopped pecans

In a heavy 2-quart saucepan combine sugar, corn syrup, water, and coffee powder. Cook over medium-high heat to boiling, stirring constantly with a wooden spoon to dissolve sugar. This should take 5 to 7 minutes. Avoid splashing mixture on sides of pan. Carefully clip candy thermometer to side of pan.

Cook over medium heat, without stirring, till the thermometer registers 260°, hard-ball stage. Mixture should boil at a moderate, steady rate over the entire surface. Reaching hard-ball stage should take about 15 minutes. Remove saucepan from heat. Remove thermometer from saucepan.

In a large mixer bowl immediately beat egg whites with a sturdy, freestanding electric mixer on medium speed till stiff peaks form (tips stand straight).

Gradually pour hot mixture in a thin stream (slightly less than ⅛-inch diameter) over egg whites, beating with the electric mixer on high speed and scraping the sides of the bowl occasionally. This should take about 3 minutes. (Add mixture *slowly* to ensure proper blending.)

Continue beating with the electric mixer on high speed, scraping the sides of the bowl occasionally, just till candy starts to lose its gloss. When beaters are lifted, mixture should fall in a ribbon, but mound on itself and not disappear into remaining mixture. Final beating should take 5 to 6 minutes.

Drop a spoonful of the mixture onto waxed paper. If it stays mounded in a soft shape, it is beaten properly. Immediately stir in the nuts. Quickly drop from a teaspoon onto a baking sheet lined with waxed paper. Store tightly covered. Makes about 40 pieces.

D. R. Sarkisian, Inman, South Carolina

Crunchy Nut Fudge

The crunch in Mildred's fudge comes from sugared peanuts. Use the extra peanuts as an added treat on your holiday candy tray.

1 egg white
½ teaspoon water
¼ cup sugar
¼ teaspoon ground cinnamon
1½ cups dry roasted peanuts

2 cups sugar
½ cup butter *or* margarine
½ cup evaporated milk
1 teaspoon vanilla

Beat egg white and water till foamy. Combine the ¼ cup sugar and cinnamon. Stir sugar-cinnamon mixture and peanuts into egg white mixture. Spread mixture evenly in a buttered 13x9x2-inch baking pan. Bake in a 325° oven for 15 minutes. Stir nuts. Bake about 15 minutes more or till coating is brown. Cool in pan. Chop *half* of the nuts. Store remaining sugared nuts in an airtight container.

Line an 8x8x2-inch pan with foil, extending foil over edges of pan. Butter the foil. Set pan aside.

Butter the sides of a heavy 1½-quart saucepan. In the saucepan combine the 2 cups sugar, butter or margarine, and evaporated milk. Cook over medium heat to boiling, stirring constantly with a wooden spoon to dissolve sugar. Carefully clip candy thermometer to side of pan. Cook, stirring frequently, till candy thermometer registers 236°, soft-ball stage. Mixture should boil at a moderate, steady rate over entire surface.

Remove saucepan from heat. Cool, without stirring, to lukewarm (110°). This should take about 1 hour.

Remove candy thermometer from saucepan. Add vanilla to fudge. Beat vigorously with the wooden spoon till fudge just begins to thicken. Add chopped peanuts. Continue beating till fudge becomes very thick and just starts to lose its gloss. This should take 7 to 10 minutes total.

Quickly transfer fudge to prepared pan. While fudge is warm, score it into 1-inch squares. When candy is firm, use foil to lift it out of the pan. Cut into squares. Store tightly covered. Makes 48 pieces.

Mildred Ringler, Virginia Beach, Virginia

To make this baked-on frosting the right consistency, use real, not imitation, chocolate pieces.

Chocolate-Covered Cherry Cookies

1½ cups all-purpose flour
½ cup unsweetened cocoa powder
¼ teaspoon salt
¼ teaspoon baking powder
¼ teaspoon baking soda
1 10-ounce jar maraschino cherries (about 48)
½ cup butter *or* margarine

1 cup sugar
1 egg
1½ teaspoons vanilla
1 6-ounce package (1 cup) semisweet chocolate pieces
½ cup *sweetened condensed* milk

Combine flour, cocoa powder, salt, baking powder, and soda. Set aside. Drain maraschino cherries, reserving juice. Set aside.

In a large mixer bowl beat butter or margarine with an electric mixer on medium speed for 30 seconds. Add sugar and beat till fluffy. Add egg and vanilla and beat well. Gradually add dry ingredients and beat till combined.

Shape dough into 1-inch balls. Place about 2 inches apart on an ungreased cookie sheet. Press down center of each ball with your thumb. Place a drained cherry in the center of each cookie.

For frosting, in a small saucepan combine chocolate pieces and sweetened condensed milk. Cook and stir over low heat till chocolate is melted. Stir in *4 teaspoons* reserved cherry juice. Spoon about *1 teaspoon* frosting over *each* cherry, spreading to cover cherry. (Frosting may be thinned with additional cherry juice, if necessary.)

Bake in a 350° oven about 10 minutes or till edges are firm. Remove and cool completely on wire racks. Makes about 48 cookies.

Mary Pickard, Tampa, Florida

Anise Cookies

Eve's unique cookie recipe was passed down from her great-grandmother.

2 eggs
1 cup sugar
¾ teaspoon anise extract
1 cup all-purpose flour

In a small mixer bowl beat eggs with an electric mixer on high speed about 4 minutes or till light. Gradually add sugar, beating on high speed about 10 minutes or till thick. Add the anise extract. Add flour and beat till combined.

Drop dough by rounded teaspoons onto a greased cookie sheet. Cover cookie sheet loosely with waxed paper. Let stand for 12 hours or overnight to dry.

Bake in a 350° oven for 10 to 12 minutes. Remove and cool completely on wire racks. Store in an airtight container for 2 days before eating. Makes about 60.

Eve Shore, Williamsburg, Iowa

Molasses Butterball Cookies

By adding molasses, Ruby turned an old cookie favorite—sandies—into a new and special taste treat.

1 cup butter *or* margarine
¼ cup molasses
2 cups all-purpose flour
2 cups very finely chopped walnuts
Powdered sugar

In a large mixer bowl beat butter or margarine with an electric mixer on medium speed for 30 seconds. Add molasses and beat till fluffy. Add flour and beat till combined. Stir in nuts.

Shape dough into 1-inch balls, using about *1 tablespoon* dough for *each* ball. Place on an ungreased cookie sheet.

Bake in a 325° oven for 20 minutes. Remove and cool completely on wire racks. In a plastic bag, gently shake a few cookies at a time in powdered sugar. Makes about 40.

Mrs. Ruby B. Kassner, Vicksburg, Mississippi

INDEX

D-E

T-Z

Have BETTER HOMES
AND GARDENS® magazine
delivered to your door.
For information, write to:
MR. ROBERT AUSTIN
P.O. BOX 4536
DES MOINES, IA 50336